I Never Met

Jerry Baker

a House Plant
I Didn't Like

Literary Consultant   Dan Kibbie

Illustrations by Dot Cohn

Simon and Schuster

New York

SBN 671-21767-4
Library of Congress Card Number: 74-13906
Designed by Edith Fowler
Manufactured in the United States of America
        3   4   5   6   7   8   9   10

Acknowledgments

When I was a youngster most people thought that growing things *outdoors* was a very useful and educational activity for young boys. Growing things *indoors,* however, was thought to be pretty much the exclusive province and pastime of maiden aunts and nice young ladies who would one day become maiden aunts. The males who became the exceptions to these unwritten rules of the day were not mere dabblers in the potting arts. On the contrary, they were "experts" and "horticulturists"—mostly doctors and preachers, I suppose.

Luckily, three people taught me early in life that Mother Nature and her plant children needn't be left locked outdoors when it was time for a boy to be at home. The first of these was my Grandma Putt, who was my gardening mentor in those formative years. She didn't believe in society's foolish segregation of the sexes. My Aunt Jane—a very young girl to be an aunt—was required to do her share of hoeing and rehoeing the bean patch. And I had to do my share of potting and repotting the house plants! Then, too, my Mom, Mildred Baker, has always had a very special knack for growing plants indoors, and when I was a boy she never hesitated to assign me the task of helping make her cacti, flowering, or leafy friends feel like part of the family. The third influence in making me a semiknowledgeable "house plant homemaker" was a nurseryman named Sid Trueheart. You see, I was sentenced to a term at hard labor in Sid's greenhouse to work off payment for some broken windowpanes! Looking back to those early beginnings in acquiring some know-how on the care and culture of house plants makes me extremely grateful to Sid, Grandma Putt, and most of all to my mother.

In the course of producing this book I came to realize that the proper culture of house plants in American homes is a subject so vast and so complex that no single person and no single book can treat it with adequate authority or detail. It is my intention, then, to present an easy-to-read, constructive guide to growing which will point up the proven fact that house plants treated with the common sense, respect, and affection usually reserved for *people* will flourish under the care of the most inexperienced home gardener. It is my hope that this basic guide will encourage you to learn how to grow house plants and gain confidence with experience.

This book, perhaps more than any I have written so far, is the product of the hard work, patience, understanding, knowledge, and love of gardening of a good many people. I particularly want to thank my friend and attorney Henry Baskin, who persuaded me to write it, and Louise Riotte, an avid and expert gardener, who helped me research every technical facet of the material and contributed her enormous energy and talent to the project. And I wish also to thank my friends and advisers Dan and Mary Kibbie and Dot Cohn, who helped me put the book into what I hope is a readable form.

To my dearest wife, Ilene

*While I have been "growing" this book
she has been raising my children and
"growing" another little Baker!*

Contents

Introduction

It was my Grandma Putt who first taught me the important fact that plants are like people and that each living, growing specimen, from the smallest patch of grass to the tallest oak, is a child of Mother Nature who needs the same sort of individual love, care, and attention that you would give to a child of your own.

As you read this book—and as you begin to enlarge your circle of house plant friends—you will quickly begin to recognize the unique personality traits and characteristics that set off each plant from its fellows. Learning about these traits and characteristics and how to live with them can become a fascinating and rewarding part of your life. Before long you'll feel delighted when a particular plant thrives or shows off its flowers, just as you are exceedingly pleased when your children behave properly before company. You'll learn that, like your children or your friends, each plant will need special handling or disciplining or coddling in order to get the best out of your mutual relationship.

When Will Rogers said that he never met a man he didn't like, he said something that's important for each of us to think about every once in a while. Usually the men we don't like belong to some group classification or stereotype. But when we begin to look at each person as an individual, the hated group characteristics begin to disappear and the person becomes unique, more likable, sometimes even lovable. So it is with plants. In order to get a houseful of plants to grow and thrive under your care, you will have to forget about treating them as a group and begin to look at each one as an individual with its own special habits, requirements, and abilities for rewarding and pleasing you. Then you too will truly say, "I never met a house plant I didn't like."

1

Getting Acquainted

Not so long ago my son Jeff was reading *The Swiss Family Robinson* and described to us the part about the family building their house in a giant mangrove fig tree. That reminded me of a California man I once met who told me he had a coral tree growing in his living room. He said that when he bought the land where his home now stands, he and his wife fell in love with the tree. Because it was too old to be moved, they decided to build around it. The coral tree has since become one of the largest, oldest, and most spectacular house plants I've ever heard of.

When I think of that coral tree and the thousands of varieties of plants that abound in nature, I begin to realize that there are literally thousands of reasons for growing plants indoors. Probably one of the most reasonable reasons for bringing any plant into your home is that you happen to like it or that someone who likes *you* happened to like it and gave it to you as a gift. And, I think, the reason most of us do like house plants is simply that they are *alive*.

It isn't just their beauty that attracts us—dried flowers and some artificial plants have a certain beauty. What it is, then, is that very evident spark of life that gives them the ability to transform the coldest and most sterile room into a warm, friendly place where compatible living things reside. We enjoy their beauty, but we are also comforted by their presence. Even on a cold winter day, there is a promise of spring to be felt just by glancing in their direction.

People who live in apartments find that growing house plants is a delightful way to enjoy the happy and healthy hobby of gardening. For them it is a rare opportunity to come into contact with nature. That contact is becoming harder and harder to achieve in the crowded confines of most city parks, which are the only available resources for many urbanites. My friend John Campbell, whose business it is to know about these things, tells me that by the year 2000 A.D. more than 90 percent of the people in this country will be living in an urban concrete jungle. So it looks as though we're all going to have to find ways to get back in touch with Mother Nature, and growing house plants can be one important way to do just that.

If you add a bird feeder to your apartment window garden, you'll bring a little bit of country living right into the city—which is all the more important if you have youngsters. And speaking of youngsters, giving your child the responsibility of caring for one or more house plants can be an important part of his early education. Just make certain that he understands that plants are like people—they need definite daylight activity and nighttime rest.

House plants can also add immeasurable joy to the lives of the elderly or the physically handicapped who don't have the strength for outdoor gardening. If your fingers are stiffening with arthritis, plants can provide therapy. Working in warm soils is as comforting as working in warm water, relaxing stiffened joints and making you feel better all over. You'll discover that ministering to the needs of your plant friends and making them comfortable will often do the same for you. You'll also find that house plants can be a tonic for your mind as well as your body, cheering you up with their presence on those blue days when the rest of the world seems pretty dreary. And if you are a member of the working world, with only a few minutes each day in which to attend to your gardening, there are plenty of easy-to-grow plants that give a whole lot in return for a very little attention.

Obviously, then, your reasons for wanting to grow indoor plants will vary according to your circumstances and your life style. Some folks, like my friend and house plant adviser Louise Riotte, are natural master gardeners and enjoy growing things so much during the outdoor growing season that they would feel lonesome without lots of indoor plants around them during the colder months of the year. Others, like my mom, take a great deal of pleasure from the feeling that their plants are dependent on them for care and comfort. My mother looks forward to that few minutes of interest and fun each day when she weeds, waters, and feeds her plant friends—always giving them that quarter turn to the light that helps them grow straight and strong. I guess those plants are like her children now. At least they don't ever sass her back when she sets them straight, as my brother and I used to do from time to time!

On the practical side, there are other reasons for having house plants. It is possible to reflect the entire color scheme of your room or its accent colors by careful selection of the right plants. Also, you can choose plants to harmonize with the style of your furnishings. If your room is contemporary, you can accent the simplicity you like with Philodendron, Caladium or Dracaena—all have interesting leaf patterns that go well with this style. Begonias and geraniums are excellent with Colonial maple, and Helxine, Fittonia, or Maranta look right with eighteenth-century furnishings. If you're on a Far East kick or feel at ease in an Oriental setting, try a bonsai tree or a cyperus.

More and more people, however, are refusing to commit themselves to only one style of interior design. The new concept is to mix furnishings of different styles and match them to your own personality and the personality of your family—which certainly goes with my approach to selecting house plants. I just pick out the ones that seem to belong with me or one of my family. I would no more want to be limited to one or two varieties of house plants than I'd accept being limited to listening to one or two kinds of music!

The increased use of house plants to accent interiors has stimulated an enormous demand for new and unusual leaf variations. New species and varieties are constantly being introduced. Unusual and exotic plants from China, Brazil, Hawaii, Mexico, South America and elsewhere are now available all over this country. Don't hesitate to take advantage of their decorative possibilities. Go into the florist shop or nursery every once in a while and browse around—you may see something in one of the newer importations that is exactly right for a particular place in your house. But be careful to find out as much about its habits and personality as you can so you can make it comfortable in your home.

In my Grandma Putt's day most people grew smaller house plants than they do now. They were especially fond of those that would fit on the kitchen windowsill or that small plant table placed where it would receive southern exposure. These days larger plants with larger leaves have been increasing in popularity. They seem much more appropriate to contemporary interiors. But the small plants are still in fashion. Their delicate flowers and foliage continue to look well in the period settings that have become so popular. Actually, some plants are so adaptable that they look well in any location. And if they are well placed and properly lighted they'll make an interesting addition to almost any setting.

Mother Nature is great when it comes to proper placement of the things that grow *outdoors.* Her natural selections always seem to fit in with the requirements of light, temperature, soil, moisture, and compatibility with the plant and animal neighbors growing close by. I believe you should take the same sort of requirements into consideration when you select plants to grow *indoors.*

When you are attracted to a plant and want to purchase it, first find out all the names by which it may be known in addition to its botanical name. Look it up in a gardening encyclopedia under its Latin name and you will likely learn some surprising and helpful things about its family tree. But don't let those big, unpronounceable Latin names throw you. I'm the world's worst when it comes to remembering them, although I can usually remember a plant by its face or nickname. The reason these names are important is that very often people in different parts of the world will get to know a plant by its local or regional name. That's how we get confused. So no matter what you or I or someone in Afghanistan may call a particular plant, its official botanical name is in Latin.

Basically, there are five types to choose from: foliage plants, flowering house plants, flowering pot plants, bulbs and corms, and cacti and succulents.

The foliage plants usually grow rather slowly and change least of all. They are quite likely to become truly permanent residents.

Flowering house plants, such as African violets, are permanent, so choose your colors carefully. Think about whether they will contrast or harmonize with the area in which they will be placed.

Then there are the flowering pot plants and the bulbs, which may be considered temporary visitors in the house. If you grow fond of them, you may want to replant them out of doors after they flower. Some of these, like chrysanthemums, will grow and prosper elsewhere, so you can enjoy them in two different worlds. Bulbs also may sometimes be saved to use again in an outdoor setting.

Cacti and many types of succulents are the fun plants of your indoor garden. They often become collectibles for children and others who delight in their funny forms and faces. Jeff has an "old man" cactus with woolly white hair near the top.

The real fun of indoor gardening starts with choosing the best possible plants for you. We have discussed the fact that we must consider plants as individuals, each with its own definite personality. Therefore, before you invite them in as guests, eventually to become family members, there are some ground rules to consider.

Ground Rules of House Plant Selection

1. Make sure the plants you select really have appeal for you or for the member of the family who will be responsible for them. Don't pick them just because you saw them growing in the house of a friend or because a book or a seller recommends them.

2. Be sure they are suitable for the conditions they will have to live in. It's your home—remember? They will be happiest—and so will you—if you both enjoy the same type of environment. You were there first, so if you like your house warm, choose tropical plants or something hardy in a foliage plant such as the fiddle-leaf fig or that old favorite the India rubber plant. If you like a cooler temperature, there is plenty of choice here also.

3. Be sure they won't require more time and experience than you will have to offer. If you are a beginning gardener, it is comforting to realize that there are many easy and inexpensive plants to choose from. Most good plant stores carry specimens from all over the world. It is usually a good idea to find out all you can about a plant's cultural requirements *before* you buy it. If those requirements are exotic, and you don't have the time or inclination to provide them, pass that plant up and get something less temperamental. Why not start off with something easy and undemanding?

If you consult your local florist about plants that are easy to grow, he will in all likelihood tell you that he sells more philodendrons than any other house plant. This is because they are tolerant of the warm conditions found in most modern homes. In addition, they can stand poor light better than almost any other type of house plant. However, if they are placed in a well-lighted window from October until April, they will grow better. Then, when the sun's rays become strongest move them back a little from the light for the remainder of the year.

4. Another thing to consider when you purchase a plant is its stage of growth. If it is a flowering plant and there are many buds or a great deal of foliage, the plant will require more water for its full development than one that is already in full bloom or one whose leaves are even more fully matured.

Some Pertinent Questions

Here are some questions you should ask yourself before selecting house plants:

1. What shape do I want—upright, bushy, trailing, or climbing?

UPRIGHTS: aphelandra, codiaeum cordyline, dracaena, *Ficus elastica* (rubber plant), *Ficus elastica decora, Ficus lyrata,* grevillea, pandanus, and sansevieria (mother-in-law's tongue).

BUSHY PLANTS: adiantum, azalea, begonia, coleus, fatsia, fittonia, maranta, neanthe, and saintpaulia (African violets).

TRAILING PLANTS: *Begonia glaucophylla, Campanula isophylla,* columnea, *Ficus pumila, Fuchsia pendula,* helxine, *Saxifraga sarmentosa,* tradescantia, zebrina.

CLIMBING PLANTS: cissus, *Cobaea scandens, Ficus pumila,* hedera, hoya, *Philodendron scandens,* rhoicissus, scindapsus, and tetrastigma.

2. Do I want the plants to be permanent residents of the room they'll be put in? If the answer to this is yes then you should avoid flowering pot plants. After a short period of bloom indoors they often look bedraggled. Some even lose their leaves.

3. Do I want a plant with colorful foliage? Many house plants have colorful variegated leaves—that is, the leaves have multi-colored edges, stripes, or spots. These plants do best if given plenty of light. If variegated plants are what you want, choose from sansevieria, *Peperomia magnoliaefolia variegata,* dracaena, *Hedera helix, Zebrina pendula,* or *Ficus pumila.* Other colors are available with nidularium, maranta, coleus, *Begonia rex,* codiaeum, cordyline, aphelandra, and *Cissus discolor.*

4. How much time and effort will I be able to give? Some house plants, like sansevieria are almost indestructible, while others are best left to the more experienced indoor gardener. I suggest that you choose at first from the "easy" group—plants that

Hedera helix variegata
Variegated English Ivy

will stand a little cool weather, a certain amount of neglect, or even poor management.

The easy-to-care-for foliage plants include *Cissus antarctica, Rhoicissus rhomboidea, Ficus pumila, Ficus elastica,* sansevieria, *Philodendron scandens,* chlorophytum, tradescantia, cyperus, grevillea, tolmiea, *Saxifraga sarmentosa.* Easy flowering plants are billbergia, clivia, geraniums, impatiens, fuchsia, and all of the cactus plants.

Placement and Plant Parenthood

When you buy a plant you probably already have a pretty good idea of where you want it to reside in your home or apartment. That's good. Proper selection and placement are two important factors in plant parenthood that are interdependent and immensely important when it comes to ensuring growing success.

Since I am the father of five children, you may be surprised to learn that I'm all for planned parenthood, or at least plant parenthood. I just believe it's a good general rule to know where your plant is going to be placed before you select and buy it. Of course, as with kids, plants do have a way of coming into our lives by surprise (as presents or the result of some impulse you just couldn't resist). These gifts of nature should be all the more loved, because they keep us from getting into a rut with our planning.

Many people have the mistaken idea that house plants will thrive only on a warm, sunny window ledge or in a room built especially for them, like the old-fashioned conservatories or sun porches. This is absolutely untrue. Despite the fact that all plants need some light to live, there is a plant for almost every room in your home. I have successfully raised plants in the basement and in darkened hallways, and I even kept a poinsettia in a closet for several weeks (to make sure it would bloom in all its glory at Christmastime).

Before selecting a plant for placement check the particular location you have in mind for it. Try to determine the amount of light your new plant will get, what the average 24-hour temperature range will be, what the normal humidity is, and what the air circulation is like. Each of these factors is important to your plant's well-being, but all of them combined will help you predetermine what kind of plant can survive and prosper in that specific environment. If you make friends with your nurseryman or florist and tell him about the location you have in mind, he will no doubt be happy to suggest certain plants for certain places.

Here is a general description of growing conditions that we might find in almost any home or apartment and some of the plants that will best fit those conditions:

DIM AND COOL: aspidistra, dizygothica, fatshedera, fatsia, ferns, *Ficus pumila,* hedera, helxine, maranta, and philodendron. When I say cool I mean in the 50–55 degree range— not cold, like 40 degrees.

BRIGHT BUT NO SUNLIGHT: *Cissus antarctica,* columnea, fuchsia, *Monstera deliciosa, Rhoicissus rhoboidea,* scindapsus, tetrastigma, tolmiea. These also include foliage house plants with variegated leaves and most of the holiday plants.

SOME SUNLIGHT EACH DAY: chlorophytum, cordyline, *Ficus elastica decora,* peperomia, sansevieria, and most flowering house plants.

BRIGHT, SUNNY WINDOW: beloperone, cobaea, coleus, genista, geranium, impatiens, passiflora, cacti, and succulents.

LITTLE HEAT IN WINTER: aspidistra, billbergia, *Cissus antarctica,* chlorophytum, fatshedera, fatsia, hedera, *Philodendron scandens, Saxifraga sarmentosa,* zebrina.

GAS HEAT: Least affected are thick-leaved foliage house

plants. All flowering plants (except impatiens and billbergia) should be avoided.

POOR HUMIDITY, DRY: aechmea, billbergia, chlorophytum, clivia, *Ficus elastica decora,* grevillea, pilea, sansevieria, vriesia, zebrina, cacti, and succulents.

Don't hedge on your evaluation when you go shopping for plants. If you're uncertain whether the climatic conditions in your home are appropriate for a particular plant, choose another one. This will save both your feelings and those of a plant that might be chosen unwisely.

Other Factors to Consider

Another thing to realize is that house plants are raised in greenhouses where the air is warm and humid. They are not accustomed to the world outside. Try to buy from a reliable supplier who makes sure that his plants have been properly "hardened off" and will not be too shocked by a sudden change of environment.

You can buy house plants at any time of the year, but it is best to purchase any of the more delicate varieties in the spring or summer. It is easier to transport them safely and they do not have to adjust to ups and downs in temperature in your house. Be sure to look the plant over carefully before buying. It should be sturdy, not spindly, have no discolored or damaged leaves and be free of insects.

If it is cold outside, wrap your new plant well before leaving the nursery or florist. You'd be surprised at the enormous number of plants that get frostbite on their way to their new home and never recover.

Plants are like people, and another bit of supporting evidence that scientists have come up with lately is that when you purchase a plant in one part of the world and take it home by airplane, you are quite likely to disturb its normal rhythm, or 24-hour cycle. Plants, it seems, can feel the effects of jet lag as much as people.

Your new plant will be coming to an environment completely different from the one it has been accustomed to. Treat it gently for about a week after you bring it home. Don't put it with your other plants right away; first make sure it's healthy and pest-free. Keep it out of drafts and direct sunlight. Don't give it too much water or allow it to become overheated. If it gets off to a good start and continues to do well after this critical first week, place it in its permanent location and treat it normally.

Certain plants, such as azalea and cyclamen, if purchased during the winter months, require different treatment. Put them in their permanent quarters at once and treat them normally. Give them as much light as possible.

Remember, you invited your plants to live with you—they didn't ask to move in. So treat them like welcome guests. Pay particular attention to each new plant until it is comfortable and a bona fide member of the family. One way to focus your attention on a newcomer is to give it a personal name or nickname. That's right, a plant should have three names: the Latin name, the common name, and the personal or affectionate nickname you give it to let it know you really care about its well-being.

Plants Can Keep You Young and Healthy

People used to have some sort of queer idea that having plants all over the house was unhealthy. They were supposed to use up the oxygen in the air, or something. Actually, we now know that just the opposite is true. Plants produce oxygen. So, in addition to giving us pleasure they contribute to our physical well-being.

Did you know that house plants can also bring their owners good health and help them hold on to a youthful appearance? I'm not putting you on. House plants have two basic living requirements that happily coincide with your own needs: a need for mild temperatures and adequate atmospheric moisture.

Most of us, unless we are ill, would be more comfortable in a cooler atmosphere than is the norm for the majority of American homes. On the whole we tend to keep our homes too warm and dry. We'd be far less susceptible to the discomfort of colds and other winter inconveniences if we would just accustom ourselves to a little less heat.

Also (and this should interest the ladies particularly) if you would adjust the atmosphere of your rooms to the moisture requirements of your plants, you'd begin to see that your skin won't dry out as easily as it tended to in the past and you won't develop those ugly crow's feet associated with premature aging. You don't have to believe me—just try it out for yourself. Turn your home into a cooler, moister place to live in and you will soon see that creating an atmosphere of humidity that will beautify your plants will also result in a prettier you.

Englishwomen have been famous for centuries for the beauty of their complexions. But when they are transplanted to America they soon develop dry skins and fall heir to the same appearance problems and difficulties we have in our warmer, drier indoor climates. Check the counter where the beauty preparations are sold some day and you will probably be struck by the large number of "moisturizer" creams and lotions that are being offered. You won't need them if you just keep cool! Now, isn't it a nice thought that when we create healthy, *moist,* and *cool* conditions for our house plants we will benefit as well?

Scientists in California researching the aging process have discovered that by lowering the body temperature of mice just one or two degrees they are able to extend the normal life-span of the animals. These scientists now feel that if it were possible to lower human body heat a few degrees, we might live ten or twenty years longer. Of course, this will be a very difficult thing to do and cannot be accomplished merely by our living in a cooler environment. However, that may well be a step in the right direction. So plants not only improve our mental attitude by providing us with beauty and pleasure, they also improve our physical well-being.

2

The Secrets of Growing Success: The Basics

If you're like me, you're curious about people. I know it's not very polite, but I like to find out as much as I can about a new friend or a new neighbor and try to learn what makes him tick. You can learn a lot about anyone if you take the trouble to find out about his background, where he grew up, his likes and dislikes, and so on. I suggest that you treat your house plants in the same way. Learn all you can about them. Where did they come from? Do plants of this type still live in the wild—and under what conditions? Knowing some of these things will help you make your plants feel comfortable and help your friendship flourish.

There are three basic things to learn about your plants before you can be successful: what *temperature* range they grow best in, how much *light* they require, and how much *water* they need. Once you learn how to fulfill these three basic requirements for each of your house plant friends, you will be well on your way to becoming a successful green-thumber. Don't be discouraged if at first this knowledge seems too technical or too hard to acquire. Since gardening is not an exact science, your knowledge of your plants' basic needs will come more from trial-and-error doing than from reading books like this one.

Proper Temperature and Other Conditions for Your House Plants

While it's difficult to generalize, most house plants need a temperature range of from 60–70 degrees in order to grow right and look their best. A continuous temperature of over 70 degrees will result in plants becoming leggy (having long, weak-looking stems) and much less resistant to insect pests and diseases. Even the flowers they produce will be of poorer quality.

Most of us find 68–72 degrees very comfortable, and if we lower this temperature for the sake of our plants, we're quite likely to become uncomfortable. And whenever that happens we begin to resent the presence of plants in the house. Believe it or not, your house plants will sense your displeasure and react— they'll feel and look terrible! After you work with house plants for a while you'll see how quickly and obviously they react to your resentment, displeasure, or inattention.

The best way to solve the problem is to compromise. Plants have to adjust a little bit to *our* living conditions. When you retire at night, cut down the temperature to somewhere between 60 and 70 degrees—the closer to 60 degrees the better. This simple procedure will save your plants—and will also save you a little money in the family budget. If this is not possible, and your plants are in containers of an easily movable size, move them to a specially cooled room during the night and return them to their accustomed place during the day. Like other members of the family, they will be rested and refreshed after a good night's sleep and will reflect this in increased vitality and beauty.

If you do decide to move your plants before bedtime, try using a hostess cart or tea cart. This may even serve as a handy plant stand during the day; the plants will already be on it and ready to move in the evening. If you have children, as we do, they are constantly growing out of their toys. My mother uses one of Jeff's old toy wagons to move plants to the glassed-in sun porch so they'll have a cool place to sleep.

Needless to say, some plants are more sensitive to temperature than others. If you are one of those people who feel that they must have all the rooms warm all the time, choose plants from among the tropicals and they'll enjoy living the way you do. Foliage plants will usually grow very well in most homes because these plants normally thrive on high temperatures. African violets like a warm room. They will grow well in a temperature of 65–70 degrees during the night and the same or even 10 degrees higher in the daytime. Keep these warmth-loving beauties out of cool rooms, especially at night.

If you prefer a cooler atmosphere for your family, choose from among such plants as hydrangea, cineraria, cyclamen, and primrose. These plants will not do their best in a high temperature. What they like is 65–75 degrees in the daytime and 55–60 degrees at night. These flowering plants will last much longer if you will put them in a cool location at night or turn down the thermostat so the house itself will be cool.

When plants are placed near windows you should take precautions against their freezing on cold nights. Pull down the venetian blinds, shades, or curtains, or place a layer of paper between the plants and the window. Heat radiates from the plant leaves to the cold glass, and this causes a chilling of the leaves. African violets are particularly sensitive to this type of chilling. Forgetting to keep a check on the outside temperature can be painful to you and your plants.

Another extremely bad position for a house plant—and one that's just as harmful as a chilling window—is near a source of heat. Don't put plants near radiators or hot-air vents. If you do, the leaves will dry out and the plants will quickly take on a very unsightly appearance.

Fumes from manufactured gas and coal combustion may also injure house plants. If you have this kind of heating, some ventilation with fresh air will probably be most helpful.

Light

The amount of light needed by different varieties of plants varies quite a lot. Some do well in partial shade, others require full sunlight to thrive. Also, the light-heat balance is important. Sometimes a plant does not get enough light to balance the heat it is subjected to, and it gets leggy. Of course, using indoor lighting—growing plants under fluorescent light—will alleviate this problem to some extent, and I will go into that later.

Part of the answer is simply to grow shade-loving plants such as the very popular African violets, but many people want to grow other species as well. There are so many plants to choose from that it is difficult to lay down hard-and-fast rules—the best I can do is offer suggestions.

Generally speaking, all flowering plants—with the exception of African violets—will do best if given full light, especially during the winter if you hope to have them blossom. Tropical foliage plants, like rex begonias, are at their best in partial light.

In my Grandma Putt's day it wasn't unusual for a house to have a bay window, a sort of glassed-in outward extension of the room which was an ideal place for growing most of the house plants that were popular then. Here they were cooler and—most important—received good light. The present-day descendant of the bay window is the picture window. If you are fortunate enough to have such an area that receives good light for at least a portion of the day, it is an ideal spot for a windowsill garden.

A windowsill was in all probability the first spot that the first grower of house plants chose when he decided to bring a few plant friends in from the out of doors to brighten the house during the cooler months of the year. It is still a good place to start your indoor garden if you will remember a few do's and don'ts.

Many of the plants that thrive best in our homes are natives of warm or even tropical climates. They will do well in partial shade because their native environment is the jungle floor, which is shaded by trees. They also like the warmth and moisture that the tropical climate provided. To have them do well for us we must reproduce these conditions as nearly as possible. Such plants, of many different species, have common needs and will usually do well if grouped together.

For a north window, with no other than natural light available, you can expect to be reasonably successful with grape ivy, philodendron, African violets, dieffenbachia, wandering Jew, English ivy, and piggyback plant.

For a south window choose flowering plants such as geraniums, amaryllis, and fibrous-rooted begonias. Cactus will do well here and so will brilliant-leaved coleus. Coleus, by the way, will

Dracaena Fragrans massangeana
Corn Plant

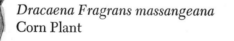

Ficus elastica
Rubber Plant

Dracaena sanderiana
Sander's Dracaena

root readily as softwood cutting, or slips, and this particularly beautiful plant may be easily increased.

If your most convenient window is exposed to the east or west, choose some of the fancy-leaved caladiums, whose attractive foliage is their most outstanding asset. Rubber plants will do well here as well as ferns, palms, dracaena, or aluminum plant.

If you don't happen to have a large picture window, or even if you do, you can often manage to get an attractive window display or indoor garden effect by utilizing plant stands or racks. Grow your plants on progressively smaller tiers, with the largest almost touching the floor and the smallest even with the windowsill. Be sure to place the light-loving plants at the top where they will receive the most sun.

This effect may also be achieved by using a plant cart, which has the added advantage of mobility. If necessary, during the day you can wheel the cart to whatever window happens to be receiving the best sun, and at night you can move it into a cool portion of the house. This will enable your plants to get the light they need during the day and the complementary darkness and coolness they need at night. Most plants need 10-12 hours of light each day. They also require the night's darkness. You know how you feel when you don't get your proper rest at night. Similarly, a good night's sleep in darkness will keep your plants fresher-looking for a longer period of time.

In summary, it's safe to say that all plants—especially flowering house plants—can use all the light they can get, so long as they are not scorched by the heat from the light source, whether it's sunlight or artificial light, and provided they also receive a good night's sleep in darkness.

Creating a Moist Climate in Your Home

I know I've said this before, but I can't emphasize too strongly that moisture in the atmosphere of your home will benefit both the plants and you. How do we go about creating this moist climate in our homes? That will depend to a great degree on the various species of house plants you have decided to grow.

With some plants you can create the proper moist atmosphere by spraying the foliage once a day. (This practice does not, however, apply to African violets. They don't like moisture on their leaves.) Another way to supply moisture is to use a galvanized iron pan about two inches deep, filled with pebbles on which the pots can be placed. Put enough water in the pan to barely cover the bottom surface. If you water your plants in this way, there is little danger of overwatering and making the soil too soggy, because the evaporation of the surplus water from the pebbles will keep the humidity higher. And if the pots are of porous clay, they will be able to absorb some of the moisture from the pebbles as well.

If you have a hot-air furnace, you can increase the humidity, or the amount of moisture, in the air by making sure that the water reservoir attached to the furnace is always filled with water. In the winter, when the furnace is burning continuously, you may need to fill the reservoir at least once a day—possibly more often. If you live in an older home or apartment, there are specially constructed galvanized pans that can be placed on the backs or tops of radiators. These, filled with water, will add a great deal of moisture to the air. If you have nothing else, use a bread pan or a cake tin. Fill it with water and set the plants on pebbles or bricks—something to keep the bottoms of the pots from being in contact with the water.

A metal tray of gravel and water placed on a windowsill will serve a double purpose. It can hold your plants and increase the humidity. If you happen to own an electric kettle, you might try letting it steam away in the plant room a couple of times a day. I remember that when I was a youngster living with my Grandma Putt, she had a kettle steaming all day long during the winter months. Ilene and I use the children's vaporizer for this purpose.

Probably the best way to be really sure that you and your plants are receiving the correct amount of moisture is to use a mechanical or electrical humidifier. This appliance will usually solve the problem once and for all. Humidifiers are generally not expensive, and since they will benefit the rest of the family as much as the plants, they are a good investment.

Time out for the Water Bucket

Perhaps the most misunderstood and worst performed indoor-gardening chore is watering. All plants need water to live and flourish. They lose water through their leaves regularly by a process called transpiration. So in order for them to produce a good root system it's very important to keep soil at their feet moist. With such a system they will be able to replace the water they lose through the leaves. Having an adequate supply of water available to the plants at their roots is an excellent way to offset the effects of low humidity in your house. The soluble portions of the soil will be more readily dissolved in this soil water, so that it can be more easily absorbed by the roots, and later by the entire plant.

Proper watering may be compared to the proper way to feed children. After a while you'll be able to establish a regular schedule and your plants will thrive on this regularity. Of course the schedule will vary from season to season, so you'll want to adjust it as the needs of your plants change at different times of the year or in periods of heavy growth or rest.

Lack of water at proper intervals will cause your plants to starve and wilt, and this will eventually result in hardening and woodiness of the tissues. On the other hand, too much water will reduce proper aeration of the soil and cause root injury. The ladies, bless 'em, are probably the worst offenders when it comes to overwatering. They literally kill their plants with kindness, often watering them every day.

Oxygen is just as necessary for the proper functioning of the roots as water. When you overwater, the soil cavities become saturated and there is no place for the oxygen. Then the roots will decay, and it will soon become apparent even to the most inexperienced gardener that the plant is in trouble. Because of this, never allow your plants to stand in water all the time.

Once you get to know your plants, you'll see that some of them require more water than others. Slow-growing plants such as aspidistras, sansevierias and Christmas and Thanksgiving cacti require far less water than such rapid growers as begonias, cinerarias, ferns, fuchsias, and the palms. If any of your plants come from a desert region—and this will include many of the succulents and cacti—they will need less water than those whose ancestors originated in a tropical rain forest. These plants have spent the past several thousand years adapting themselves to the necessity of getting by with almost no water at all and they will quickly rot in a too moist environment. I will deal with their special watering requirements in another chapter.

Easy-care geraniums will get along quite well with a good watering or soaking only once a week. Too much water is likely to cause them to grow leggy and be very stingy with their blooms.

Consider your plants as individual friends even if they are of the same species or even the same color within the species. Plants do have different characteristics and needs just as much as people, and you will probably notice that their shape, leaves, and blossoms are quite variable; their need for water may differ also.

Watering, then, will depend on many factors—the type of plant, the type of soil it grows in, the season of the year and the atmospheric conditions under which it is being grown. Knowing when to water, what kind of water to use, how much to use, and how often to water are very critical. But don't let all this discourage you. Just remember that most gardeners are made, not born, and knowledge and skill sometimes evolve slowly—but they do evolve. Here are some helpful tips to help you with your watering.

The actual water you use should be considered. Rainwater or melted snow is very desirable. My Grandma Putt used to keep a rain barrel for collecting the high-nitrogen-charged water provided by old Jupiter Pluvius. With the current interest in collecting antiques, you may find a rain barrel outside a useful conversation piece. Your plants will bloom with appreciation!

If rainwater is unavailable, using distilled water is a good idea, especially if your tap water contains a high concentration of soluble salts. (Since plants don't have teeth, they don't need the fluoride.) Also, use water defrosted from your refrigerator or collected from a dehumidifier for watering your plants.

If you must use tap water, place a layer of agricultural charcoal—which you can buy at any dime store—over the top of the soil in the pot. This will filter out such additives as chlorine and fluoride. In winter, water from the cold-water tap may be colder than you realize. It's a good idea to let it stand until it reaches room temperature, or to use half cold and half hot water.

Give your plants a beer every now and then if possible.

After a party or backyard picnic at which you've served beer, collect leftover beer in the cans and let it stand overnight. Then mix ten parts of water to one part of beer and water your plants with the potion. Believe me, they'll really appreciate the pick-me-up—and one nice thing is they won't be driving after drinking!

In most cases it really doesn't matter whether you water a plant from the top or allow the water to rise from a saucer through a hole in the bottom of the pot. As a matter of fact, changing the procedure sometimes can be a good idea. It helps make sure that the whole soil mass is moist. It also helps avoid the buildup of a layer of soluble salts on the very top surface of the soil. These buildups can block out needed oxygen.

Some pots have an automatic watering wick in the bottom, and these save you work and are also practical if you must be away from home for a short period of time. Just make sure to check the wick occasionally, and do add water to the surface of the soil at least twice a month.

For the times when you have to leave your plants for a period of a week or so, you can make your own automatic waterer that will handle a number of plants at the same time. Just place several plants in a circle on a table or counter top. Water them thoroughly. Then place a large fruit-juice can full of water in the center of the circle. Cut a clothesline wick, making sure to fray both ends, for each plant. Saturate the wicks with water and run them from the water can to the soil surface of the plants. As the plants need more water they will draw it through the wicks.

In watering, the actual pot itself has to be considered. Small pots dry out faster than large pots, and moisture will evaporate more quickly from clay pots than plastic ones. If the plant is a rapid grower and the pot dries out too quickly, you should consider repotting. Also, think of where the pot will be placed in your home. At floor level a plant may need less water than one placed on a stand. A hanging basket will probably need more water than either type.

Should you use those automatic watering pots that are available at garden centers? Well, it's up to you. The gadget consists of a pot with a glass wick or tube. This wick hangs in a reservoir of water and enables the water from the reservoir to moisten the soil. Louise Riotte, who has one of the best house plant collections I know of, says this method of watering is good for many plants, especially African violets. It is also good for starting seed.

If you don't want to use an automatic watering method, use your own good common sense. Keep the soil just moist enough so your plants won't wilt, but not so moist that growth becomes exceedingly active. To begin with, try watering thoroughly just once a week. Check every day to be sure the plant is not wilting. If the plant appears to be in good condition when the week is up even though the soil is quite dry, water again.

One of the best investments you can make is an inexpensive one. Purchase a sprayer that can be used for watering fragile plants or misting pesticides. Most plants enjoy a morning shower and a kind word, which will get you both off to a good start for the day.

Twice a month give your plants a bath—whether they need it or not. Use warm water with a small amount of soap (biodegradable dishwashing liquid is best—1 tablespoon to a half gallon of water). Wash the leaves top and bottom to remove any dust or grime that is stopping up the pores. Mix a tiny amount of mild tea into your plants' bath or shower water. According to old-timers, it will give the leaves strength and a deeper color. The soap and tea-and-water mixture will act as a surfactant on the surface of the leaves, making it easier for the plant to breathe and carry on photosynthesis.

Grandma Putt used to laugh at her contemporaries who would wash the leaves of their foliage house plants with milk. She was right. Milk, "plant wax," and all the other so-called leaf cleaners combined don't do as much for your plants as an occasional soap-and-water bath. Use a liquid detergent, about a tablespoon to a half gallon of water, and wash the leaves top and bottom. Foliage plants breathe through their leaves so don't let them get all clogged up with dust. Hairy-leaved plants can be "dusted" with a soft-bristled paint brush, they don't like water on their leaves. Getting back to the "bath," do this about once every two or three weeks unless your home gets extra dusty. In between regular bathing, you might give them a quick whisk with a dampened paper towel to freshen their little faces. When you give your plants their morning shower make sure that you have the water at room temperature and that the mist is gentle. I carry my plants right into the bathroom and turn on a nice mist. Plants are like people, and they generally don't like a shower that's all icy needles. Most garden centers and nursery-supply houses have misters available that release an aerosol-type mist when you apply fingertip pressure.

The atmosphere of the room where a plant lives has an important bearing on the amount of time between waterings. If the room is excessively dry, there will be greater evaporation from the surfaces of the leaves and more water will be needed at the roots to overcome the low humidity.

After the thorough soaking mentioned above, don't water again until the soil becomes dry. Wetting just the top of the soil frequently is like snacking or "noshing" between meals with cookies and candy. Your plant children will suffer just as your own youngsters would, and you won't be happy either.

You can make many of your plants happy by giving them a steam bath every once in a while. Just place a brick or wooden block in the middle of a bucket and place the plant on it. Then add steaming water to the bottom of the container. Don't let the water touch the pot or the plant. Allow the plant to relax and luxuriate in this improvised Turkish bath, or sauna, for five or six minutes, then return it to its favorite spot, refreshed and happy.

And here is another hint. When watering your plants, place a small flat stone or a plastic bottle cap on the top of the soil and let the stream of water strike the stone. Do this slowly so the water will not splash off in all directions if the pot is small. This method will prevent holes being made in the soil, thus exposing the fine hairlike roots close to the surface.

Always remember that it's a good idea to have a nice little chat with your plants every day. They should never be allowed to wilt because of need for water. If you just take the time to talk with each of them a minute or so each morning or afternoon you'll always know when they're ready to be watered. When water *is* needed, do the watering thoroughly. For most plants the way to do this is to saturate, then to allow the surplus to drain away before putting the plant back in its accustomed place. And the best time of day to water your plants is early morning. But whatever time of day you choose, just be sure that the excess water is drained away. Don't ever let any of your house plants stand with their little feet in mud or water over a long period of time.

If you have been careful about all the watering points I have raised and your plants still seem to be suffering from a soggy condition, check to make sure the drainage vents in the pot are not clogged. Sometimes, if you don't repot a plant after you bring it home, you won't realize that no crock shards have been placed in the bottom of the pot for drainage. As you begin to notice that the plant soil stays soggy too long after watering, remove the plant and clean out the pot. If it doesn't need a larger pot, put in some broken potsherds (pieces of a broken clay pot, or pebbles, or bits of broken brick). Now put the plant back into the pot. Water if necessary, and check to see that the drainage is working.

Feeding

A secondary consideration, but an important one, in plant care is proper feeding. Potted plants obviously can't reach out their roots beyond the allotted space of their containers, and sometimes they try desperately to maintain their health in a state of semi-starvation. If you want them to keep up their health and good looks, you'd better start them on a regular feeding program. They need feeding just as much as anyone else in the family, though fortunately not as often. Fish emulsion is an excellent fertilizer for foliage plants. Use it as directed on the label and work out a regular schedule.

Now that I've made you thoroughly miserable by taking up all these little nit-picking details, I'd like to say some comforting words. Actually, watering plants isn't all that much of a big deal. Just remember that plants are a whole lot like people. When you get thirsty, your mouth and throat feel dry, so you take a drink. A plant is much like you. Its soil gets dry, and if this goes on too long, its thirst will be reflected in its leaves and blossoms. After it has been watered, it will be as refreshed as you feel after taking that first thirst-quenching drink.

Plants do have definite personalities, and there is no doubt that we grow fonder of some than others—just the way we get to feel about people. Do our plants know this? I believe they do and that they respond to us in the same way. I believe they have feeling and will produce better (fruit or blossoms or prettier foliage) for someone they like. And they may even pout and become stubborn if they build up a dislike.

When you are in close contact with people, animals, or plants you become sensitive to each other. They grow accustomed to your way of caring for them, the little daily routines of feeding and watering. Soon they will adjust to your way and come to depend on it. You will notice that when you perform your chores with gentleness and affection your plants will almost react positively. Believe me, your plants will grow best in a feeling of mutual love and friendship.

As you continue to take care of your plants this mutual respect and love begins to increase. You will learn their language and begin to interpret their needs—they will be constantly telling you something by the way they look and act. No one who sees a plant wilting and bending over can fail to realize it is suffering, or that a perky, upstanding one, whether in bloom or not, is happy.

As time goes on, you and your plants will prosper and you will gain a reputation as a knowledgeable green-thumber. Your plants will have confidence in you. I think this is especially true of gift plants, for they are nearly always a gift from a loved one to a loved one. With that kind of an auspicious beginning the atmosphere is cordial to begin with, and likely to continue that way. I believe that plants, like children, feel this and grow best in a happy home.

3

Gifts That Go On Giving:
Flowering Pot Plants

As I have said earlier, good gardeners are made, not born. Most of us find out the secrets of growing house plants through experience. But while it is true that experience is the best teacher, it can also be a very high-salaried one. I hope that in the next few pages I can save you from making some of the more common mistakes with the house plants you have just bought or received as gifts.

Like most of us, plants can't live on love alone, though admittedly it helps. If the giver as well as the gift means a lot to you, that Christmas, birthday, or anniversary plant is going to receive all the TLC you can shower on it. The question is: How, and how much? Let's consider those key questions in terms of some of the most common gift plants—the flowering pot plants.

POINSETTIAS

Just about everybody who thinks of giving a plant for Christmas thinks first of poinsettias. Florists know this and prepare well in advance, because they know this favorite will probably never go out of style. New colors have been developed, and while red may always be the greatest in demand, we can now choose from varying shades of white, pink, and even marbled.

Poinsettias can be enjoyed longer if a few simple suggestions for their care are faithfully followed. Check the soil every day, and water when it feels dry to the touch. Don't allow it to dry out completely—or remain soaked. Quite likely the poinsettia you

Euphorbia pulcherrima
Poinsettia

received is all beribboned and in a fancy foil-covered pot. If so, check to be sure the drainage hole is not plugged. Do this by poking a wire or long nail into the hole at the bottom. If it hits something hard, that's fine. If you strike nothing but soft earth you are in trouble. Water the plant carefully, and when time permits, repot it correctly. You'll find easy-to-follow instructions on how to do this in a later chapter. If everything is all right (lucky you!), place your plant near a warm, sunny window, but don't let it touch the glass. Keep your poinsettia away from any extreme of heat or cold and out of drafts.

All this care is a lot more worth while than it used to be back in the old days when poinsettias were just poinsettias. Now the one you receive is very likely to be a hybrid, one of the long-lasting type that may still retain its colorful bracts well into late spring. The multiflowered poinsettia plant is now in vogue. By following a program of pinching off new growth and treating with a growth retardant, you can keep these plants looking beautiful far longer than the older type, but you must do your part too.

If the plant continues to do well and you still find it a pleasure to behold, feed it a soluble fertilizer after a month or so. When the day finally comes that you find you and your plant are getting a little tired of each other, you can prepare to enjoy it for another season by doing this. Stop watering the plant and wait for the leaves to fall off. Then store it in a cool, dry place where it can rest undisturbed. In the spring, water it again and cut the stems back to six inches. Keep the stems pinched back as new leaves begin to form. From early October until blooming starts, place the plant in a dark closet (without a single flash of light) for twelve hours each day (8 P.M. until 8 A.M.) and keep it in a sunny window for the other twelve hours of the day. Fertilize during active growth with either dry or soluble garden food.

Believe me, it's twice as nice to see that Christmas gift blooming back at you the second year!

CHRYSANTHEMUMS

Chrysanthemums are another favorite gift plant, and with good reason. They are usually the longest-lasting flowering house plants. Another reason they have become so popular is that there are so many color choices now available.

Keep your plant in a good light—be sure it's getting enough sunshine—and in the coolest spot you have. Night temperatures of 60–65 degrees are especially important to chrysanthemums, and one way to give the plant a cooler atmosphere is to set it on the floor when you go to bed. Just make sure that it's not in a draft.

Water your chrysanthemums well and frequently—about every other day, or when the soil becomes dry. If the plant is in a soilless medium (some are now grown that way), give it a soluble fertilizer feeding after it's been in your home for about a month. This is a plant that enjoys a daily spray with water or a mister. Keeping its leaves clean will make it prettier and more comfortable.

After your plant has bloomed, cut it back to about eight inches and keep it moist but not wet. Hardy varieties can be planted outside, but many are tender and must be planted in well-protected spots and covered closely if you intend to carry them over the winter.

AZALEAS

Azaleas—both single and semidouble varieties—are popular gift plants. The color choices range from white through pink to deep red. Some new varieties are salmon-colored or orange.

You'll have better luck in keeping your azaleas if you will remove the foil or other gift covering from the pot and submerge the pot in a pan of water every other day for fifteen to twenty minutes and then allow it to drain. These plants like a cool, moist environment, so spray the foliage with water three or four times a week.

Azaleas need bright light but not strong sun. The soil should be evenly moist, and the temperature should be kept between 55 and 65 degrees. Again, this may mean putting them on the floor at night or in a cooler room.

To get azaleas to bloom another year is not the easiest gardening job you'll ever tackle, but it can be done. They need a cool treatment of around 40 degrees for a period of about six weeks. A specific plant climate of this sort is not easy to create in a home atmosphere, but if the plant means a lot to you and you want to try, here's how. Give the plant a chance to replenish its strength after it has finished blooming. In the summer set the pot in the ground in semishade where it is protected from hot, drying winds. Water it regularly and feed with special fertilizer for acid-loving plants. Bring it inside in the early fall and place it in a cool, light place, keeping the soil moist but not wet. When buds show activity, provide more sun, water, and fertilizer.

EASTER LILIES

Lilies like it cool, so keep your plant well out of the sun and check it daily to see if the soil is drying out. When your lily seems sandy on the top of its soil, water well, being sure the pot drains properly.

To keep it looking neat, remove blossoms as they fade and pinch out the yellow anthers as new buds open. After the last blossom falls, you should still keep your plant watered and in good light. Eventually it will die down. When the weather warms up, plant it outside in a sunny place.

If you want to try to get your lily to bloom again indoors, plant the bulb in a pot with only two inches of soil beneath the bulb. Place it in an unheated place (garage or shed) until December, then bring it indoors to a temperature of no more than 60 degrees.

HYDRANGEAS

Hydrangeas will bloom for a long time if you keep them well watered and out of the direct sun. Water at least twice a day or submerge the pot in a pan of water daily and then drain. After your plant has finished blooming, cut back all the stems with flowers and then plant it in your garden in a shady spot. The stems that have not bloomed will often produce blooms during the summer.

If you bring the plant back inside for winter, cut it back severely after it has bloomed and repot in fresh planter mix. Keep it in full sun and give it a great deal of water, feeding it with fish tablets once a week.

CYCLAMENS

If someone presents you with a cyclamen, you really have a plant worthy of cherishing. It is not a difficult plant to keep and care for despite its reputation of being hard to grow. Experienced growers keep it in a temperature range of 50–60 degrees and in a place where the humidity is high. Because these conditions are difficult to duplicate in the average home, many of these great-looking plants die very quickly after being received from the florist.

If you want to prolong your pleasure and extend your cyclamen's life, keep it in a cool, bright place. Pay particular attention to giving it a cool temperature at night—about 55 degrees. This will enable it to stand a warmer 70 degrees in the daytime, so you both can be comfortable. When your plant needs watering, stand the pot in a basin of water until the top of the soil shows dampness, then allow it to drain. Cyclamens will do best in an eastern exposure. Given good care, these beauties may continue to bloom —often from Christmas until May.

Keep in mind when growing cyclamens, as well as other gift plants, that they are really what you might call florists' plants. They were grown in well-lighted greenhouses under ideal conditions of temperature and humidity. Duplicating these hothouse conditions at home is not always possible even for the most experienced and knowledgeable gardener.

If your cyclamen fails, don't lose heart. If you like these plants well enough to try again, you might consider the alternative possibilities of raising them from corms or seeds. These two methods can be very interesting and are far less expensive than buying new full-grown plants. Whether you buy corms or plant the cyclamen seeds, the potting mix will be the same. Corms will bloom within a few months, seeds the following year. Both should be planted in August if possible. If this is not convenient, they may be started at any time during the summer.

Use 5- or 6-inch pots for corms, with plenty of drainage material and a rich soil. Cyclamens are natives of the Near East, tender plants that enjoy a mixture of garden loam, sand, and leaf mold in about equal parts. A little fine charcoal will help keep the mixture sweet. Firm the soil and plant the corms so they are about half within the soil and half above it. Place the pots in a shady window and keep the soil just moist.

If you plant seed, the soil should be sterilized. You can do this and be a gourmet cook at the same time. Place the soil you intend to use for potting in an aluminum cake pan. On top of the soil place an Idaho potato, and set the oven at 200 degrees. When the potato is baked tender, the bad guys in the soil will be finished. Eat the potato for dinner and then go about your potting chores. After the soil is cool, moisten the soil and the pot by standing it in water. Allow to drain off before planting the seeds. Sow them thinly, about an inch apart, and cover lightly.

As I've said many times in my horticultural life, all growing success is dependent on the three P's—practice, patience, and persistence. In this case you'll have to be patient, as the germination of seedlings is often irregular. But once up, they transplant easily. You can pot them when they are about two inches high. Keep them in a cool, shady place and do not overwater.

An important thing to remember about cyclamens is never to water in the center of the plant. Lift the leaves and water around the edges of the pot. The corms should be kept dry.

These plants should not be fed until just shortly before the flower buds begin to appear, then give them a feeding by watering with weak liquid manure. At flowering time, sprinkle the soil with a good general house plant fertilizer; do not get any of this on the corms. Generally speaking, all flowering plants are working at their hardest when they are in bloom. This is the time when they need a little more food.

When your cyclamens cease flowering, the leaves will begin to turn yellow. Many people who see this mistakenly believe their plants are dying. Actually, it is just a signal—in flower language—that the plant wants to rest. Clean away all the dead growth from the corms and reduce the water supply. Around the end of May, cease watering the plant entirely and expose the corms to full light until about the first of August. At this time watering should begin again. When you notice young leaves developing, repot in the next size container and return the plants to their favorite windowsill.

GLOXINIAS

Gloxinias are a distant relative of the African violet but are much more flamboyant. They have large velvety flowers in many deep dramatic colors. With proper care they will last for months. The tubers can be saved for repotting. Gloxinias should never be placed directly in the sun. They do best in an east or west window. Keep the soil uniformly moist. This is best done by setting the pot in a pan of water and letting it seep upward. If you must water from the top, don't wet the foliage.

Gloxinia

Most of the gloxinias you buy at the florist will be two-year-old plants, raised from seed or cuttings, but older tubers may be grown for many years. These plants are tropical and you should never put them where the temperature will drop below 50 degrees. The best growing medium for gloxinias consists of equal parts of peat and good soil into which should be mixed a little well-decomposed manure and a little sand. Shake the tubers free of the old soil in February or March and place them in a shallow box on a bed of peat moss and sand, but do not cover them completely.

The gloxinia tubers, kept in a humid atmosphere and at a minimum temperature of 65 degrees, will soon root, and when the shoots are about one inch in length the tubers should be potted separately. Use 5- or 6-inch pots, and set the tubers so their tops are level with the soil. This should be about three-fourths of an inch below the rims to allow space for watering. Keep the soil moist but not waterlogged. Never wet the leaves, but a moist atmosphere for these plants is essential. Apply liquid fertilizer when the flower buds start forming.

Gloxinias are propagated by seeds and cuttings of shoots and leaves as well as by division of the old tubers. You may want to try some of these possibilities if you have an especially beautiful gift plant.

4

A Greening of America: Small Foliage Plants

Philodendron oxycardium
Philodendron

Back in the 1930s, a Florida nurseryman discovered that the tropical heart-leaved philodendron (*P. oxycardium*) could be an ideal house plant—one that required little care, little light and gave more than a little beauty to the part of the home where it was placed. In the three and a half decades since, commercial growers have searched the world over to bring back attractive and house-hardy small foliage plants suitable for growing in homes or apartments. Because flowering plants have limited blooming periods and life spans indoors, more and more folks are finding out that small foliage plants are in many ways more practical for indoor cultivation. These plants come in so many shapes, sizes, leaf patterns and color shadings that you can easily find specimens to add interest and beauty to any indoor location.

Availability Is No Problem

Today, the availability of good-quality small foliage house plants is so widespread that the shopper can't enter an antique shop, bookstore, dime store, ladies' boutique, gift shop or supermarket without facing an inviting array of plants arranged and integrated with the more expected merchandise. In addition, stores other than traditional florist shops that deal exclusively in foliage plants have sprung up in almost every city block and suburban shopping center. Names like "Mother Earth," "The Greenery," "The Plant Orphanage," "Deborah's Garden," etc., etc., cast their eye-catching lures to catch every house plant fancier who happens by! These shop owners have found they have little or no trouble keeping foliage plants green and healthy in even the darkest corners of their stores. In the past two or three years, sales of these plants have boomed beyond the wildest hopes of most commercial growers. It seems safe to say that the small foliage house plant is an idea whose time has come!

There are hundreds of types and varieties of attractive small foliage plants being sold today. Each year, more and more are discovered and placed on the market. Here are a few of the most popular.

BABY'S TEARS OR PADDY'S WIG

Helxine solieroli is known by a number of common names including "creeping nettle." It makes an interesting addition to your small foliage plant collection with its densely matted, tiny green leaves on creeping stems. Baby's Tears may be grown in pots, terrariums or hanging baskets. It requires high humidity and a fast-draining or sandy soil.

BOXWOODS

Boxwoods are good growers both outdoors and in. They prefer a cool location with temperatures in the high 60s during the day and five to ten degrees cooler at night. The thick shiny foliage grows quite slowly and can be kept pruned to the size and shape you desire. Plant in 8-inch pots in porous soil that is fairly fast-draining. Feed in the spring with a 5–10–5 fertilizer.

Buxus microphylla
Japanese Boxwood

COLEUS

Anyone who thinks green is the only color choice available in small foliage plants has only to be exposed to these colorful members of the mint family to have his mind changed for him! You can find coleus specimens with green-and-pink leaves or various combinations of yellow, maroon, red, and dark purple. Coleus adapts well to both outdoor and indoor cultivation. Inside, the plants require a bright, sunny location but have been known to do quite well in curtain-filtered sunlight. Temperatures should range from the low 60s at night to the mid-70s during the day. These plants are fast growers, and to keep them to the size and shape you prefer, pinch off the tips of the stems where new growth occurs.

CROTONS

Crotons, members of the Codiaeum family, have been popular foliage plants for a long time because of the unusual shapes and color blends of their leaves. They need high humidity and warm temperatures (into the 80s). They should be kept out of drafts because they are susceptible to leaf drop. Plant in soil composed of half sand and half organic material (leaf mold or humus). Keep soil moist at all times. Give plants four to eight hours of sunlight per day. Feed sparingly, in the spring and fall only. These are fast growers; keep well pruned or they will grow too large.

Codiaeum variegatum
Croton

Fittonia verschaffeltii
Red Fittonia

FITTONIA

This low, ground-hugging creeper, with its pretty green leaves, veined white, is a decorative and exceptionally appropriate plant to use as a table centerpiece. The flower of Fittonia is a white spike that arises erect from the creeping plant, and many think it resembles the rattle of a rattlesnake. Don't let this put you off—Fittonia is an attractive, silver-green plant that's pretty enough for any indoor landscape. Grow Fittonia in a low bowl and it will add a note of elegance to the most simple setting.

This plant needs a little pampering and will want higher humidity than is normally found in our warm rooms. If the air is too dry, it may react by dropping its leaves. Fittonia is an excellent plant for terrariums. It grows best in one part potting soil, one part leaf mold, one part sand and a half teaspoon of superphosphate fertilizer. It requires warm daytime temperatures of 75 degrees and above and nighttime temperatures down to 65 degrees. Place in a north window on a shallow tray with pebbles and water to provide humidity. Propagation is by cuttings.

KENTIA PALM

This is an elegant, graceful house plant that does well in indirect sunlight—a north or east exposure is ideal. Palms are

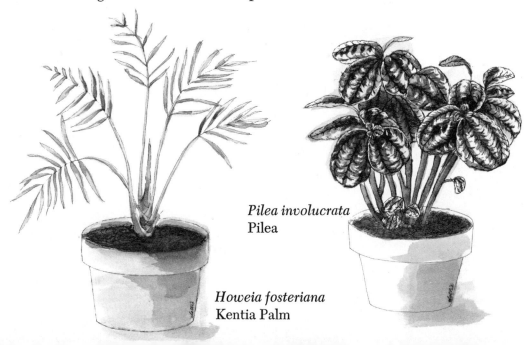

Pilea involucrata
Pilea

Howeia fosteriana
Kentia Palm

easy to grow, but many people overwater them and the poor results give them the idea that they require special care. Simply pot
them in a rich potting mixture, water well once a week, and you'll
find this rapid grower a delightful addition to your home. Spray
with a mister once a week to keep it in tip-top condition.

PILEAS

Plants in the Pilea species include the popular aluminum plant
(or watermelon plant), Creeping Charlie and the South American
Friendship plant. Most pileas grow no more than a foot tall. They
require bright, curtain-filtered sunlight and a humid atmosphere.
Keep the soil moist at all times. The aluminum, or watermelon,
plant is so called because the leaves are striped like a watermelon
and the lighter portions have the color of aluminum paint. They
grow to about 10 inches. Creeping Charlie (*P. nummulariaefolia*)
is a tender perennial with creeping stems, not to be confused with
Lysimachia nummularia of the Primrose family. The bronze-
leaved South American friendship plant grows about a foot tall, is
colorful and easy to grow.

PEPEROMIA

These members of the Pepper family make ideal small foliage
specimens for indoor growers. Most types grow no more than 6–10

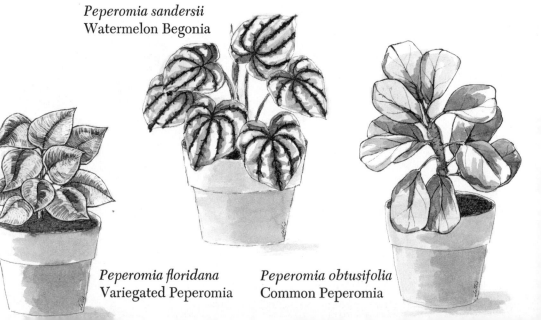

Peperomia sandersii
Watermelon Begonia

Peperomia floridana
Variegated Peperomia

Peperomia obtusifolia
Common Peperomia

inches tall and the leaves range from 1 to 2 inches. Place in a bright location or in a room with white walls, which will reflect light. Peperomias will grow well in any general-purpose potting soil (see Baker Mix #1). Water thoroughly only when the soil is dry to the touch. The most popular small foliage peperomias include the watermelon peperomia (*P. sanderii*), emerald ripple (*P. caperata*) and blunt-leaved peperomia (*P. obtusifolia variegata*).

PHILODENDRON

Philodendrons are one of the few plant families known to millions of beginning gardeners by their Latin name. It's a paradox that these *large foliage* plants from tropical rain forests of Latin America have become the best-known and most often cultivated *small foliage* plants in North American homes and apartments. Those little darlings that you buy at the neighborhood dime store grow to huge proportions in their native tropical habitat. However, the dry, poorly lit conditions and cooler temperatures in most American homes keep the foliage small. Theoretically, all you have to do is to turn up the light, heat and humidity in order to create a monster that will eventually take over your home! Actually, most of the 225 or more varieties sold in this country are hybrids which have been developed to grow small leaves and to be house-hardy.

Philodendron dubium
Dubium

Philodendron hastatum
Philodendron

They may be trained to grow as trailers or climbers although many of the self-heading varieties make excellent self-supporting pot plants. The most popular types include: heart-leaved (*P. oxycardium*), velvet-leaved (*P. micans*) and *P. florida*, the Florida philodendron with leaves from 4 to 8 inches.

Philodendrons need moist, well-drained soil and will grow in almost any location where they get a little light and warmth. For best results, feed several times a year and keep in a warm, humid, well-lit location.

SCINDAPSUS

Plants often mistaken for philodendron and called under various common names like devil's ivy, ivy arum and pothos are all members of the genus Scindapsus. Like philodendron, the leaves are generally club-shaped or heart-shaped, and the plants seem to grow continuously under good conditions. They can be grown in pots or as climbers and trailers.

Despite their deceptive resemblance, scindapsus plants are completely unrelated to philodendrons and the foliage is generally much lighter and more mixed in color than philodendron leaves. Scindapsus plants require much less light (subdued or indirect light is fine) and need very little moisture. Water thoroughly, then allow the soil to become almost completely dry before rewatering. They should be placed in a warm, dry location.

Scindapsus aureus
Pothos

Syngonium (Arrow or arrowhead plant)

These very common and easy-to-grow house plants come from tropical America, where they reach enormous size. They can get to be pretty big even indoors, but most people cut them back to obtain new plants. The leaves are shaped like an arrowhead, or they are deeply lobed, with either three or five lobes. Two types are found in most plant stores—a solid green and a green-and-white variegated. Both do well in shade at normal room temperature. Syngoniums (sometimes sold under the name nephthytis) are often combined with other plants in planters. Use any good all-purpose potting soil. Syngoniums can also be grown for a time in water, but after a while they look a little pallid and bedraggled.

Wandering Jews

Inch plants and Wandering Jews are the common names of plants of the genus Tradescantia and the genus Zebrina. Although of different families, the plants are very similar to each other. They are creepers and their growth characteristic is that they seem to inch their way along. The plants are very easy to grow indoors or out, and very easy to propagate from stem cuttings. Perhaps this is why they have been popularly named Wandering Jews—because they have wandered into so many homes and gar-

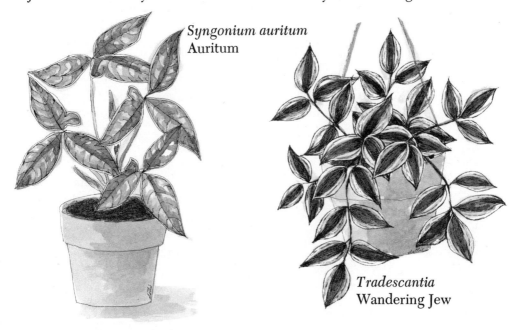

Syngonium auritum
Auritum

Tradescantia
Wandering Jew

dens! Tradescantia Wandering Jews have leaves that are 3 inches long when fully developed and about ¾ to 1 inch wide. The leaves are striped from stem to tip with alternate dark green and creamy green. The white velvet Wandering Jew (*T. sillamontana*) is an off white with a pale-green cast, with a velvet, or wooly, feel.

These plants do best when planted in a soil mix that contains equal parts of humus and sharp sand. They prefer homes where the daytime temperatures are kept slightly cool (by American standards)—in the high 60s. And they will enjoy temperatures down into the high 50s at night. They require bright indirect light. If your plants seem to be losing leaf color, increase the intensity of the light that reaches them. Water thoroughly then allow the soil to become dry before rewatering.

Wandering Jews of the Zebrina genus are also creepers, but the dark green stripes on the leaves alternate with pale stripes with a reddish purple or pinkish cast. They grow well in soil that's half sharp sand and half humusy loam. Zebrinas should be well watered and the soil kept slightly moist all the time. This is in contrast to the dry soil conditions preferred by Tradescantia. Zebrinas like indirect, bright light and slightly higher temperatures than the other types. Daylight temperatures in the high 70s and nighttime temperatures in the high 60s get the best results.

Let Your Foliage Plants Have a Little Light

People who grow plants indoors often keep the blinds drawn during the day as a precautionary measure to keep the sunlight from fading drapes and furniture. While I can sympathize with you ladies, this is not good for your plants. Leaf drop or yellowing of the leaves of house plants is a symptom of insufficient light and must be remedied in some manner or eventually the plant will die.

Arrange, if you can, for your indoor foliage plants to have a summer vacation outdoors. A change of scene works wonders.

Check the Water, Please

One way to check if these plants need water is with what I call the "dip-stick method." If the top of the soil seems dry, but you are not certain of the condition of the rest of the planting medium, slide a wooden stick down the interior side, like a dip-stick that helps check the oil level in your car. When it comes out, you can see how far the moist soil extends.

5

Hanging Gardens

There is something about a hanging basket that appeals to most house plant lovers. One that is well grown, with its trailing tendrils, often covered with flowers, can make a dramatic picture. These are the spellbinders of your indoor garden, and there are many places where they will look and do well.

A hanging basket adds a note of aristocratic elegance to an entryway or foyer. It can lighten up a breezeway, stairway, porch, or veranda. You can even attach one outdoors to a tree branch during the summer months. Suspend a hanging basket from the eaves or rafters and you have put it in an excellent position to enjoy light. Place it above the sunny windowsill where you have your plant garden and you have added another dimension to your arrangement.

There are bracket holders of all sorts for hanging baskets. They may be placed on walls and even hooked onto stairways. And containers for basket growing have come a long way from the old-fashioned type composed principally of wire and sphagnum moss in which plants seldom could be grown successfully outside of a greenhouse, where moisture and temperature could be controlled.

Various Types of Hanging Baskets

Many hanging baskets now come with separate liners, and some have attached interior saucers that permit watering so drainage can be handled without dripping. There are also clip-on saucers available for baskets not so equipped. Redwood baskets may be purchased in a number of different shapes and forms, and other containers are made of clay and fiber glass. The open-slatted redwood basket is the type most commonly used for growing orchids. This kind allows for sufficient air circulation without rapid loss of moisture. It is inexpensive and lightweight and well within an economical price range. Brass and copper containers are exceedingly handsome and often add decorative accents to a room. If you use them, consider liners of some type to make them more practical.

In some ways a plastic pot has more advantages for hanging plants than for ground-level plants. It will hold moisture longer than the traditional hanging baskets, and even during hot weather a thorough soaking once a day will often be all that is necessary. You can convert an ordinary plastic pot into a container for a hanging plant by attaching the wire forms that are available at most garden centers. Plastic containers are of a much lighter weight than clay and so much more easily handled.

If you like them, you can probably still obtain the old wire baskets. They are light and usually quite large. I don't recommend them, because they are inclined to dry out so quickly. During warm weather it may be necessary to add water as often as two or three times a day if you would keep the plants from wilting.

When it comes to size, don't select a small container for hanging plants, no matter what type of material it's made of. Small containers dry out too quickly when exposed to the warmth of the upper air in a room or when hung outside in the sun and wind. A heavy container will require a secure arrangement whether it's placed inside or outdoors. Remember, continually moistened soil will make it heavier, no matter how lightweight the material of the container. Give some consideration to this, especially if a basket is to be hung outdoors in summer in a location where it might be exposed to wind or sudden storm. If you live in an area where heavy thunderstorm activity is the norm, take your hanging basket down during that time of the year. I have seen wind and a hard rain do tremendous damage to delicate blossoms.

What to Plant

What should you plant in a hanging basket? Generally speaking, the best plan is to put plants of just one kind in each basket, but you can vary this by planting those having like soil culture and soil requirements. For instance, the combinations of ivy and white marguerites or geraniums and trailing white petunias give pretty effects. Or try plants of the same species but of different colors.

Plants suitable for hanging include ivy, geraniums, tuberous begonias, lantana, and fuchsia. Others you might like are Christmas or Thanksgiving cactus, wandering Jew, and spider plant. If you don't like the looks of a flowering plant after it has bloomed, pot it up—if you still want to keep it—and put it somewhere else. Replace it with a foliage plant such as golden archangel or zebrina or even a lush fern. Ferns make excellent hanging plants and, depending on the variety chosen, are among the easiest to care for. One of my favorite hangers is lavender. It is especially nice in a bathroom for keeping the room smelling fresh.

If you have extra annual plants well started in your seedbed, here is a place to use some of them. Annuals with a trailing growth will look well in hanging baskets and should bloom long enough to make them worth while. Annual possibilities include trailing petunias, sweet alyssum, trailing nasturtiums, or ivy-leaved geraniums.

Whatever you plan to grow in a hanging basket, be sure it is suitable for this type of culture and has a trailing characteristic of growth. Many plants of the same species now come both upright and trailing, and a mistake could prove embarrassing to both you and the plant—so check first. Another point to consider carefully is the proper height for your hanging basket. If it is too far above eye level it may defeat your purpose, as it will not be readily seen. If you place it too low a taller member of the family may have to duck to get by it. I'm kinda tall, so I know what a pain this can get to be!

Proper Soil, Watering, and Feeding

If you buy your hanging basket already growing, it will be supplied with the correct potting soil. If you pot up the plants yourself—which you will probably do when the first plants are spent—it's good to know just how to do this. In general, you should follow the same rules given for house plants of similar requirements. Plants with fibrous roots—roots having many fine hairlike growths—such as fuchsias and tuberous begonias, need a soil well supplied with humus. Make a mixture of equal parts of fine sand, compost (leaf mold or peat moss), and good garden soil. Add to this a small amount of fertilizer and mix all the ingredients well. This is also a good mixture for ferns of all kinds, many of which are acid-loving plants.

Hanging baskets need feeding on a regular schedule. If you buy your hanging basket already planted and ready to hang, find out from your florist the correct plant food for that particular species or planting. This additional care, administered every two or three weeks, will help make its stay in your home mutually enjoyable.

Now for the watering. This is something you've got to plan for. Get yourself a three-step ladder or step stool and a long-beaked watering can. If you want to water in a way that will eliminate dripping, use ice cubes. Place three or four cubes around the edge of the hanging container. When I first learned about this method I had my reservations, but my mother has been using it for years without any harm to her plants, so I know it works, and you don't have to make the difficult choice each time between having your rugs drenched or taking down the baskets. Just the very fact that these baskets are *hung* causes a quicker evaporation of moisture. The reason for this is that if they are hung in a room, they are constantly enveloped in hot, dry air. It is almost impossible to give them the proper moist atmosphere that is so much easier to provide for plants that are near to ground level.

Hanging basket plants can be beautiful, but they are not the easiest type of indoor specimens to keep looking their best. If your time for gardening is limited, or you must be away from home fairly often, or you simply want a more carefree type of planting, they are not for you. Consider these things, and if you still feel you want to do it—go ahead.

6

Room Dividers That Grow

Not everybody wants to put plants in a window—or even has a window where the conditions are favorable to plant growth—yet there are house plant addicts everywhere who long for the sight of something green and growing. And whether homeowner or apartment dweller, everyone can derive a tremendous amount of pleasure from his indoor plants during the colder months of the year. One way to do this is to divide a good-sized room with a living indoor hedge or room divider.

Plants used as room dividers can add a whole new architectural dimension to your home without the expense and bother of tearing down or building up. Actually, in many modern homes provision is made for plantings of this type, and indoor planters are often a part of the construction. If they aren't, you can make them appear to be by building them of woods that match the rest of the room. But if you build such a planter, make it movable, so that if you get tired of the arrangement, or it becomes desirable or necessary, you can simply move the whole thing somewhere else and start over.

Of course, the problems of growing plants indoors are always present, but aside from requirements of temperature, humidity, soil, and so on, the greatest problem appears to be giving your plants the proper amount of light. It is now possible to purchase attractive indoor lighting for almost any location (and we will go into this later on), but for many plants it somehow spoils the effect to have something hanging above. It detracts from the look we want to achieve of natural and free-growing beauty.

As I mentioned above, these plants will grow well in locations where there is a low light level. However, they do need *some* light. Curtain-filtered sunlight will help them to thrive under your care.

The "Fear of Failure" Syndrome

Many indoor gardeners have a "fear of failure" syndrome which makes them think twice about investing their hard-earned money on large foliage house plants. This, of course, is sheer nonsense. Large plants are just as easy to take care of as their smaller cousins. And the chances are that a beginning gardener will be less likely to overwater and overlove a large plant.

MONSTERAS

If a north light is all you have to offer your plants you can still have Monstera. This is a tropical evergreen climbing plant with ornamental fruits and foliage. It belongs to the arum group and is found growing wild in tropical America, Mexico, and Costa Rica. The kind most frequently grown as a house plant is *M. deliciosa*, sometimes called *Philodendron pertusum*. In the tropics this type will produce edible fruits, but this seldom occurs with plants cultivated indoors. We grow this plant principally

Monstera deliciosa
Monstera, Swiss Cheese Plant

because of its ornamental divided leaves. These are large, leathery in texture, and perforated with large holes. The leafstalks are one to two feet long and they sheath around the stem at its base. I have never seen the fruit, but if you're lucky and produce some, you will find it to have a taste between that of a pineapple and a banana.

Since this plant is large, it is most suitable for a large room as it matures, but young specimens in smaller sizes may be grown almost anyplace. The bold foliage will give a carefree tropical feeling anywhere you place it, and when it grows too large, it can be moved or replaced. This plant is a climber, and a wire or trellis should be fixed in place so the shoots can be trained on it.

Monsteras are not fussy. They do best in a temperature range of 60–70 degrees but will be agreeable and get along in one a little warmer. Soil for these plants should be a mixture of compost and garden loam with a little coarse sand and, if possible, some well-decayed manure. And even though they will grow in low-light areas, they will benefit from a summer outdoors if you can manage it. So give them a summer vacation out in the yard, at first placing them somewhere in deep shade so they don't go into shock.

You can propagate monsteras by taking stem cuttings. Each cutting should have three or four joints. They must be kept in a propagating case (described later) with a temperature adjusted to 75 degrees. When well rooted they can be potted separately in 4-inch pots. When they outgrow these, shift them to pots of 6 or 7 inches.

DIEFFENBACHIAS

There are several varieties of a group of plants called dieffenbachias, or "dumb cane," which will adjust well to high temperatures and subdued light. Like the monsteras, these, too, make fine room dividers and are also good to soften corners. The dieffenbachias are tropical plants with very ornamental foliage. You often see them in office buildings and stores, but they are also great for homes and apartments.

There are so many different kinds of Dieffenbachia that I will mention only a few: *D. amoena* has broad, dark-green leaves with white feathering; *D. chelsonii* has deep, satiny green leaves

Dieffenbachia bausei
Dumb Cane

Dieffenbachia amoena
Dumb Cane

Dieffenbachia picta

with gray feathering; *D. fournieri* is black-green with white spots
—very dramatic; *D. imperialis* has leaves of shining green with
light-yellow blotches; *D. longispatha*, dark green with light midribs; *D. picta*, green blotched with white; and the delightful *D.
picta jenmannii*, which is green with a herringbone pattern of
white veins. With all these variations, and many more too numerous to mention of green, cream, white, yellow, and bronze, it is
possible to find a dieffenbachia plant to suit just about any color
scheme for any room in the house.

Dieffenbachias are among the "tough" plants and face up
well to difficult growing conditions. They are only moderately
large, growing to about four feet in height, which makes them
very well suited for a room-divider planter box that's elevated a
few feet from the floor. The large, usually oval-shaped leaves are
spotted and lined with cream or white. The leafstalks sheath at
the base and encircle the stems.

Dieffenbachias should be planted in a rich mixture of equal
parts of peat, loam, coarse sand, and well-decomposed manure.
While they can stand considerable heat, you must not let the
winter temperature go below 55 degrees. These plants also will
benefit from a summer vacation outside. Older plants sometimes
get leggy (leaves too far apart on the stem), and you're usually
better off replacing one of these with a young plant.

To propagate, sever the stems just below the bottom leaves

and place as cuttings in a propagating case following the same procedure as for monsteras (above). Another way to produce new plants is by air layering, which is described in a later chapter. Still another possibility is to cut up pieces of stem into two-inch lengths and insert these in pans of moist sand. If the pans are placed in a propagating case in spring or summer, the stems will soon root and form new plants.

FERNS

Ferns are almost always a satisfactory choice for low-light locations because that's where you will find them in nature. These plants, which I will deal with in greater detail later on, are tender perennials with underground fleshy roots. They may be of erect or climbing growth. The dainty, airy growth of ferns is particularly delightful as a contrast to the heavier, thicker leaves of many other indoor plants.

One of my favorite varieties of fern is *Asparagus sprengeri*, from Natal. It has long-branched stems with narrow leaves and bears small white flowers followed by red berries. This is an excellent plant for hanging baskets, room dividers, or as a single specimen. The ornamental kinds of asparagus fern are grown for their leafy graceful shoots, which are often cut by florists and combined with flowers.

Nephrolepis, or Boston fern, is probably the most commonly seen in American homes and apartments. Its enormous popularity doesn't necessarily mean it is easy to grow indoors, but if you are successful you may soon find that one of these plants can become very large and bushy. They probably do best near an east window where they can get plenty of curtain-filtered sunlight, but my friend and fellow gardening enthusiast Cindy Dunne has one that is handsome and thriving on her white brick fireplace, where it receives only artificial or reflected light. If you choose to grow one where there is little natural light, compensate with several hours of artificial light—about 600–800 footcandles. (A footcandle is the light of one candle falling on a surface one foot away from the candle.) If someone in your family is an amateur photographer, like Cindy's husband Peter, you can probably borrow his light meter to check the light levels your plants are getting at various times in the day. Remember, these levels change with the seasons, so check the light several times during the year. If pho-

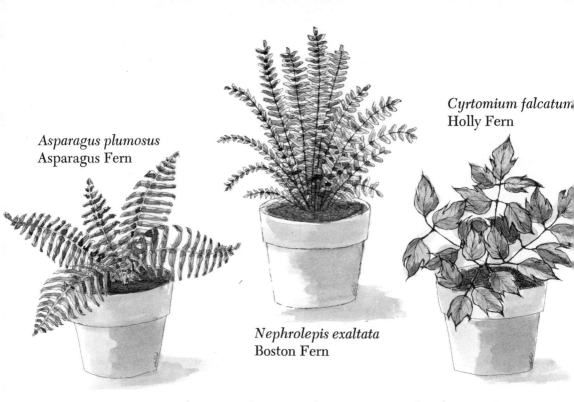

Asparagus plumosus
Asparagus Fern

Cyrtomium falcatum
Holly Fern

Nephrolepis exaltata
Boston Fern

tography is not a long suit of anyone in your family, an inexpensive light meter that reads in footcandles is still a great gift for you or your favorite gardener. Be sure to get one that measures in footcandles and not F-stops!

Although ferns can be found growing wild in almost every corner of the world, the ones that have been most successfully adapted for indoor growing originated in the tropics. They do quite well in the 70 degrees or more of most American homes during the daytime, but at night they prefer to sleep in much cooler surroundings. They like nighttime temperatures in a range of 40–50 degrees. That can be a real problem for most of us. I suggest putting them near a cool window so they can get a comfortable night's sleep.

Don't pay attention to those gardening experts who tell you to set your potted fern in water. It is true that these plants dry out quickly and need lots of moisture and humidity, but it's been my experience that their roots rot when they're wet all the time. Watering depends a great deal on the dryness of your home. Keep the soil moist but not soggy. Use a mister on the leaves and give them their morning shower as a part of your daily routine. And don't feed your new fern until you've had it for several months. Then feed it regularly with plant food once or twice a year.

Our fern friends like soil that's made up of lots of organic material. I usually pot them in pure humus and sphagnum moss mixed together about 50-50. The moss holds moisture and helps prevent the soil from drying out too quickly.

Thriving ferns grow extremely fast. Before long you may have to move them into larger quarters. You can do this at any time of the year. Use a humus-rich potting soil, sphagnum moss, or some of your precious compost to fill in as needed. A teaspoonful of superphospate growth stimulator added to the soil won't hurt.

Schefflera (Umbrella Tree)

A handsome foliage plant with glossy leaves which can get to be the size of a small tree, the schefflera is ideal for the amateur indoor gardener. It needs good light, but not direct sunlight. Although it can survive a certain amount of neglect, it will reward you if you give it just a little attention. Water well and then allow soil to dry completely before watering again. Wash leaves once a month with a solution of water and any biodegradable dishwashing liquid. Use any good standard potting soil.

Schefflera actinophylla
Schefflera

The Norfolk Island Pine

Another indoor plant that can withstand low-light levels is this small handsome tree. If you go to the florist or nursery you

Araucaria excelsa
Norfolk Island Pine

may find it there under the name of Araucaria. These delightful trees belong to the family Pinaceae, one of the cone-bearing groups. They are also found in Australia, New Guinea, New Caledonia, and the Norfolk Islands.

In the United States the Araucaria is hardy in the far south and on the Pacific Coast, and it even grows in Great Britain and the milder parts of Europe. It is the pattern of growth that makes these trees such interesting house plants. They are neat and compact and have regular tiers of flat, soft-leaved branches. In the house they are generally grown in pots and will attain a height of three to five feet. Male and female cones are usually produced on different trees, but sometimes are produced on the same tree. When mature, the female cones are the size of large coconuts. As a house plant, however, your tree will probably never attain the size to produce these, so you will have to take my word for them.

Give your Norfolk Island Pine a good foundation to grow in, with a compost mixture of two-thirds loam, one-third leaf mold, and a scattering of coarse sand. Annual repotting is usually necessary until they are placed in 7- or 8-inch pots. Hold them as long as possible at this size, and rather than continue repotting, remove some of the old soil each spring and replace with fresh compost. A sprinkling of fertilizer each month from March till September will also help to keep the plants healthy.

One way to discover whether these plants need water is to use the "dip-stick method" described on page 54.

As I mentioned before, these plants will grow with little light

—so just make sure you let them have *some* light. People who grow plants indoors often keep the blinds drawn during the day as a precautionary measure to keep the light from fading drapes and furniture. While I can sympathize with you ladies, this is not good for your plants. Leaf-drop or yellowing of leaves is a symptom of insufficient light and must be remedied or eventually the plant will die. Arrange, if you can, for your indoor plants to have a summer vacation outside.

You may sometimes take root cuttings of Araucaria if they are inserted in sandy soil outdoors in the spring. Sow the seeds in March and place in a propagating case at 50 degrees.

Pinching Off, Pruning, and Trellising

If you have given your plants proper care and lots of love and attention, they will want to please you and reward all your good care with a tremendous surge of new growth. As with small children, this seems to take place almost overnight, but it is actually a continuous process that is going on all the time.

However, it's of paramount importance to keep your living room landscape in balance—don't let it become a jungle! Many times inexperienced gardeners become so overjoyed to see their plants growing that they miss the forest because they're looking at a new leaf, flower, bud, or branch that's forming. But eventually you will stand back and see that you are running out of space. This is the time to say, *Enough already!* Now it's time to send your plants to school, to give them proper training.

Don't let the words "pinching," "pruning," or "training" frighten you. Just think what you would look like if you didn't cut your fingernails occasionally! Plants are the same; they need to be manicured, just as your hands do.

Pinching a plant won't get you slapped. All it means is simply removing the tip of a growing shoot. This is usually done by pressing it off with the thumbnail and finger. Of course, it can be done with a pair of clippers, but I am inclined to think both the plant and you will prefer the personal contact rather than the touch of cold steel. The reason for pinching is to restrain the overenthusiastic plant and promote a compact, bushy habit of growth, which is always more desirable in a house plant than a long, attenuated one. Pinching will check the strong shoots and stimulate the buds that might otherwise have remained dormant into growing. "Disbudding," which is another form of pinching, refers to the removal of flower buds, which forces the plant to conserve its energy until the time we want it to bloom. Florists use this technique to get flowers to bloom for special holidays.

You can use the very same methods to train climbing and trailing plants. These may send out too many shoots, or the shoots may become undesirably long. Cutting some of them back will give the plant a far more attractive appearance.

One of the greatest "cuts" in the fabled history of opera is said to have taken place at La Scala, where a faulty American tenor was being cheered into encore after encore. Finally a wise-acre in the audience shouted, "Encore—and this time get it right!" Well, gardening is not very much like the opera, but plants do have a way of performing poorly as a result of improper training. When this happens, you may have to do some cutting of your own. If so, pruning can be used to stimulate new growth from the plant at its base. Sometimes a plant that is in poor condition can be saved by cutting it back completely. This operation should be combined with such other measures as careful feeding and watering. Also, this time around train your plant to grow and perform in a way that will please its severest critic.

Pruning is generally more severe than pinching and involves cutting back to a greater degree. It may also mean root pruning as well as pruning the upper growth. Whichever is in order for a particular plant (both may be), prune with a sharp knife or pruning shears. Never hack at a plant with dull tools. Keep in mind that a clean cut will heal much more quickly than one that is bruised and chewed.

When pruning back a branch, make your cuts just above a leaf that has in its axil a bud pointed in the direction that you want the foliage to develop. If a branch needs to be completely removed, cut it closely to the trunk or parent branch—don't leave a stub. If you need to prune back a diseased portion, cut back to healthy tissue. After such an operation be sure to disinfect your tools with denatured alcohol before using them again.

Many healthy indoor plants will benefit from root-pruning, which reduces the size of the root ball so that it can be replanted in the pot it came from instead of in a larger one. The best time to do this is in the spring, when growth is most active and wounds heal quickly. The day before you intend to perform this operation, water the plant patient, so you will have a fairly compact ball to work with and the soil won't fall away from the roots.

Knock out the plant and place it on the potting bench (or your kitchen counter). With a sharp knife trim portions from all around the root ball. Shape the root mass so it will fit reasonably well, with about an inch or so of room all around when it is returned to the pot. Now repot, using new soil.

The plant should be kept for a while in a warm, humid atmosphere to give it a chance to recover. The humidity can be achieved easily by covering it with a large plastic bag. Keep it out of the sun until new roots have had a chance to form. This will take ten days to two weeks.

Of course pinching and pruning are all a part of training, but in the case of climbers and trailers this may also involve providing them with suitable supports. If you choose these carefully you can achieve interesting and unusual effects and at the same time enable your plants to look their best.

Such tropical foliage plants as monstera and others of the arum group with creeping rhizomes will attach themselves to supports by their aerials if given some rough material on which to climb. This may be a plant stake (Figure A) wrapped with moss or osmunda fiber held in place by wiring, or an unbarked length of red cedar (Figure B) with a trunk about two to two and a half inches in diameter. These supports should be installed with the plants when they are potted and should extend right down to the bottom of the pot. Pack the soil firmly around them so they will be firmly set. Obviously, small pots are not suitable for this purpose, so this treatment is generally given only where large plants needing at least an 8-inch pot are used.

Talk to your plants encouragingly during their hour of need. Give them assistance if the shoots seem to be swaying about aimlessly. In time they will find their targets, but you can help this along by tying them to the support with some soft material that will not injure the stem. You can try wool yarn, but check every now and then to make sure your plant isn't allergic to wool —plants *are* like people, you know! Use of a spraying device will encourage the air roots to take hold on the new support.

Some Humble Cousins

Don't overlook the possibilities of some of the humbler plants for training on trellises indoors or around window frames. The morning glory, the pea, peanut, potato, and sweet potato can be a lot of fun—especially for children—and can look terrific in an attractive container. Choose a south window where they can obtain plenty of sunshine. Explain to the kids that these will probably be only temporary visitors to your indoor garden.

A Sweet Potato Vine

Growing a sweet potato is utter simplicity; you can even use a pickle jar for the container. Since sweet potatoes are often treated with some material to retard sprouting, either use a home-grown one or find one in the supermarket that shows some signs of life.

If you are in any doubt about which end to insert in the jar, lay the potato on a moist bed of peat or sphagnum moss and leave it in a warm place for a few days. When growth starts, insert it in the jar with its lower end just touching the water. (A lump of charcoal in the water will help to keep it sweet.) As water evaporates, add more.

A mass of roots will soon form inside the jar and sprouts will start coming out all over the upper part of the potato. These sprouts may grow to a length of several feet, especially if you pinch them back to just two or three of the strongest. Placing the container in a bracket and letting the runners trail downward will display the plant very well, or you may train the runners around your window as a frame for the other plants. Several sprouting sweet potatoes placed in a bowl can make a very attractive centerpiece for your table.

Beet roots may be grown in the same way as sweet potatoes.

Carrot and Rutabaga Tops

To grow a carrot or rutabaga top, cut it about three inches from the top and insert in a bowl that is shallow but deep enough so the top can stand upright when it is covered with pebbles, with only about one-quarter to one-half inch exposed. Cover the pebbles with water and continue to add water as it evaporates. You will get an abundance of pretty fernlike foliage from the carrot and interesting leaves from the rutabaga.

ENGLISH AND GRAPE IVIES AND KANGAROO VINE

English ivy, grape ivy, and kangaroo vine (*Cissus antarctica*) are also easy to train. The kangaroo vine, a native to Australia, is an attractive but relatively little-known foliage plant. It deserves better press. My friend Louise Riotte says the best kinds are *C. antarctica*, a green-leaved plant for a cool room; *C. discolor*, with ovate, velvety green leaves variegated with silvery white and red-purple beneath; and *C. capensis*, with kidney-shaped leaves, rust colored beneath.

Pruning and training consist of thinning out and shortening the vigorous shoots in March or early spring. You may wish to propagate more plants by inserting cuttings of young shoots in sand. This is best done in a propagating case in spring and summer.

Cissus rhombifolia
Grape Ivy

Cissus antarctica
Kangaroo Vine

7

Gardening in a Dish

Up to this point we've been more or less concentrating on proper culture for the full-size plants that occupy the main part of the indoor gardener's world. Some of them can become gargantuan in size. But if you are a creative plant lover with space problems in your home or apartment, you may want to think about growing miniature plants in dish gardens.

Dish gardens are attractive shallow containers holding groupings of tiny plants that have similar requirements of soil, moisture, and temperature. They can have tremendous appeal. If you have developed an interest in ecology, you'll get a big kick out of creating some miniature natural environments in a dish—they will present you with a real challenge! All the joys of gardening on a larger scale may be experienced with fewer headaches—and all under artificial lights.

These gardens can take you anywhere you'd like to go—to the Orient, the tropics, the desert, a woodland, a bog, a swamp, or perhaps an open meadow. If you have small children, you can add excitement and fantasy to the scene by a special style of container or tiny figures depicting people or animals. Just be careful not to let the ornaments detract from the main point of interest —the plants.

Half the Fun Is in the Finding!

You'll have a great deal of fun searching out the miniature plants for your dish garden. You aren't likely to find them all at the first florist or nursery you visit, but patience will in time reveal many small wonders that you may have overlooked when preparing other indoor gardening projects.

Select your little plant people with care, because with this kind of gardening each individual is important to the over-all look. Many enthusiastic dish gardeners regard their plants with much the same fervor as a jeweler gazing through his magnifying glass or a scientist viewing one of life's small miracles through his microscope.

You can increase your dish-garden enjoyment by turning your entire family into sharp-eyed plant scouts and going on weekend treasure hunts for attractive additions. Some of these might be small lichen-covered rocks. At the seashore you may find interesting shells. In the woods there are bits of decomposing bark and logs covered with attractive and unusual mosses. On such a hunting trip in Colorado my dish-gardener expert Louise Riotte tells me she found some very odd lichens (mossy cup) shaped like little trumpets. She brought them home and kept them alive in a dish garden for several months.

If you are fortunate enough to have access to a woods, an abandoned field, or a country roadside, there will be an abundance of material to be gathered for the taking. Of course, you should be mindful not to trespass or dig up some wild thing that is one of the plants protected by conservation laws. But you may come upon a spot where many tiny plants are growing together, and taking one or a few of these may give them a beneficial thinning. You may even find some young firs or spruces of a suitable size and all sorts of ferns, mosses, and small flowering plants. Sometimes a grayish lichen (Cladonia) will provide an excellent contrast with something more brightly colored. Like other arrangements of plants and flowers, our dish gardens shouldn't be monotonous—the unexpected focal point can be as exciting in miniature as anywhere else.

Dig out these found plants with as many roots as possible, keeping a little ball of earth about each one if you can. Fold each one as you gather it in a moistened piece of paper towel and put it into a plastic bag or cardboard box so it will not dry out. You can easily moisten a supply of toweling before you leave the house and put it in your container to be used as necessary. Also take along something to dig your plants with—nothing is more disconcerting than to find yourself without tools. Pulling up plants is a no-no! Take with you a small trowel, a jackknife, or even a

Hedera helix
English Ivy

broad-bladed putty knife. You will find that enough plant specimens for a dish garden can usually be gathered like this and enclosed in a quart-sized bag in an hour's time.

Some of the plants you will use are natural miniatures, such as *Sinningia pusilla*, a miniature gloxinia. Some are the results of hybridizing, and these include *Sinningia pumila* and begonia "China Doll." Others, such as peperomia "Pixie" and *Hedera helix* "Needlepoint," have occurred as mutations.

Perhaps you will want to use cacti. If you do, use *all* cacti, and make provision for the correct soil mix accordingly. Generally speaking, cactus plants that are nursery-grown will give you better and longer-lasting results, but if you live in an area where cactus plants are easily obtainable in nature, there's nothing in the rules that says you can't use some of these.

Arrangements of cacti can be both enduring and endearing, and they are among the most satisfactory plants for dish-garden use. Succulents—which take a little more water than cacti and a little less than other types of plants—are also very suitable candidates for dish-garden culture. There are succulent miniatures that don't grow very large at maturity. Cacti and succulents usually cost less, are easier to care for, and last longer in arrangements than most other plants.

Experiment!

When you begin to collect miniature plants indoors, there is always something even more exciting just ahead that you may want to try out. One such individual is *Erythrodes nobilis argyro-centrum*, a tongue-twisting name for a very lovely orchid. This plant, sometimes called the silver orchid, is cultivated for its foliage, the striking silver network on its shining, satiny green leaves giving it its name. In midwinter the plant may reward you for your ministrations by sending up a small spike of white flowers. Because of its need for moisture, it is best grown in a closed case.

There are hundreds of miniature orchids in cultivation now and many more are being hybridized. Growers are constantly working to provide us with plants of easier culture, increased vigor, and larger and more colorful flowers which will blossom over a longer period of time. *Cattleya walkeriana*, for instance, has lovely fragrant flowers with a pleasing rose color that appear on plants only four to six inches tall. Other orchids grow only two to three inches tall, and many of these have tiny flowers—white, yellow, brown, and orange.

Did you know that there are miniature African violets? Well, there are, and if you happen to be fond of these lovely plants but don't have much room for them, relax and grow them in a dish garden. Miniature African violets are tremendous space-savers, and will do well if grown on a windowsill that faces east. The morning sun and afternoon shade are ideal for their healthy culture. Someone has figured out that you can grow fifty miniature varieties in a space in which only about a dozen of standard size would be comfortable.

To restrict these little fellows to a desirable size (and this goes for many other miniatures as well), they should be kept in small pots, preferably 1¼ to 2½ inches in diameter. Be a little stingy in your program of watering and feeding them. The object is to maintain good health and good appearance rather than to encourage additional growth.

Miniature begonias are another great favorite for indoor culture and are especially complementary in an Oriental setting. Try the rhizomatous one, "Baby Perfection," which has pink flowers, "Baby Rainbow," a rex, *Begonia dregei*, or *Begonia lulandi*.

Miniature geraniums are always as delightful as the larger ones. And just like their bigger brothers and sisters, they need sun, or at least light, for they may be grown very easily under fluorescent illumination. Keep your geraniums moist but not muddy; the soil should be just damp to the touch. These plants need a temperature of 65–75 degrees in the daytime, dropping to 55–65 degrees at night. Actually, geraniums are very pleasant plants to have around, because they will thrive in the same conditions of light, warmth, and humidity as we do. So if you're looking for a miniature that's pretty and easy to grow, try geraniums.

There are even roses for dollhouse gardening, and these small woody plants are actually of the same royal blood as those hybrid teas and floribundas that reign as queens of your outside garden. Their perfectly formed buds may be no larger than a pea or even a grain of wheat. The tiny, often fragrant flowers bloom almost continuously. Like geraniums, they require all the possible light you can beam their way. During the winter months place them where they can get natural sun or indoor lighting. In summer they also require good light but should not be placed in direct sunlight. They have a need for moisture, especially because they have a tendency to dry out quickly in their tiny containers. Too much warm air or sunlight will dry them out too quickly.

Finally, you might consider the little trees of the bonsai type, which will be described more fully later on. They have a timeless Oriental charm and often last for years. If you shape and prune them, they may even improve in appearance, grace, and dignity as they grow older. They remind me of wizened Oriental wise men.

Gardeners can do just about anything they want to with miniature plants. And some miniatures are hardy enough to withstand even cold winters. Some of the very small, needle-bearing conifers, or evergreens, grow very slowly and sturdily. They are beautiful, long-lasting and require little time.

Plan Before You "Do Your Dishes"

The first step in any hobby is to organize your tools, your materials, and the space where you intend to work so that you have everything ready and handy to use. Before you actually plant anything, give some careful thought to planning your dish garden. What you will use for a container is strictly up to you. Just be careful to match the plant or plants to the dish. The container should be large enough to hold a group of at least three or four plants. It should be small enough so that it will be appropriate for the place you plan to put it. You may use a simple wooden salad bowl, a basket lined with moss, a dish made of glass, pottery, or metal. Once again, don't let the container be so ornate that it takes interest away from the plants.

Place your little potted plants (if they came from the florist) in the container you have chosen and move them about. Eventually you will create an arrangement that is most pleasing to you. As you work out your design, remember that this is a landscape in miniature, and a flat landscape is usually monotonous. Create some hills and valleys and shape the contours to esthetic proportions. Do not put the largest plant in the center. Placing it over to one side of the dish will nearly always result in a more interesting composition. This will become your accent plant; arrange the smaller ones around its base. The possibilities for achieving distinctive effects with miniature plants are innumerable. And one of their greatest charms is their suitability for growing conditions that would be impossible for large plants.

You should give some thought to the soil you will use even though a dish garden has a very short life expectancy. If you use cactus, you will want to use the type of sandy soil recommended for these plants (see Chapter 11). If your miniature garden plants are "woodsy," use leaf mold or compost mixed with a little sand.

You should also make provision for drainage. If your container doesn't have small holes underneath for allowing moisture to escape, use some drainage material in the bottom, such as exceptionally porous soil. If you chose the latter method, be sure to water with extreme care to avoid waterlogging. My friend Louise Riotte often leaves a small opening down one side of her dish gardens. This permits the insertion of a meat-baster syringe to draw off excess water. Drainage material may also be broken potsherds, bits of crumbled brick, small pieces of charcoal, gravel, coarse sand or cinders. On top of any of these media put a layer of sheet moss to prevent the soil from sifting down and clogging the drainage.

Miniature compositions are always a little more difficult to create because they are more closely examined than larger ones. When you have everything planned out, remove your plants from their containers as gently as possible—they are more easily damaged than their larger cousins. Work the soil loose around the sides of the pot and tap the plants out, but use great care—*never pull them out*. This done, you can begin to follow your original plan. A small rough drawing of the design you liked best could be of help, or you may move the plants around a little more until you are completely satisfied with their arrangement. If you're a woman who likes to rearrange furniture in her home, you'll like this part the best.

When you are ready to plant, firm the soil around the collar of the plant so it will be well supported. Be sure the roots are well spread out and covered. Any trailing material or ground covers should be planted last. Water the dish garden just enough to moisten the soil, and keep it in the shade. Let it rest for a few days until it becomes established and then put it in the light.

Caring for the garden to keep it attractive as long as possible can be a bit of a problem. Obviously there is no hard-and-fast rule for watering. Just keep it moist at all times. (This goes for everything except cacti.) You'll have to judge for yourself when it's time to rewater, as soil, room temperature, number of plants, and so on all enter into this decision. Poke your finger down into the soil occasionally, and if you find it bone dry underneath, water. When you do water, *gentleness* is again the watchword. Small plants are easily dislodged, so use care. Use of a mister will help keep many small plants fresher-looking by washing off dust. But use of a mister does not take the place of regular watering. The plants need thorough watering to provide the necessary fluid for absorption by the roots.

As with any kind of gardening, indoors or outside, you should remove blooms and blossoms that are beginning to fade. The experts call these blasted blossoms. The plants will continue to feed these has-beens, wasting precious food that could be going to the more important new buds and blooms. When you pick them off, grab the petals and take only what comes away easily, leaving the rest to set new flowers. Also remove any faded leaves, and if some of the plants begin to grow too tall, prune them back.

In Sum . . .

A miniature garden is another place where you don't need the proverbial green thumb, where you can learn by doing. The balance of plants will create a pleasing picture, and I believe a garden you have arranged yourself will give you far more pleasure than any you might buy already completed. Although you may feel a bit clumsy working on a small scale at first, don't let that discourage you—remember, expertise comes with practice, patience, and persistence. Like the gardener who works with a larger landscape, you will soon develop skill and imagination by working carefully according to *plan*.

If you make mistakes, correct them the next time around. A miniature garden is not forever. Its length of life will depend on the plants used, the soil, temperature, and humidity to which it is subjected, and to your own personal cultural practices. For example, if you have gathered plants in a cool, northern section of the country while on vacation and have brought them home to the atmosphere of a warm, dry room, their lives may be short. Nevertheless you may enjoy them enough for that short period to make it all worth while.

Remember, too, this garden is yours—you can do what you want with it. As with all gardening projects, it should provide personal pleasure and be a delightful experience. And if you don't like the final result, you can change it much more easily than you can replant trees and shrubs outside that somehow don't seem to be quite at home where you have planted them.

8

For Carefree Gardening, Try Terrariums

If you liked growing dish gardens but have trouble keeping them alive over a long period of time, you might want to join the hundreds of thousands of folks who are making terrariums the hottest-selling items in the gardening industry. Terrariums are the best idea yet for the inexperienced gardener. If you fit into that category, here is a specialized indoor-gardening hobby that's just meant for you. If everything else you try to grow indoors fails, don't give up—I'm willing to bet that with one of these little gardens that grow inside glass you will achieve a measure of green-thumb success! And if you are an accomplished indoor gardener who's looking for new worlds to conquer, you can create such a world inside a glass bowl and make it flourish with your green thumb tied behind your back.

It is the glass enclosure that makes your terrarium different from the dish gardens we have just finished talking about in the preceding chapter. In its simplest terms, a terrarium is a glass-enclosed garden that may contain plants only or both plants and animals.

If your life has seemed too busy and complicated to consider growing house plants, you are probably ready for a terrarium, because it is a complete environment. And as such it is an easy, satisfactory way to grow plants indoors without the usual headaches of watering, feeding, and constant attention. Your terrarium will keep the life-giving conditions your plants require for survival in almost perfect harmony. In a sense, it bottles up the climate, providing a moisture-perfect, dust-free space where plants will thrive. Here they have no problems of drafts or gases and are seldom bothered by insects. You may even ignore them for a time and they will still continue to do well. But a terrarium does not really deserve to be ignored. It can be a window through which you and your children will be able to watch Mother Nature at work.

Terrariums can be any shape you may choose, provided they are clear containers. They can be tall or short, fat or funny—even a baby's discarded bottle can be used. A fruit jar, a glass dish, a brandy snifter, even glass cookware may serve. Plastic may be used, provided it is clear. However, if you start with a small container you may soon become so enthusiastic that you will want to graduate to something larger, such as a ten-gallon aquarium tank, or one even roomier.

Like dish gardens, these microcosmic environments may be of several different types, such as woodland, desert, tropical, or semiaquatic. The kind of plants you keep in your terrarium will largely determine the kind of enclosed climate you will want to set up. While most terrariums need a glass cover and should be provided with one, an exception should be made with a desert environment of cactus plants. These are not generally covered.

Observe the same elementary rules of conservation when you go out to search for your terrarium plants as apply when taking wildflowers and plants for any gardening project. Gather only as many plants as you will need. Carefully consider which ones will fit nicely into the size and shape of your container.

Select plants that take much the same type of culture (for example, do not mix cactus with woodland plants that like acid soil and need a closed-type container). Pick only those that will grow in harmony together. Try to dig up plants where you find several or a clump. Follow the same procedure for preserving the plants as suggested for dish gardens. Don't forget the trowel or some tool for digging and a supply of wet paper toweling and several plastic bags.

FERNS AND MOSSES

Ferns, which are sometimes hard to grow in a dry home, are especially nice for terrariums—particularly maidenhair, ebony spleenwort, Christmas fern, and the walking fern, *Camptosorus rhizophyllus*. Low-growing mosses are ideal for a terrarium. A wall-to-wall planting of moss under glass can look great. Mosses, cut and shaped, may also make a fine lining for your container, or you may want to try draping them over small rocks. Club moss, *Lycopodium obscurum*, and shining club moss, *Lycopodium lucidulum*, are excellent choices. So are the liverworts, which are small green plants similar to mosses. These grow on damp ground, in water, or on tree trunks, and are so named because the main leaflike part of the plant resembles the human liver.

Many plants such as maranta, fittonia, and ferns will actually grow better in a terrarium than exposed in a room. Such plants as the selaginellas and sinningias, which prefer high humidity, will thrive in a covered garden. Even a pickle jar can provide them with an attractive home. And don't forget the old goldfish bowl for cacti and succulents. These can live on happily and healthily for years in such an environment.

Fungi Are Fun Guys!

Plants sometimes overlooked as possibilities for terrarium culture are the fungi. This group lacks chlorophyll, and so its individual members do not have any green coloring. They cannot manufacture their own food, and exist by absorbing their nutrients from whatever decaying or living matter they grow on.

Some fungi obtain their food from living plants and these are called parasitic. Others, such as mushrooms and toadstools, get theirs from decaying matter and are saprophytic. Considering the current craze for mushrooms—which are being designed into everything from saltshakers to wall plaques—they are certainly a most interesting possibility for terrariums.

The vegetative part of a fungus consists of finely branched threads. These do not form roots and leaves as in higher plants. They penetrate the tissues of the host and take their nourishment from it. They reproduce themselves from spores, sometimes in vast numbers. When gathering fungi, take them on the stick or piece of bark to which they are attached. Otherwise they will die.

Don't *ever*, unless you know exactly what you're doing, eat any of the wild mushrooms you find growing in the woods. There are many, many species and some of them are very poisonous. So if you are an inexperienced forager, play it safe. Don't be tempted into eating any wild mushroom unless you are certain it is an edible species.

What we have been talking about up to now are fungi for

ornamental purposes, but if you want edible mushrooms, you can buy them from nursery supply houses in preplanted kits (or you may buy the spawn and plant your own). These come in both large and small sizes, and all you need to do is add water according to the directions. You might even be lucky enough to get several good pickings.

LICHENS

Lichens, which often form an attractive growth on rocks, are part fungi and part algae, which live together symbiotically. They form a flowerless plant that grows on bare rocks and tree stumps throughout the world, mostly in waste places. They are found in such cold regions as Antarctica and also in the tropics. They grow on beaches as well as on mountaintops. Scientists are aware of at least 20,000 different kinds. In color they may be gray, yellow, brown-green, blue, or black.

Each lichen consists of an alga and a fungus, which live together in a kind of partnership. The green alga produces food and the fungus part absorbs and stores water. Lichens have no roots, stems, or leaves, and they consist of layers of irregularly shaped extensions called thalli. Lichens of the foliose type resemble leaves; the crustose type resembles shells, and these may cover large rocks with delicate patterns of grays and greens. The fruticose lichens resemble moss or tiny shrubs, and they grow in clusters on barren ground. These plant formations multiply by means of fragments, a special kind of structure, that "breaks" from the plant. Carried by the wind, they may travel considerable distances, or they may simply drop to the ground and establish a new plant.

Plants of this type do not require soil for growth. They often exist where other plants cannot grow. As they break down, lichens help to form soil and produce acids. They are Mother Nature's way of breaking down rocks. Some types of lichens are considered valuable food for man and animals—one such is reindeer moss. Wherever you happen to live, it is quite possible that you may find some lichens on rocks or decaying bark, and because of their odd and interesting shapes and forms you'll enjoy seeing them planted in your terrarium.

Woodland Terrariums

Tiny shrubs and trees that are just starting to sprout from seeds will serve you very well if your terrarium is to be a woodland type. Look for cedar, white pine, and hemlock. Also, seedlings of deciduous trees such as maple and oak may be used. Simply remove and replace them when they outgrow their quarters. Low-growing plants and vines, creeping fig (*Ficus pumila*, an evergreen creeper), and partridgeberry (*Mitchella repens*, another evergreen trailer) are also candidates worthy of your consideration.

Gather all your necessary tools and planting materials and set them out conveniently in your working area. Arrange the plants you have decided to use in several ways before you place them in your planter. This will help you decide on the most interesting silhouette and design. Doing this *before* you place them inside will help you avoid moving them around too much during the actual planting operation and thus smearing the glass unnecessarily. I might note here that keeping the glass—or plastic—clean is the first rule of terrarium planting. No matter what the container, make every move carefully to avoid touching it. These surfaces are difficult to clean after the plants are in place.

When you choose your tools, make sure they are a few inches longer than the height of your container. A small rake, trowel or just an iced-tea spoon, scissors, kitchen tongs, and a bottle or percolator brush for cleaning are all good instruments to use in terrarium building. For bottles you will need a metal or paper funnel for putting in the soil, a ¼-inch wood dowel or piece of stiff coat-hanger wire, with a cork attached to one end for tamping the soil, and a plastic straw or peashooter to help you move rocks. A watering funnel with a rubber hose is another item to include on your list of tools.

Use a layer of charcoal at the bottom of the terrarium. Since this will be a planter with no drainage, you'll need to use about half an inch of agricultural charcoal to keep your terrarium "sweet." Now start with the "soil." You can use a commercial mix if you prefer. Such mixes are available for both woodland- and desert-type plantings. Use warm water to thoroughly moisten the mix in its own bag. Squeeze the excess moisture from the bag. Each planter is a different size and type, but a good rule of thumb is to fill your terrarium about a fourth of its height with soil.

Work with the utmost care so you don't smear the glass. Tilt the container so that the mix level is higher on one side than the other. This will create a natural "hillside" inside the container instead of just a flat foundation. Also, mounds in large containers will give more root space to the taller plants. Low spots become open planting spaces for sprawlers and trailers. As you work, have all your tools handy and reachable. Get your plants ready by removing each one in turn from its pot. Shake off any excess soil. Don't unpot the next one until the first one is planted. Always try to take extra care to keep the plant roots from drying out.

If you want, you can line the bottom and part of the sides of your container with moss. Do this by cutting a thin piece of moss with scissors. If any bits of the old soil are still clinging to the moss, remove them with tweezers. Continue until the area you have decided on is "mossed over."

If some of your plants are taller than others, plant these first. Dig the hole off center on the uphill side to give more root depth, and spread the roots evenly. Then cover with the potting mix. Tamp with the cork-ended dowel or coat-hanger wire.

As you plant, spray the plants lightly with water. A small, bulb-type mister is just right for this job. This may be purchased at florists' and is also included in terrarium kits specifically for this purpose. Let the earth soak up the water. Don't overdo this spraying—use just enough water to help anchor down the plants and keep air pockets from forming. Make this simple test. If a small amount of moisture comes out when the material is pressed down, you've watered enough. Continue planting toward the foreground, with the small ground covers being put in last.

Remember to leave open spaces—let Mother Nature have some of the fun. Don't fill it all up so your plants have nowhere to spread. After the plants are in place, arrange the rocks you have chosen to complete your landscaping scene. If some of these are lichen-covered, they will add another note of natural beauty. You can also put in a small twist of driftwood or a few seashells.

Within twenty-four hours after you finish planting, the closed terrarium will have a slight mistiness around the top. This is normal. Give your microclimate a little time to get into proper balance. If a tightly covered container continues to be sopping wet all around the top, remove the cover for a while or slip it back to let in some air. Chances are that you overwatered in planting.

For most terrariums the ideal temperature is 70–75 degrees

during the day and somewhere close to 60 degrees at night. You may give them an hour or two of sunlight either in the early morning or in the late afternoon. However, for the greater part of the day the woodland terrarium should be placed in a shaded spot. If you allow too much sun on the glass the moisture action will be speeded up. Try good, strong light instead.

Desert-Type Terrariums

For a desert-type terrarium planted to cacti and succulents, mix fine sand with the soil and fill the terrarium to a depth of approximately two inches. Aloes and agaves may also be used in a container in which this type of landscape is desired. Very small cacti may be left in their flowerpots and buried directly in the sand.

These desert plants will need sun in summer and warmth in winter. Don't neglect the watering of your desert terrarium. Just spray both the plants and the sand about once a week, using a mister. Keep the bottom layer of sand moist and the top dry. Minimum watering will assure beautiful specimens that will probably give showy blooms.

If you, like my friends Dan and Mary Kibbie, live near an area where cactus plants are easily obtainable, you might try gathering your own. Mary, who has been a cactus collector for several years, gets many of her best specimens from the high desert near Victorville, California. She says cactus-hunting is a lot more fun than you might at first expect. If you go searching during the summer months, she cautions that you do so early in the morning or late in the afternoon. Digging cacti during the heat of the day is for "mad dogs and Englishmen"! Also, it's not a very good idea to dig plants when it's hot—their mortality rate is too great. She tells me that nursery-grown cacti are generally more dependable growers than those you find in the desert. Still, the pleasure of seeing one bloom that you raised from a wild youngster is quite a thrill. Wear gloves—cactus spines can smart.

You'll find that this type of planted environment does best in a daytime temperature of 75–85 degrees and a nighttime temperature that doesn't get much lower than 65 degrees. These plants will enjoy long hours of sunlight, and they need it—especially during the winter months. Remember, though, that since the action of the sun will dry out an uncovered terrarium more quickly, it needs to be checked regularly. Never let the mix dry out completely. Warning signs for a too dry condition will show up in the browning and dropping of leaves and buds.

Water your terrarium if at all possible with rainwater, melted snow, or refrigerator defrostings. All of these are good choices as long as the water is at room temperature. Cold water for terrariums—either woodland or desert types—is an absolute no-no. Also, avoid using water which has softener in it (this is true for any plant). Most softened water contains harmful salts. Try using bottled water if you can obtain no other type that meets the necessary requirements. If you must use tap water, and it is heavily chlorinated or treated, allow it to stand overnight in an open container before using.

These gardens under glass may go as long as six months without watering, because the moisture is retained inside and evaporation is held to a minimum. Water only when moss or small ferns show signs of drying. Use a kitchen baster (the kind sold for basting turkeys) or the funnel-and-hose apparatus suggested earlier. These will allow you to get the water to the proper spot without dislodging or drowning small plants. If you get splash marks on the bottle, fasten a small cotton swab to a dowel and wipe away. If yours is a terrarium with a vented top you will need to water more frequently. The vent, which is usually no larger than a silver dollar, admits air and permits a certain amount of evaporation to take place.

To find out the moisture condition of the soil in your terrarium, take a cotton swab and affix it to the end of your dowel tool. Press it into the soil as deeply as possible and leave it for about ten seconds. The condition of the swab when removed will let you know whether your soil is soggy, damp, or almost dry. If necessary, add water *carefully*.

Some General Suggestions

For the first few days after planting, keep your new mini-greenhouse out of bright light. After this waiting period, move it to its new environment. Keep in mind that direct sun is only for the desert family. But don't fail to provide enough light. You may notice after a few months that some of the plants are growing leggy (too much space between the leaves). This means that they are reaching for the light. In that case, try a new location. And never allow your terrarium to remain in one position day after day. The plants will lean toward the light and become lopsided. So be sure to shift the container a quarter turn once a week. Remove fading leaves and flowers. Your terrarium should always look well cared-for, even though the plant people inside can put up with a certain amount of neglect.

You can prune most plants with manicure scissors or kitchen shears. Prune back any leaves that touch the glass. If the plants begin to outgrow their location, don't be afraid to remove them. You can pot them up and use them elsewhere or start a larger terrarium. Replace the plants you remove with another variety— experimentation is the name of the game. Aggressive plants that begin to crowd out their neighbors must be ruthlessly pruned or exiled.

How long can you expect a terrarium to last? By following the simple steps outlined above, you can have one indefinitely.

9

Fishbowls Without Fish:
Indoor Water Gardening

If you are one of those people, like me, who have a hard time keeping fish alive in an aquarium, there is no reason why you can't do away with the fish completely and have a water garden. That idea may sound funny at first but remember that with terrariums you are creating balanced environments without animals —so why not do the same thing under water without fish?

If well planned a water garden can be very beautiful. Because many submerged gardens will do very well in subdued lighting they are ideal for those locations in homes or apartments where other growing things would not flourish. They will add a great deal of interest, for instance, if they are integrated as a portion of a room divider along with other plants that enjoy the same conditions.

Of course, plants for a submerged garden are different from those planted in a terrarium, and while many of them do resemble grass, there are really no true grasses used in such plantings. One of these grasslike plants is *Vallisneria spiralis*, commonly called eelgrass or tape grass (though entirely unrelated to the grass family). Its pale-green translucent leaves often attain a length of two or three feet, so it will be suitable for only a rather large aquarium. Eelgrass is easy to grow and pretty for framing your planting. Set a few plants at each end of the container and let them arch over and meet in the center.

Other water plants include the various arrowheads, or Sagittaria. While the hardy types of this plant are frequently used for planting in shallow pools, what you will want to use is the tender type, *S. sinesis*, which grows about a foot or so high. The ribbon arrowhead and the awlleaf arrowhead are even smaller varieties good for your purposes.

Fish grass (*Cabomba caroliniana*), a submerged aquatic plant, is native from southern Illinois on down to Texas and Florida. It's often grown in aquariums as an oxygenating plant. This is a strange plant with hairlike submerged leaves. It also may produce floating leaves—although this is not likely—which are narrow, brittle, and not hairlike. This plant will not live very long in water unless it has soil in which to take root. Plant it so that it can't float freely. Fish grass, also called Washington plant and water shield, is easily propagated by seeds, cuttings, and divisions. Remember to do all your propagating under water. Sounds like a scene in *From Here to Eternity!*

Water milfoil, also an oxygenator, has similar growth habits. Another good plant is the perennial anacharis. This one belongs to the frog's-bit family, the Hydrocharitaceae. These plants are easy to grow and are increased by cuttings, sometimes by winter buds, and they will grow in any ordinary soil beneath a foot or so of water. The most easily obtainable is *A. canadensis*, a rampant water weed if you allow it to grow unchecked. It's easy to grow, but you must prune it back occasionally.

Since all of the above plants have narrow leaves, for contrast you will probably want some with different growth habits and physical characteristics. You might try Ludwigia, which belongs to the evening primrose family. It is identified by its rather small round leaves, which are slightly pink on the underside and dark green on the top. *L. mulerttii*, believed to be native only to South America, has trailing stems and yellow flowers. It is easily propagated by either division or cuttings.

Nuphar, or yellow pond lily, is another interesting plant for water gardens. It belongs to the water lily family and is a hardy flowering perennial. The floating leaves resemble those of water lilies and the flowers are mainly yellow. Propagation is by seeds or root division. These plants must also have their roots in soil.

Other flowering plants include Nymphoides, or floating heart, the water poppy, and water snowflake. Their culture is essentially the same as for Nuphar. Water poppy (Hydrocleys) is another tender perennial aquatic plant from South America, belonging to the family Butomaceae. They have thick, heart-shaped leaves and bear yellow three-petaled flowers, two inches in diameter. Water poppies may be planted in soil covered with shallow water at the margins of natural ponds or in pots of fertile, loamy soil, with the soil surface submerged six to nine inches beneath the water of a natural or artificial pool.

Another method of cultivating these plants is the following. Place a few inches of soil in a container 12 to 18 inches deep. Set the plants in this, cover the soil with an inch or two of clean sand, then fill the container with water. Containers or tubs planted in this way may be kept out of doors during the summer and moved indoors for the winter. Propagation of water poppies is by division in the spring. This plant flowers over a very long period in summer and fall.

Water plants that float freely on the surface are mostly ferns or fernlike plants such as water fern, Salvinia, and Azolla. They are generally of easy culture. *Pistia stratiotes* (water lettuce) is a floating plant native to South America and the southernmost United States. The leaves, about two inches long, are pea-green, velvety, and rather wedge-shaped. They grow in attractive rosettes. The inconspicuous flowers are small, green and arumlike. The rooting type of plants are most likely to be satisfactory, and these can often be obtained at fish supply stores or pet stores.

When you plant your submerged garden, put the strongest growers at the rear and at the ends, planting the rooted ones first. Do not use too many plants, for they are likely to increase quickly and become too dense to be attractive. When you need to remove plants or parts of plants, try to select the oldest ones first. Dealers in aquarium supplies have a small tool called a plant snip, which you may find handy for grooming your water babies.

You may think everything is all set and growing beautifully and then one day you begin to notice something green and scummy forming on the glass. So you thought this submerged garden was one place you wouldn't have to worry about weeds? Yes, underwater gardens have weeds too, I am sorry to say, but just as on terra firma, there are measures you can take.

Algae make their appearance, sometimes growing on the glass, sometimes floating freely in the water, and usually as a result of too much light. One means of controlling this is by placing the garden where the light is more subdued. Or the growth of many algae may be checked by the introduction of a few fresh-water snails—they are scavengers and this is their natural food.

10

Exotics: Romantic Travelers From Faraway Lands

Now let's take a look at the "immigrants" of the plant world that will help you earn your reputation as a topnotch indoor gardener. These are the exotics—plants from the far corners of the world, plants that have romantic appeal, rare beauty, and unique requirements and characteristics of growth.

Exotic plants are not new—many of them have been known and grown in this country for more than a hundred years—but for years lots of people have shied away from them, thinking they are too difficult to cultivate in the average home. That's a lot of baloney, perpetrated by so-called experts who like to play the one-upmanship game! Some people just naturally want to look down their noses at us ordinary house plant gardeners. They like to pretend that a plant they "specialize" in growing is beyond our humble abilities. I believe that it's more difficult to grow and provide for the welfare of many different types of plants than for just one type. Once you try your hand at exotic house plants you'll learn that, with the possible exception of the carnivores, these plants are as easy to grow successfully as their more common cousins. The three P's—practice, patience, and persistence—will have your successes outnumbering your failures.

Here are a few of the most common exotics. Have fun.

ABUTILON: FLOWERING MAPLE

Flowering maple is a tender shrub having large deep-green leaves with a striking white margin. This fellow is normally grown indoors as a house plant but makes an excellent border or window-box specimen during the summer. In the winter it is transferred to the windows or to a greenhouse for a display plant. The pendent bell-shaped flowers are rosy-orange and form during the summer and fall. New growth begins in the spring, and plants may be transferred to a slightly larger pot if root-bound. The potting soil should be made rich with two-thirds potting soil and one-third leaf mold and decayed manure. After repotting it's important to keep the plants in a warm and damp atmosphere for several weeks and spray the leaves often with a mister.

In their permanent location the plants require full sun and free air circulation. The dropping of the lower leaves indicates a need for fertilization. To meet this, make biweekly application of Ra-Pid-Gro during the summer. The soil should be maintained in a drier condition during the winter, but the stems should never be allowed to shrivel from lack of moisture. For pot culture, the top few inches of soil are removed annually and replaced with fresh potting soil. Plants grown in pots are pruned in March by shortening the growth of the past year by half. They should be kept in a moist atmosphere with the temperature between 55 and 60 degrees. If a climbing habit is desired, all the side shoots on the main stem should be pruned back to within two or three buds of the previous year's growth. All new shoots are fastened to supports as they progress.

The flowering maple is active nearly the entire year, and cuttings may be taken in the spring or fall. The pruned new wood may be used in March and will yield blooming plants by fall. Place cuttings in a propagating case and follow directions in Chapter 21.

The plants grow rapidly and will need shifting to larger pots from time to time. When you have your new plant in the largest pot you can conveniently handle, let the plant become root-bound. Fertilize twice a week to make up for the restricted growth, and prune to develop a more symmetrical, compact plant. Flowers are produced on new terminal shoots, therefore the more new growth you have, the more blooms you will get.

Amorphophallus

If the unusual is your bag, don't overlook Amorphophallus. The krubi, *Amorphophallus titanum,* is an immense inflorescence. It is the largest plant of this type known. The flowers, more correctly called inflorescences, appear before the leaves. They resemble the arum lily in shape. The flowers are mainly of a reddish-purple color. Most of these plants become huge, so I suggest you select one of the smaller types. *A. campanulatus* when in bloom is not more than 18 inches tall. The spathe is purplish-pink and the handsome stem is spotted. These plants are natives of Sumatra.

The corms, or bulbs, are potted in March in a rich soil with plenty of humus. They should then be placed in a warm sunny spot where the temperature is constantly above 55 degrees. Water sparingly until the flower spike has withered and the new growth of leaves begins to show. The soil should now be kept moist until growth ceases in the fall. In autumn the watering program should be gradually discontinued. Leave the soil completely dry for the winter. Small corms will appear on the older ones. Pot these in the spring and they'll flower in a few years.

If these strange plants interest you, keep a program going, once you have obtained the original plant, of repotting the corms. You can be bringing on new plants as the older ones become unmanageable or flower and deteriorate.

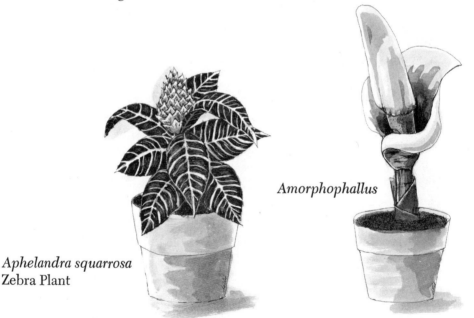

Amorphophallus

Aphelandra squarrosa
Zebra Plant

APHELANDRA—THE ZEBRA PLANT

In my travels around the country I've been surprised at the new interest in aphelandras, sometimes called zebra plants because of the zebralike white stripes on their shiny emerald-green leaves, which give them their distinctive appearance all year. In the fall and winter, when it's in comfortable surroundings, the plant will burst into bloom, producing one or more spikes of yellow flowers. This type *A. squarrosa* is interesting because it is indeed square—its flower spike is definitely four-sided! Imported originally from South America, these plants vary in height from nine to twenty-four inches. *Aphelandra aurantiaca* has orange-scarlet flowers; *A. aurantiaca roezlii*, rich scarlet; *A. tetragona* (cristata), scarlet; *A. nitens*, orange-scarlet, with very handsome glossy foliage.

Fresh plants of Aphelandra are raised from either cuttings or seeds. Their first "baby shoes" should be 3-inch pots, from which they can be gradually moved forward as they grow. The soil mix should be a compost of equal parts of loam and peat, with about another one-fourth of sand, and the pots should always be well drained. Keep the atmosphere around them humid by placing them in a pebble tray filled with water, as you would camellias.

During the summer zebra plants do best in a cool atmosphere of 65–70 degrees, and atmospheric conditions must be kept moist. It's not a good idea to pinch off the tips of the shoots, as the real aim is to produce only one stem with one large spike of bloom. However, if you want more but smaller blooms, pinch away.

As the plant grows, water the soil only when it is moderately dry. Overwatering will cause the lower leaves to fall off, so do your watering operation carefully. Be sure that there is good drainage. After the plant has flowered, and during the winter months, water should be given only occasionally.

With a large older plant, remove side shoots in the spring with a bit of heel (a piece of the old branch) attached. Insert this in sand in a propagating case. You may also sow seeds in pots of sandy peat and loam in a temperature of about 70 degrees. The best time to do your seeding is in the spring.

BROMELIADS

The Bromeliad, sometimes called the air plant, is a plant belonging to the pineapple family. It makes an ideal house plant. If you have ever cut off the top of a fresh pineapple and inserted it in a pot, where it obligingly grew, you have been growing a bromeliad. But this plant, however interesting it may be, is not at all as dramatic as some of the more colorful types of bromeliads now available for house plant culture. *Billbergia nutans,* for example, has blue-edged petals, conspicuous golden stamens, and striking red bracts.

Bromeliads, being native to the Central and South American jungles, thrive on warmth, and room temperatures can be kept as hot as you like. Further, they have developed water-retaining powers that are perfectly suited for the dry household conditions in most of our homes. In their native habitat they grow on tree branches and are accustomed to very little light. This, too, makes them ideal for our darker rooms.

Billbergia nutans is an evergreen plant from Brazil. It has long, rigid, pineapplelike leaves that rise in the form of a rosette straight from the rootstock. The flowers are spikes, or panicles, and appear in the centers of the rosettes in winter.

The temperature for billbergias should never be allowed to drop below 55 degrees. Potting is done in spring in a compost of peat, loam, sand, and leaf mold, with the free addition of chopped charcoal. Or they can be potted in orchid peat (osmunda fiber) alone. These are relatively shallow rooting plants, so fill the pot halfway with drainage material. Billbergia needs a fairly moist atmosphere, with abundant water at the roots in summer, but less during the winter.

The bromeliads are quite an extraordinary family, interesting and infinitely varied. They range from the slender droopiness of the Spanish moss that hangs from the trees in the South to the hohenbergias, harshly upright in growth. Some, like the pineapple, are terrestrial.

PINEAPPLE PLANT

Pineapple plants are easy to grow and will give the youngsters in your family an opportunity to watch Mother Nature at work. Just purchase a pineapple at your local produce store and enjoy the fruit in any one of a thousand ways. (I, for one, like pineapple upside-down cake.) When you cut up the fruit, save the top foliage with a thin slice of the fruit attached.

Plant the pineapple top in a shallow dish containing a soil mixture that's half sand and half packaged potting soil. This plant will not bear fruit, but if you give it at least four hours of direct sunlight a day, a day-night temperature range of 75-55 degrees, and keep it moist, it should bloom in a year or two. Fertilize the plant once a month.

Most bromeliads are air plants, but they seem to thrive very well when their roots are placed in a coarse planter mix. Also, most plants of these have pointed leaves that rise in a whorl. This center forms a natural vase and must be kept full of water at all times. Save rainwater, refrigerator drippings, or use bottled water for this purpose. Avoid hard water or water that is heavily chlorinated.

Cryptanthus

Cryptanthus is closely related to the "friendship plant," Billbergia. In their native South America these plants grow wild on trees. The rather thick, heavy, spiny leaves form a dwarf rosette. The flowers are in terminal spikes with conspicuous bracts. The name Cryptanthus means "hidden flower"—the flowers are partly concealed by the bracts. The flowers are red or white.

Cryptanthus requires a large amount of drainage material, and the pots should be half-filled with crocks, broken brick, or large gravel. The leaves of the Bromeliad are exceptionally attractive and richly colored. Propagation is accomplished by removing the suckers, or offshoots, in spring and placing them in small pots. As with other types of bromeliads, they should be put in a propagating case, preferably the type with bottom heat.

Other bromeliads include Nidularium, a group of tender, tree-perching Brazilian plants which are also suitable for cultivation in terrariums, and Tillandsia. Most tillandsias have leaves that are smooth, rigid, and leathery, rising straight up from the base of the plant. This is a common characteristic of growth except in the case of *T. usneoides*, Spanish moss.

Spanish Moss

This form bears no resemblance to the other kinds of Tillandsia. It is simply composed of long, gray filaments, often several feet in length. These hang from trees in great masses and grow naturally from Virginia to Florida and Texas. They are also found in South America from Argentina to Chile. Spanish moss is more than just a curiosity—my friend Buck Ray, at Florida's Silver

Springs, says it is used in the manufacture of a number of products, including women's lipsticks.

CALCEOLARIAS

My Grandma Putt used to grow some beautiful pot plants
she called "lady's slipper" but that I have always known as
"Grandma's pocketbook." They were at their height of popularity
back in the 1940s, but lapsed into undeserved obscurity. Calceolarias are now making a comeback and many florists sell them as
Easter gift plants. The purselike or slipperlike blooms are often
speckled, and only three—yellow, orange, and deep red—come in
solid colors. A deep, speckled-red variety, called "Strawberry," is
often a favorite of the ladies, florists have found that men prefer
the solid colors. Calceolarias are mostly tender perennials of herbaceous or shrubby growth and are principally natives of Chile
or Peru in the Andes. They belong to the snapdragon family,
Scrophulariaceae.

These plants should be purchased full grown and in bloom,
as it can be difficult to get them to flower. This is done best
by professional growers in a greenhouse. When you bring the
plant home, it should bloom for quite a long time, since the
growers usually sell them when the blooming period is just beginning.

Place your calceolaria in a bright east or west window or
where it will get strong indirect light. Use a maximum-minimum
thermometer, which gives you the high and low temperature in a
24-hour period. This plant needs to be placed where it will be in
the cool 50s at night and in the cool 60s in the day. When the
flowers begin to wilt and turn brown, it is important to pinch them
off before they go to seed. If you do this, a second set of blooms
will come up through the center of the plant.

The best way to water your calceolaria is to set it, pot and all,
in a shallow pan and let it stand for about an hour. Remove it and
allow the excess water to drain away. Don't water again until the
soil is dry to the touch. Don't water from the top, as the leaves will
rot. Don't feed the plant while it is in bloom; the florist will have
put in plenty of food to carry it through.

Both the herbaceous and shrubby types of perennial or bi-
ennial calceolarias can be grown in a home greenhouse. The herbaceous, or soft-stemmed, kinds are raised from seeds sown

annually in early summer and are grown in pots for spring and early summer. The shrubby kinds may also be raised from seeds but are usually propagated by cuttings.

Seeds of the herbaceous types may be sown from early April until late September. From the earliest sowings, plants may be grown out to finish in 9–10-inch pots. While in flower they may measure as much as two to two and a half feet high and spread as far when staked out. A fair-sized plant in a 5–6-inch pot may be raised from a sowing made as late as August 1. Seeds should be sown on a screened mixture of two parts compost, one part peat moss, and one part sand. Make a level surface by pressing the mixture down so it is moderately firm. Before seeding, soak the soil thoroughly, and sow seed as soon as it has drained. The seeds should be scattered evenly and thinly over the soil surface. As they are very tiny, don't attempt to cover them with soil. However, it's a good idea to cover the container with plastic wrap to conserve moisture, and put a piece of newspaper over that. Change the plastic wrap every day to remove excess moisture. Do not let the soil dry out.

When the seeds start to germinate, remove the paper and put the container where it can receive light but not direct sunlight. Remove the plastic wrap from time to time to allow the seedlings to receive air; in a few days remove it altogether. Seedlings may be transplanted after the first two leaves have formed. The first shift may be to a flat, where they should be placed two or three inches apart in sandy soil mixed with humus. After about six weeks pot them up singly in 3-inch pots. They should be moved progressively to larger pots as growth continues. You can give your perennial calceolarias a summer in the outdoors. They do well in light soil and partial shade. Repot them and return them to a north windowsill in the house before frost.

Although most calceolarias are either biennials or perennials, there are some very good annuals. My favorite is *C. mexicana*, a visitor from south of the border. This is a bushy plant that grows to a height of only about one foot. Its miniature half-inch flowers are yellow.

The shrubby calceolarias are mostly propagated by root cuttings taken from the new growth, which starts soon after the flower heads are cut off. The stem cuttings root readily in sand. They should be kept in shade in a moist atmosphere. After the roots form, take care of them in the same way you would the herbaceous types.

CAMELLIAS

Even if you never become a member of the Camellia Society, like so many of my friends down in Ocala, Florida, and southern California (where these plants flourish outdoors), you can have good results growing these plants indoors or in greenhouses.

Camellia flowers are among the most beautiful in the plant kingdom. I've known them to bloom up to six weeks. The blooms, depending on the variety and where you live, appear from September to May—although most seem to disappear around income-tax time. The flowers appear in clusters, but if you want large blooms, pinch off all but one bud in each cluster. Colors range from white to red. Pinks and other mixed colors are very popular. Blooms can be as large as five inches across. They are so beautiful that they're worth a little extra trouble.

Camellias make fine indoor plants. They need cool temperatures and high humidity. A temperature of 65–75 degrees during the day and in the low 40s at night will suit them very well. They are much the same as azaleas in their cultural requirements. Like azaleas, they also need an acid soil mix, rich in organic matter such as leaf mold and peat moss. Add a generous amount of charcoal to the soil and use cottonseed meal as a fertilizer.

Soil for camellias should always be kept moist. Use a mister on hot days to prevent bud drop. Camellias drop buds when night temperatures reach the high sixties. Put the plants where they can get curtain-filtered sunlight or in a bright east or west window. After blooming is finished, prune to keep the plants to three feet or less. These plants will need root pruning from time to time.

CHINESE HIBISCUS

This variety of hibiscus is a native of Hawaii, where it is the state flower. It's a "tropical" and likes warmth, sunshine, and a moist atmosphere. The gorgeous flowers come in single pink ("American Beauty"), double carmine ("Celia") and double bright yellow ("Peggy Hendry").

If you intend to raise one indoors, you should give hibiscus a sunny location and a winter temperature of 45–50 degrees. A temperature of 55–65 degrees should be maintained after the plants are started into new growth after the annual pruning. When the atmosphere is extremely dry, the plant has a tendency to drop the flower buds before they are fully developed. Avoid this by providing water in an open container near the plants and by frequently sprinkling the foliage.

When you bring your new friend home, put it into a 4-inch pot, using a potting soil consisting of two parts of loam to one each of sand and humus. The humus may be peat moss or decayed leaves (leaf mold) to which some well-rotted manure has been added. Set your plant where it can get strong light—but not against a sunny window, where the foliage may burn. The plants, which can be grown outdoors in mild climates, may be set outside in summer but must be brought in before the first frost. After the blooming period is past, cut them back to encourage new growth and more flowers.

Propagate your Chinese hibiscus by inserting 3-inch cuttings in sand and peat moss in March and April. Place them in a propagating case (in a hothouse if you have one) and keep them there until roots have formed. Pot separately in 3-inch pots and gradually shift them to larger ones. Pinch back the main shoot as soon as the plants are six inches high, and do the same to the side branches to encourage bushy growth.

GARDENIAS

Whether you call these plants gardenias or Cape jasmines, they are truly exotic plants, with an air of romance and mystery. The summer-blooming type is often called the "mystery gardenia." And when you add to the romantic name the heavy sweet fragrance of their scent, you know for sure that these are something special! Gardenias are one of the more difficult house plants to grow, but close attention to their needs will help you bring them to bloom.

G. jasminoides, the winter-blooming type, is the one most often offered by florists for growing as pot plants. These plants require a minimum winter temperature of 60 degrees. Like camellias, the gardenia needs a humid atmosphere. Less water is required during the winter months, but try never to let the atmosphere or the soil remain dry for any period of time. Water freely and heavily during the summer.

These plants need up to eight hours of sunlight a day, with a minimum of four hours to keep them healthy. Feed them with a liquid fertilizer once a week during the summer and monthly at other times of the year. Cut the application dosage to half what is recommended on the container.

Potting compost should consist of peat, loam, and well-decomposed steer manure in equal parts, laced with a free addition of sand and a small quantity of crushed charcoal. The mix should always be loose and porous (not like the hard-packed soil I recommend for geraniums). Gardenias are acid-loving plants, and when the soil mix becomes alkaline from the accumulation of hard water salts, iron does not get to the roots. It can be provided in the form of iron sulfate or a diluted teaspoonful of patented tonic. You can tell when the need for iron exists—the top leaves will turn yellow.

Remove the flower buds during the summer and the plants will bloom in autumn and winter. Old plants should be repotted in February, and pruning of any shoots that have become too long can be done at this time.

GERANIUMS

Geraniums have been grown in the United States for so many years that we don't think of them as exotics. But these plants originally came from South Africa and they are a pretty cantankerous bunch. There are certain things they like and certain things they dislike. Meet these needs and then let them alone and this independent plant will bloom well for you. Many species have scented leaves—lemon, nutmeg, rose, and peppermint.

The correct botanical name for geranium is Pelargonium. The most common types of geraniums are zonal pelargoniums and ivy-leaved pelargoniums. Zonal pelargoniums are named for the markings on their rounded leaves. They have upright growth and flowers that range from deep red to a salmon or pink color. These plants are extremely popular as pot and window-box plants. As you would expect, ivy-leaved pelargoniums have ivy-shaped leaves, are less hardy than the zonal types, and the flowers are mostly pink in color. They have a hanging characteristic of growth and are very charming as hanging-basket plants.

Unlike so many plants we discuss in this chapter, geraniums like just an average potting soil, one not overly rich. Plan on using one part each of sand and humus (peat moss or leaf mold) and two parts of garden loam, with a small amount of finely ground bone meal or superphosphate.

Geranium

Geraniums love the same sort of hot bright sun and lack of water that their ancestors knew in the African veldt. You should spray their leaves every once in a while, but be very stingy with water on the soil. Give them only the minimum amount of water needed to keep the plant in healthy condition. Do not spray leaves when the sun is on them or they will burn. They are great plants for a sunny windowsill, window boxes, and hanging baskets.

When feeding your geraniums don't use fertilizers high in nitrogen or you will get more foliage and fewer flowers. Only when they're getting ready to bloom do they want food; the rest of the time they want the soil packed firmly around their roots. At blooming time add any plant food to the water, and water a little more often, but try not to splash the water on the flower buds, because they tend to rot very easily.

As I have said, geraniums love the sun and will enjoy all the sunshine they can get, especially in the winter. While you can't really expect them to be in flower the whole year round, this obliging plant will permit you to choose its flowering season—winter or summer. You can let the plant rest in the other season. Remember, in South Africa the seasons are reversed from those in the United States. If you want *winter* flowers, pinch off any summer flower buds. If you want *summer* flowers, don't let any flower buds form until after March.

One thing is absolutely necessary if you plan to force your geraniums into bloom and that is to let them become pot-bound. This means that the pot your plant is in will be allowed to fill itself up with roots. Of course this condition cannot go on indefinitely for in time the roots will force all the soil out of the pot. Then, having nothing to feed on, the plant will die. But the geranium, like many other plants, needs this condition temporarily to force it into bloom. So don't use any larger pot than necessary. A 4-inch pot is a good size for a newly received plant.

Place several pieces of broken shards in the bottom to make sure that the drainage hole remains open. Be sure that the soil is sifted down around the sides of the pot, leaving no air holes. In fact, it's a good idea to ram the soil down with something hard and heavy so it is thoroughly packed. This technique is called hard potting. Another method is to thump the pot vigorously on the potting table or kitchen counter after the soil has been filled in. Then water thoroughly.

One common mistake beginners make is to allow the plants to become unattractively leggy. If you want to avoid this, pinch back the tips of the stems to encourage branching. Short, sturdy branches bearing more flowers will be your reward. Long, weak shoots are the result of too much water, too much fertilizer, or too little light.

Get-Up-and-Grow *Power!*

Have you been hearing about something called gibberellic acid and wondering what it is? It is a plant hormone that speeds up growth, and many and wonderful are the results it has achieved for us. Geraniums in particular have responded well to it, their stems stretching in about one-fourth the time it would take normal plants to do this with the old hand-pruning method.

In the past it has taken twelve to fifteen months to produce tree geraniums, but experiments have shown that weekly sprays of gibberellin will bring this about in three or four months. Such application will also result in the production of larger flower heads and longer-lasting flowers. This hormone must be used in very small amounts, and the rapid rate of growth causes the plant to demand more food. In fact, the rate of fertilizer feedings should be doubled so you can compensate for the greater rate of growth.

If you want to stretch your geraniums, start with those in 2¼-inch pots. Transplant them at once to 5- or 6-inch pots and let them grow naturally for a couple of weeks before beginning to spray them with gibberellin. Spray your plant lightly each week, but only the top four to six inches. Feed it with a soluble house plant fertilizer at every other watering. As the plant grows, remove the side leaves until it reaches the height you want—you will probably need to stake it. Now allow it to form side branches, and do not pinch off any flower buds.

Many other flowering plants besides geraniums will respond to this treatment, but there is a wide variation from plant to plant. Some flower earlier, some, like the geranium, have larger blossoms, and, oddly, some don't react at all. This high-powered booster spray has also been tried on the foliage of roses with good results. If you want to experiment with geraniums or other plants, you can obtain this gibberellic-acid spray under various trade names from most nurseries and garden centers.

Martha Washington Geraniums

Martha Washington geraniums, sometimes called Lady Washington geraniums, are different in appearance and culture from other types. They resemble azaleas so much that they are sometimes called the "poor man's azalea." They produce their flowers in large clusters in the spring, and after that go into a rest period. This type also needs lots of sunlight and can take higher temperatures. When the plant is blooming it should have ample water. But after the blooms are spent, reduce the water supply, as you would with other types.

After it flowers, put the plant outdoors in May and turn the pot on its side. Cut back the shoots to about an inch above the soil line and soak the pot with water in late July. When new growth starts, repot, using a smaller pot and removing as much soil as possible. All weak sprouts should be removed and even the vigorous ones pinched back when they are six inches long. In January, repot into larger containers. Cuttings for propagation may be taken during the time the plants are in flower. Or, later, you can propagate from sliced-off pieces of root.

Red, Red Geraniums Need Complementary Plants Around Them

If you really like red geraniums, here's a tip. Red geraniums planted alone are often harsh-looking. But they can become elegant and aristocratic-looking if you mix the planting with another sun lover—Cineraria. Our grandmothers knew this secret, and Grandma Putt used "dusty miller" (the common name for Cineraria) for this purpose. Cineraria "Diamond" grows twelve inches tall, "Silver Queen" eight inches, and "Frosty" is still smaller. It is the fine hairs on the leaves of these plants that soften and absorb the brilliant red, making the entire planting far more pleasing to the eye.

Taking in Your Winter Geraniums

I think the thing people ask me most about geraniums is how to bring them in from outside and keep them successfully over the winter. To bring in and winter geraniums, jerk them up by the roots right after the first frost when they turn a brownish color. Lay each geranium diagonally across a double spread of newspaper and wrap it up. Now put your wrapped-up roots in a cool, damp basement and leave them there until March.

After March 15, take your geraniums out and unwrap them. Cut off one-third of the roots, and two-thirds of the tops. Repot in clay pots filled with a mixture of half sand and half soil. To sterilize the soil, put it in a cake tin and bake with a potato at 200 degrees. When the potato is tender, your soil is ready for planting. Hard-pot the plants as previously described.

FUCHSIAS

Most fuchsias bloom from April through September, so they can be grown in window boxes as well as indoors. They are equally at home in either location and also make a magnificent display in tubs or pots on porches and terraces and in gardens. Fuchsias are one of the best examples of a plant that is easy to grow and appropriate both indoors and out. (Fuchsias may also be encouraged to grow as "trees" by the use of gibberellic acids.)

Fuchsia

While Fuchsia plants are generally available for purchase and shipment from nurseries every month of the year, the best time to start them for house plants is November and December.

As soon as you receive your plants or bring them home from the local florist they should be placed in 4- or 5-inch pots. Place bits of broken potsherds over the drainage holes in the bottom to prevent clogging and use a rich, porous soil mixture. Here is a good recipe that may be used not only for fuchsias but for other plants with the same soil requirements:

> 1 part good garden loam
> 1 part sand
> 2 parts leaf mold, compost, or other humus
> ½ part well-rotted or dried cow manure
> 1 tablespoon of bone meal per quart of the mixture
> above (a 5-inch potful per bushel)

Your fuchsia likes the soil well firmed about its roots. So thump the pot good and hard on the table. Water from the bottom by standing the pot in a pan of water and allowing it to soak up all the soil will hold. Drain for a few minutes and stand in a light but not sunny window. Leave it in this location until the roots are well established, then give it a little sun for part of the day. Like so many house plants, they must have a cool, airy atmosphere. Give them free ventilation in mild weather.

Now hear this! Unlike some house plants, fuchsias should *not* become pot-bound. Repot them frequently, using the next larger size pot each time. They require plenty of light, but should be kept out of the midday sun. Water your fuchsias freely during their growing season, but decrease the amount gradually from late October to the middle of November. Then repot, cutting back the plants to half their height, and store them in a cool, dark cellar. Give them only enough water to keep the soil from becoming bone-dry until March, when the plants should be returned to the light and watered generously.

From March on, give them a weekly watering with liquid manure or plant food (such as Plantabbs or Ra-Pid-Gro) in solution until the first flower bud appears. Pinch back the growing tip often while the plants are in active growth to keep them compact and bushy. Watch out for red spider mite, which can be controlled by regular spraying with Red Arrow, and largely prevented by frequently washing the foliage.

Fuchsias once enjoyed a wider popularity, and Grandma Putt's collection of old gardening books and catalogues, some published almost a hundred years ago, enumerates more than five hundred varieties of fuchsias. Nowadays we have fewer varieties, but the lovely, waxy flowers (sometimes called, "lady's eardrops") are more choice, and they come in doubles as well as singles. Rose-red is still the favorite color.

If you want to increase your stock, shoots should be taken off for cuttings about three inches long. Remove the lowest leaves and sever the base of the shoot beneath a joint. Insert the cuttings in a propagating frame in the greenhouse or under glass. Here they will quickly form roots. If the cuttings are taken in February, they should be ready to be potted up in March or early April, and this may be done by placing them singly in 3-inch pots.

MEXICAN HEATHER

This plant, *Cuphea hyssopifolia,* comes from Florida. It is sometimes called "cigar flower." This is one of the most useful plants for window-garden culture that I know of; it is easy to grow and blooms constantly. Though generally grown as a pot plant in the North, it is valuable as a summer bedding plant and may be grown outdoors permanently in the far South.

This is a plant that should be grown in full sun—or at least as much sun as you can give it—as it likes light and warmth. Here is a potting mixture that will provide the proper foundation:

> 1 part sand
> 2 parts sandy garden loam
> 1 part leaf mold, peat moss, or other humus
> ½ part dried cow manure, if available
> 1 tablespoon bone meal per quart of soil mix

Plant Mexican heather in a 3-inch pot. When the plants appear to be crowding, put them in another pot at least one inch larger. However, it shouldn't be necessary to repot frequently; a five-year-old plant can remain almost indefinitely in a 6-inch pot. To keep it small you may occasionally have to root-prune.

Keep the soil about as moist as you would for geraniums. In other words, don't let the soil dry out completely, but don't let it become overly wet. In the spring, when growth becomes active, use a liquid fertilizer. At that time feed the plants once a month for two months. These plants are seldom attacked by insects or disease. You should cut them back from time to time to promote lateral growth.

OLEANDER

Oleander, or Nerium, should be potted as soon as you bring it home, using 3- or 4-inch pots and making a later shift to 5- or 6-inch pots. The potting mixture is as follows.

> 1 part sand
> 2 parts potting soil
> 1 part leaf mold or other humus
> ½ part pulverized, dried steer manure
> 1 tablespoon bone meal per quart of mixture

Oleanders are very attractive pot plants, and the fact that the stems, leaves, and flowers are poisonous if eaten doesn't seem ever to have affected their popularity. But it is something you should keep in mind if you have a baby or inquisitive preschooler. Oleanders are easily grown if attention is paid to cutting back and resting them after they finish flowering and to shaping (by pinching tips of growth) and feeding while growth is active. The blossoms are produced in summer, and the plants are often used for foliage effect during the winter. While the plants are in active growth, water them well and feed them every two weeks with liquid manure or Plantabbs. Cut back after flowering, and water sparingly until growth is resumed. Watch for scale.

Oleanders are also grown outdoors, especially for flowering hedges, in the South and Southwest.

These plants are propagated by cuttings three to six inches in length made from firm shoots cut off in the summer. Remove the lower leaves and cut the bottom of the stem cleanly across just beneath a node (joint). The shoots should then be inserted in a jar of water with their bases just beneath the surface of the water. Place the bottle in a sunny location or on a windowsill that gets the sun.

Oleander cuttings may also be rooted in a mixture of sand and peat moss or in vermiculite. Place a jar or plastic bag over them until roots are formed, or put the cuttings in a propagating case. Cuttings should be placed in 3-inch pots after they have rooted. Gradually shift them to larger pots. If you want bushy plants, remove the tips of the shoots as soon as the plants are rooted and placed in the 3-inch pots. Also prune off subsequent side shoots.

Oleanders are available in a wide range of colors. There are also single- and double-bloom varieties. The principal kinds are: *N. oleander*, red and its varieties: album plenum, white, double; "Henri Mares," rosy-pink, double; splendens, red, double; variegatum, red flowers and variegated leaves; "Soeur Agnes," white, double. *N. indicum* and its varieties also offer a choice, some of them being double- as well as single-flowered and also having very fragrant blossoms.

Most oleanders grow taller than eight feet in height at maturity. My editor, Dan Kibbie, who lives in southern California, has a clump of reds and whites that is easily fifteen feet tall. So you can see that you will have to prune your pot plants ruthlessly. By careful pruning, an indoor plant may be kept blossoming and looking good for many years. Replace these occasionally with younger plants.

MINIATURE ROSES

I have mixed emotions about putting any members of the rose family in a chapter about exotic plants. Everybody knows that the rose is the world's best-known and most domesticated flowering plant. I've never met a rose that I couldn't be friends with—even the old-fashioned varieties, which are the most fragrant. However, growing miniature roses as house plants is a relatively new pastime, and these lovely Lilliputians of the royal family are rapidly gaining in popularity.

These tiny dwarfs with miniature leaves and buds, resemble their larger sisters in every detail. They are ever-blooming, and indoors, as house plants, are evergreen. The range of colors of these miniature monarchs offers something to complement every decorator's color scheme.

Because they are so small, many people hesitate to try growing miniature roses indoors, thinking they are too delicate. Actually, just the opposite is true. They are much easier to cultivate than their outdoor relatives. Careful watering is their only special requirement. This is because of their shallow root system. Don't

Miniature Rose

overwater, and don't get their clothes (foliage) wet when you do water. These little roses need full sun and regular fertilizing and spraying. Given the moderate attention they deserve, they should be in constant bloom indoors. They are vigorous growers, and for this reason they will need frequent pruning or they will outgrow their pots. Keep them within bounds.

Take your baby roses out of doors in the spring and let them enjoy the summer. They will be refreshed and invigorated when you return them to the house in the fall. Sow seed in good garden loam and keep moist—they'll germinate in about three weeks and bloom in three months.

Starfish Plant

Stapelia, known as the "starfish plant," is a branching succulent resembling a cactus without thorns. The vaguely star-shaped flowers, nearly two inches across, are spotted yellow and brown in unusual designs. This plant needs plenty of sunlight, plenty of water with excellent drainage, and a fairly rich, loose soil. For potting use the following mixture:

> 2 parts sand, medium coarse
> 2 parts garden loam or potting soil
> 4 parts humus (leaf mold or peat moss)
> 1 part flowerpot shards or soft brick in small pieces
> 1 tablespoon bone meal or limestone per quart of potting mixture

Fill the pots about one-fourth full of drainage such as broken flowerpots or gravel. Near blooming time it is a good idea to add some fertilizer to the water.

During the fall months let the plants rest with less light and water. In early winter place them in a sunny window and give plenty of water, being careful not to let the soil become soggy. It probably won't get that way if you use the potting mixture above. Water your starfish plant frequently, but don't set it in a container of water and leave it there—the soil must always be drained.

Early in March the plants should start to bloom with their very curious, strangely brown-mottled blossoms. And the blooming season should continue well into summer. Don't repot very often as the roots need to be pot-bound to force the plants to bloom.

Propagation is by division and cuttings, and new plants may also be grown from seeds. Division is the simplest method. Just repot the roots that appear at the base of the shoots and they will grow to new plants. If a cutting is made, the cut surface should be left exposed to the air and allowed to dry for twenty-four hours. A corky skin will form at the base. Insert this in sandy soil and allow it to form roots in a shady spot. Do not water unless the rooting medium becomes dry.

SPATHIPHYLLUM

This plant, which has a white flower much like an anthurium or a calla lily and very ornamental dark-green leaves, is a native of South America. It loves a moist, tropical atmosphere, since its natural environment is near the equator on the dark jungle floor. In spite of the fact that it is tropical in origin and thrives best in a humid atmosphere, it succeeds remarkably well as a house plant, possibly because it is accustomed to receiving very little light.

The minimum temperature for these plants should be 55 degrees. In nature they have adjusted to a climate in which the seasons are so much the same that there is little need for a rest period or dormancy. For this reason spathiphyllums bloom almost constantly and thrive in a warm, dark household interior, thus making them ideal house plants. They are receiving considerably more attention than they have received in the past, and more and better varieties are now available.

Most of these plants have green, lance-shaped leaves that

rise straight up from the rootstock, varying in length from six to twenty inches. The flower spathes, which are produced on short stems, average three inches and are white or greenish-white in color.

Well-rooted plants will benefit from regular fertilizing with diluted liquid fertilizer. Repotting, if necessary, should be done in February. Remove the root ball and take off some of the old soil with a pointed stick. Repot in the next larger pot size, adding some new soil. Spathiphyllums are best propagated by division of the roots at potting time in the spring.

PITTOSPORUM

These are among the most beautiful and desirable plants for indoor culture. They are prized for their foliage as well as for the tiny white or cream-colored flowers that appear in the spring-time. Pittosporums are small evergreen trees, or large shrubs, and vary somewhat in leaf and flower. There is one variety of this species with variegated leaves.

The Japanese Pittosporum, or Tobira, is one of the best, having small white flowers in spring that smell like orange blossoms. The plant is handsome in or out of bloom because of the clean-looking dark-green leaves. In mild parts of the United States,

Pittosporum tobira

Tobira is an evergreen and may be grown out of doors. Believe it or not, in its native country Tobira sometimes grows twenty feet tall, with the leathery leaves up to four inches long and one and a half inches across! But don't let this worry you—in your home you can keep them for several years at a height of three to four feet.

The flowers are borne in dense clusters from the ends of the shoots. They are white when they first open but will yellow with age. The plants will grow fairly well in bright, indirect light but prefer up to six hours of sunlight a day. Feed them twice a year— in early spring and early summer—and prune in the spring after they have bloomed.

As I said, in the house this plant won't grow too rapidly. But after several years it will become too large, so it's a good idea to have a young one coming along to replace it. You can accomplish this by taking cuttings of the half-hard shoots. These should be about four to five inches long with a small heel of the old wood. Do this in July and place the cuttings in a propagating case. Even those placed in a cold frame outdoors will root easily. Leave the young plants undisturbed until the following spring.

11

Cacti and Succulents: The Desert Tribes

CACTI

Cacti are the weird and grotesque members of the plant kingdom. They may be small as a thimble or tall, stately, forty-foot giants that dominate the landscape. You can take your pick. And if you don't mind taking a little needling from time to time, you will get a great deal of satisfaction raising some indoor plants of the cactus family and perhaps some of their less spiny cousins from among the succulents. As house guests these plants demand much less attention and affection than some of their foliage and flowering friends.

Contrary to all the legends, cacti are not reservoirs of water on the desert. But they do store a sticky, mucilaginous, sometimes bitter juice for periods of drought. Cacti can go as long as four or five years without rainfall—how about that? If you are the type who sometimes forgets to water, maybe these are the plants for you.

You may always have thought of cactus as those spiny, spiked, stick-you-in-the-seat-of-the-pants plants that provide ouches and yeeoows in those "Roadrunner and the Coyote" cartoons. But anyone who has ever seen the desert bloom in the winter and spring, or raised a Christmas cactus at home, knows that cacti can be as beautiful as any of Mother Nature's charges in the plant kingdom. Folks who take the time and have the interest to establish a cordial relationship with these charmers wouldn't trade them for a whole trayful of African violets. A cactus in bloom is not even surpassed by an orchid—in fact the epiphyllums are often called the orchids of the cactus world. These beautiful flowering plants were first discovered in 1689, deep in the lush, tropical jungles of Central and South America. But despite their name, they are true cacti and are not related in any way to orchids.

Even prickly pear, that terror of the Texas badlands, is crowned with gorgeous, delicate yellow flowers during its annual blooming season. Some varieties of this species even produce their flowers in orange or red. And even though prickly pear—or Opuntia, if we want to be formal—is generally looked at with disfavor the rest of the year, it does have some good points. Cattlemen sometimes burn off the spines and use the fleshy parts of the plant for fodder.

Actually, the fruits of all cacti are edible, but some aren't very tasty. They are relished by birds, rodents, cattle, deer, and other wildlife. The fruit of the prickly pear is used in the making of jellies, jams, and candies. The fruit of the giant saguaro is a traditional staple item in the diet of the Papago and Pima Indians. These tribes celebrated their New Year in late June, when the saguaro fruits were ripe. And what would a delicious Mexican meal be without a Margarita or two? These refreshing cocktails are made with Mexico's national liquor, tequila, which is derived from the agave. Cacti in the wild have also been used to provide nesting places for birds and woody supports for the building of human shelters.

While many species of cacti are American, having discovered this country long before Columbus, others exist elsewhere in jungles, near lakes and seas, even on mountains, where they have adjusted to bitter cold, strong winds, and poor soil. Most prefer the semiarid regions of North and South America, Asia, and Africa, but some, like the epiphyllums, like to live in rain forests. Mexico probably has the largest number of varieties on the North American continent, but there are plenty to choose from which are native to the western deserts of the United States. Domestic or imported, cacti offer about two thousand different species to perk up your indoor garden.

Many varieties of cactus are so strange, so startling, in their infinite possibilities of spine formations on healthy, well-grown plants, that they would win flower-show awards for beauty even if the blossoms never appeared. Some members of this family are so oddly constructed and have lived so long that they warrant your investigation.

The enormous number of shapes and sizes of cacti is sur-

Opuntia microdasys albata
Angel Wing Cactus

Strawberry Cactus

passed only by the dramatic beauty, delicacy, and vividness of their colors. For example, Rudolph the red-nosed reindeer's schnoz won't stop any more traffic than "Redhead," a unique triangular cactus from Japan. This has a bold, round, bright-red cactus (Spring Hill) grafted on top. The fluted flowerlike ball has spiny tips and almost glows with color.

The blossoms of the cactus that resembles a rose appear from March to August. They run the entire range of brilliant colors, but most remain open for only one day in the low deserts. At higher elevations they remain for several days. The night-blooming cerei (saguaro, queen of the night, organ pipe, and so on) all have white flowers that open late in the evening and close the following morning. The blossoms of *Cereus hexagonus* are white, tinged with purple on their outer petals, and resemble a magnificent water lily when they come to full bloom.

For indoor cultivation cacti require a minimum temperature of 40 degrees, and 10–15 degrees higher is even better. With few exceptions these plants should be exposed to every bit of available sunlight (or should be grown under fluorescents) throughout the year. An exception to this is the epiphyllum group mentioned earlier.

Cacti are easy to grow, but for those in "captivity" the trick is to get them to bloom. Here are some ideas that may help you persuade them to step into the spotlight. One of the prime requisites is good drainage. To ensure this, fill the pot one-fourth full of flowerpot chips or pea-size gravel before putting in any soil.

Stop for a minute and think—have you ever seen a cactus

GRAVEL

POTTING SOIL

FIBROUS MOSS
BROKEN POTSHERDS
DRAINAGE

Proper Method for Potting Cacti

growing on the beach? Of course not! Succulents and cacti do not, as so many people think, grow in pure sand. They need a nutritional soil suited to their specialized needs. A mix compounded of equal parts of garden loam, leaf mold, and sand is satisfactory for most species. For desert-type cacti, add more sand and some gravel. For jungle species such as Epiphyllum and Rhipsalis, you will need shredded fir bark or osmunda fiber mixed with one part garden loam. All ingredients should be thoroughly mixed, and the texture should be loose and friable so it will easily drain water and yet provide moisture for the plant roots.

Use pots that seem too small for the plants. I know this will be hard for you to do, because it just doesn't seem a nice way to treat a plant friend. There is a good reason to do this, however. Cacti make comparatively few roots and will not bloom in larger pots. That's where a lot of cactus fanciers go wrong—they want to give these stay-at-homes too much room to roam.

Do yourself a favor. If you want to raise cacti, buy yourself a pair of good heavy gloves. Because these plants are conditioned by nature to ward off pests and animals with their spikes and spines, they may not recognize you as a friend and may decide to treat you as a foe. Cacti will take a little manhandling, so when working on them you might try folding a newspaper to encircle and grip them. If you use some of that uncommon common sense that Grandma Putt was always talking about, you won't ever need to end up with a handful of needles. Here are some specific directions for growing the most popular types of cactus that adjust well to indoor life.

Christmas Cactus

This long-time favorite blooms between November and March, but most usually in December and January. It is sometimes mistakenly called Thanksgiving cactus. Christmas cacti are the easiest things outside a terrarium to take care of, and they'll be sure to bloom if you follow these simple instructions.

Plant in a pot no larger than five inches. Use a gritty, porous soil composed of garden loam, leaf mold, and sand, plus a generous sprinkling of well-rotted or dried cow manure. Avoid using any bone meal or lime. Put the plants in a permanent place away from direct sun and drafts if they are to remain in the house. If you can put them outdoors, place them in shade from June to September. Water when necessary and feed them weak liquid manure every second or third week.

About Labor Day, take the plants indoors and place them in an east or west window. If they must be in a south window, the sun should be diffused through a curtain. If only a north window is available, protect them from too much cold during severe winter weather. Keep the soil almost dry until the flower buds begin to appear. Strong artificial light should be avoided, particularly when the plants are ready to bud. At this time the decorative, flat-jointed leaves become tipped with beautiful $2\frac{1}{2}$-3-inch multitinted red and pink blossoms, sometimes developing into two or three blooms in racemes.

The long blooming season continues from the holidays well on into late winter. Water moderately until the plants are through flowering. After they bloom, reduce the watering to give the plants a rest until new shoots start growing. During the resting period, cut off any straggly growth. Water freely while the new growth is being made in the spring.

When Christmas cacti drop their flower buds before they open, it is usually because of too much or too little watering, drafts or sudden changes in temperature, manufactured gas or smoke in the air, or too much handling. If possible, try not to move the plants while the flower buds are developing.

The Thanksgiving cactus is similar to the Christmas cactus, but the leaves are slightly different, having crablike incurved tips. The blooms are much the same except for a delicate tinge of salmon to the red.

The Easter cactus can be grown in pretty much the same way

as the Thanksgiving and Christmas varieties. It has leaves that are slightly narrower and the plant is bushier. Its large star-shaped red blooms are produced in abundance. The Easter cactus starts blooming three months later than the Christmas cactus, and will continue for three or four weeks once it has begun. This one absolutely must be potted in a container that is apparently *very much too small* for it. It should be left in this pot indefinitely or it will not bloom.

Cacti and Succulent Dish Garden

DISH-GARDEN CACTUS

These little dandies are mostly desert varieties for growing in "desertariums," or small shallow pots. You'll get a kick out of their odd and interesting appearance. Don't count on their flowering, but if you talk nicely to them they may reward you with blossoms from time to time.

Use a soil mixture of ordinary garden soil and sharp sand. Add to this a sprinkling of agricultural lime. The soil should be porous and feel gritty between your fingers. Once a year scratch a little dry bone meal into the soil surface. Never use any manure. Water sparingly, about once a week, and keep the plants in full sun.

ORCHID CACTUS

The epiphyllums will bloom in the spring—and this may be in April, May, or June, according to the variety. A 4-inch clay pot with an inch of drainage material in the bottom is the best container. The same soil mixture recommended for the Christmas cactus is satisfactory if the proportion of well-rotted or dried cow manure is increased. The orchid cactus needs plenty of moisture at the roots while the plants are in active growth, and it appreciates a humid environment. During the winter, when the plants are resting, the soil should be kept quite dry, though the tops will be benefited by a daily shower.

The plants are happiest in an east or west window where they will receive lots of light but little or no direct sun. If a sunny window is the only place you have to place them, shade the plants from the direct rays during the middle of the day or make sure the sunlight is well diffused. During the summer give these plants a summer vacation—set them out in the shade.

QUEEN OF THE NIGHT—NIGHT-BLOOMING CEREUS

Queen of the Night (*Selenicereus grandiflorus*) is a variety of cactus native to the jungles of the tropics. One of its characteristics is a trailing habit of growth; Cereus should be given supports to grow on as the plants develop. It usually starts blooming in May and will continue to bloom intermittently through the fall. The most important requirement for their successful culture is adequate drainage. The roots must never be in soggy wet soil or they will rot. Fill the pot from one-fourth to one-third full of broken crockery and charcoal. The best soil is a good garden loam to which should be added some sand, leaf mold, and a small amount of lime.

Use comparatively small pots, and water enough to keep the soil relatively moist, especially during periods of active growth. Newly potted plants should be watered sparingly until they are well established. Keep them in semishade for the best results.

Some Myths and Questions

Are the spines of cacti poisonous? No, they are not. And for those who are accustomed to handling them, cacti are not very difficult. As I said earlier, wear gloves or use some other protective device to keep your hands away from the spines.

Can cacti be grown from seeds? Easily. Cacti raised from seeds are somewhat slow, but if you are patient, this method will ensure your getting really strong, healthy plants, adapted from the beginning to indoor culture.

Place the seeds in pots of sandy compost in spring or summer and just barely cover them with this. Place a pane of glass over the propagating case until germination takes place. Cacti seeds germinate best in a temperature of 60–70 degrees. Keep the seedlings shaded from strong sunlight and carefully watered until they are large enough to prick out at an inch apart. Now put them in pans of porous compost. Later transplant them singly into one-inch pots.

What about grafting cacti? This is something that you should do for several reasons. Some kinds of cacti, such as the Cereus, are of pendulous growth. Grafting them onto a tall, erect stem makes them more ornamental. *Pereskia aculeata* is considered a suitable stock and is grown from cuttings. When it is large enough (6 to 8 inches), remove a thin slice from each side of the scion base. Cut off the top of the pereskia, then remove a wedge-shaped piece. Fit the scion into this wedge tightly. Hold the graft in place with toothpicks or one or two spines from one of the cacti. After grafting, the new "plant" should be placed in a propagating case or in a warm, sunny room until a union is formed. You may also want to graft cacti of different shapes or kinds of growth as curiosities.

Will cuttings from cactus grow? You bet. Pieces of shoot or stem taken from just about any part of a cactus plant will form roots. Also, cactus plants have a tendency to form offsets. If you remove these when they are a reasonable size and repot them, they will quickly form roots. When you take cuttings, lay them in the sun for a day or two so they can form a corky skin over the cut section. This will prevent rotting. Next insert them in pots of moist sand and peat or sand alone.

Become a Cactus Collector

Because of the amazing number of varieties, colors, shapes, and sizes, cacti make wonderful collector's items. The fact that most of them require very little care makes this a hobby that doesn't have to take up all your time.

Collectors of cacti often form a deep affection for their plants. You will find that, as with gardeners who concentrate on collecting other types of plants, the more your interest grows, the more varieties and species you will want in your collection. There always seems to be one more, down at the local florist's or in some plant catalogue, that you *must* have to round out your collection.

The following is a list of readily available cacti to help the beginning collector. Happy hunting—and try not to prick your fingers too often!

Cacti

Mammillaria elongata	golden lace
Opuntia microdasys	bunny ears
Aloe variegata	tiger aloe
Aloe gasteria	duck wings
Haworthia margaretifera	———
Cereus peruvianus	Peruvian apple cactus
Euphorbia polyacantha	fishbone
Aloe humvir	needle aloe
Kalanchoe tomentosa	panda plant
Espostoa lanata	Peruvian snowball
Pachycereus pringlei	Mexican giant
Crassula arborescens	jade plant
Chamaecereus	Sylvestrii hybrid peanut
Haworthia fasciata	improved zebra haworthia
Aloe humilis	spider aloe

The Succulents

There are many people, like my wife Ilene, who are wary about eating fish because of the bones. These folks always think they're going to get a bone stuck in their throats. Still, they don't have to eliminate seafood from their diet entirely—there are many delectable creatures of the sea, such as crab, lobster, oysters, abalone, and others, that have no bones. So it is with the succulents. If you are afraid of cactus plants because of their spines and bristles, don't give this group up entirely. There are plenty of spineless succulents. Defining a succulent is a little more difficult than defining a cactus. While a cactus is a succulent that can store moisture, not all succulents are cacti.

As I have already explained, cacti, with such rare exceptions as *Cephalocereus senilis*, the "old-man cactus," with its long woolly hair, do not have leaves. Most of them have definite spines and bristles. But the ability to store moisture, which gives the succulent group its name, is not confined to one family. Moisture-storing tissue occurs in the lily, amaryllis, daisy, milkweed, crassula, and even in geraniums. All of these, then, are succulents. Perhaps the most interesting and dramatic types of succulents occur in nature in some sort of desert or drought environment. No book on house plants would be complete without describing some of them.

Pot culture for most succulents is similar to that of cactus. If you travel a lot and take your family with you, you won't have to worry about who's going to have to stay home and water the house plants. These tough guys are the camels of the plant kingdom. But don't ignore them entirely when it comes to watering. Keep the soil moderately dry between waterings, but give it a thorough soaking when it's completely dry.

Try to give your succulents from four to six hours of direct sunlight a day unless directed otherwise by a knowledgeable nurseryman or florist who knows precisely about the light requirements of a particular species or variety. Most of these plants like temperatures of 72 degrees and above in the daytime and on down to about 55 degrees at night.

Take a tip from experienced growers of these plants and get as thorough a briefing on your succulent plants as you can *before* you buy them. Then you will be able to treat your new plant as nature has treated members of its family for generations.

No matter how much you may *think* you know about a particular plant's family background, remember that these plant people are individuals and can be as different from one another as your own children or puppies in a litter. Observe each plant closely; see how it responds to the way you are treating it. If it doesn't respond as the florists and the books say it should, try treating it differently. With careful attention and a little luck, you will probably find just the right environment and just the right program for watering, feeding, and helping it grow fat and sassy.

You can propagate most succulents as you would cacti. Take cuttings from the stems or leaves—or remove the offsets or suckers from the base of the plants—and repot them as individuals.

ALOE VERA, A FASCINATING AND USEFUL PLANT

To go deeply into detail about the different types of succulents would require a book in itself, so I will choose one group, the

Aloe vera
Burn Plant

aloes. Aloes belong to the lily family, Liliaceae, and the word "aloe" (pronounced *al*-o) is derived from the ancient Arabic name for these plants. They are mentioned frequently in the Bible, and both ancient and modern physicians have made use of their curative powers.

The best-known and most frequently grown member of this family is the *Aloe vera*, an interesting-looking plant that practically takes care of itself (see illustration). Don't let those fierce-looking jagged leaves with their intimidating spines put you off. This plant looks more ferocious than it really is. The spines are not nearly so sharp as they look, and the soft barbs do not "hook," as cactus does. Handling these plants is quite painless. The pale, cool green leaves,which grow in the form of a large rosette, are soft to the touch. The flowering stalk will spring from the center of this rosette when the plant has attained sufficient maturity. The stalk, about a foot high, will bear a dense cluster of blossoms which are small, narrow, and tubular. They may be red, white, or yellow, varying in different forms of aloe.

For centuries *Aloe vera* has been the indoor gardener's drugstore in a pot. People who live in the tropics, where this plant grows in nature, have discovered many fascinating and wonderful things about its healing properties. It is a great remedy for painful but not too severe burns. (For severe burns you should always see your doctor.) It gives almost instant relief for minor skin irritations, insect bites, minor sunburn, and chapped hands. The gel, which is the juice of the leaves, or its dried derivative, aloin, goes into salves for burns and sunburn creams. It is also a marvelous skin conditioner and is currently being incorporated into many beauty creams and skin cosmetics.

There is nothing mysterious about this. The *Aloe vera* is just another of Mother Nature's many healing gifts to mankind. Anyone who wishes may have one of these plants for his very own—they are anything but rare. Grow yours in a flowerpot summer and winter, ready for use at any time. The healing ingredient is in the plant's very thick leaves in the form of a clear salvelike juice. This juice is available at any time it is needed. Just slice off one of the leaves and put the juicy part directly on the burn or bite, using a comfortable bandage to keep the leaf in place.

My friend Mary Kibbie, who is extremely sensitive to insect bites and sunburn, says that once she placed a slice of aloe leaf on a bee sting she received in her garden. By acting quickly and applying the healing juice almost immediately she was able to get nearly total relief. The bee sting didn't even raise a blister. Louise Riotte suggests that we all keep a potted *Aloe vera* growing on the kitchen windowsill to use as a relief-giving medication for minor burns. Louise says to cut off a leaf whenever the need arises and squeeze it to extract the juice. She says you need not discard the leaf after using it, because it will seal itself over and can be sliced through and used again (within a reasonable length of time) if hung somewhere to dry.

Aloes make excellent house plants and a mature plant can survive in a winter temperature of 45 degrees or even slightly lower. When planted outdoors in the summer, aloes take much the same culture as cacti and other desert plants. Aloes of some species are treelike in form, growing as tall as five feet. Others form dwarf clumps, with clusters of leaves arising from the base of the plant. One of the most popular aloes, and also the most attractive, is *A. variegata*, the partridge-breast aloe. The green-and-white leaves are very ornamental, and it is often used as a window plant.

For pot culture, fill the container about one-quarter full of drainage material; the rest of the compost should be about two-thirds loam and one-third coarse sand. Add a little crushed limestone and bone meal. Pot the plants in the spring, and water sparingly in the summer—only when the soil becomes quite dry. From September to March give them only enough water to prevent the leaves from shriveling.

An attractive feature of aloes is their slow growth—they will not require frequent repotting. It's not unusual to keep one in the same pot for as long as ten years. Top dressing with the same soil mix is recommended occasionally if you keep the plant in the same container over a long period of time.

Aloes can be propagated by either seeds or cuttings. When in doubt, choose cuttings, because they are easier to grow. Or, as with cacti, simply detach the suckers (small plants that develop around the base of the mother plant), and insert them in pots of sandy soil. Press them well down so they make good contact and they'll develop roots. Real cuttings may be made by severing the stems just beneath a joint. Allow the severed place to dry up and form a corky-textured skin, which should take a day or two. Otherwise the cutting will rot. The cuttings, which should be approximately six inches long, can then be inserted in sandy soil. You will not need to place a glass over these as they will not droop. Apply water sparingly—keep the soil just barely moist.

Dish-Garden and Hanging-Basket Succulents

For a dish garden you may want to try some "living stones." These are curious-looking succulents from South Africa which have in the course of centuries reduced themselves to two pairs of fleshy leaves that act as water reservoirs. Their disguise is broken in summer when daisylike flowers appear. These have several different colors according to species.

If you are partial to hanging baskets, you will find a great many members of the succulents that are particularly well suited for these handsome containers. Here is a partial list of species you might want to consider.

Donkey tail (*Sedum morganianum*): Its stems may eventually reach as long as six feet. This is a great favorite for hanging baskets in southwestern gardens and in Mexico.

A. decorum: A branching type with rosettes of copper-colored leaves.

A. haworthi: A bushy plant with trailing stems of gray-green rosettes.

A. woodii: Sometimes called the rosary vine. This beauty has heart-shaped leaves marbled with silver.

Crassula perforata: Also called necklace vine. The bluish-gray leaves are in pairs and have red dots.

Hoya carnosa: Known as the wax flower. This one has lovely whorls of waxy cream-white flowers.

Sedum morganianum
Burro's Tail

Hoya carnosa variegata
Variegated Wax Plant

These are only a few of the many possibilities. There are, of course, many, many more. Succulents used in hanging containers need a moist soil, especially if hung outdoors in warm weather or under windy conditions. Put several plants of the same kind in the basket, which should look as though it is overflowing with plants lavishly cascading over the sides in a dramatic way.

One Last Tip About Care During Dormancy

Overwatering is the greatest crime you can perpetrate against your succulent and cactus plants. If you want them to bloom, show restraint! During September and October they will go into their dormant period. When you notice the plants begin to decline, *withhold water* and keep in a cool (55 degrees), dry place until you see signs of new growth. You will be rewarded with blossoms. Now spray the stems, spines, and foliage every week or so, but keep the soil moderately dry. Do not feed your plants the first year; after that feed with any house plant food at half the prescribed dosage every six to eight months.

12

All About Little Orchid Annie

Most of us who remember giving or getting our first orchid corsage still associate orchids with romance and exotic beauty. It's hard to imagine growing them as house plants. Yet many people do grow them and consider their success with orchids the ultimate sort of gardening achievement. If you've always thought of raising orchids as too difficult for the inexperienced gardener, you will be delighted to learn that some of them are really rather easy to grow. A great deal of your success with these plants will depend upon where you live, how you live, and what facilities you can provide for their growth.

In southern California, tender orchids such as cymbidiums are grown in garden beds of specially prepared soil. In Florida, epiphytal kinds (those that grow on trees but are not parasites), including dendrobiums, epidendrums, laelias, oncidiums, and vandas are grown out of doors. Of course, even in Florida, provision must be made to protect them from extremely low temperatures. On nights when such conditions may be expected, hoods of heavy cloth are put over the plants. Nevertheless, with the possible exception of Hawaii and the warm, humid states, orchid growing can be accomplished best indoors.

Orchids are more exacting in their requirements than most house plants. So it's important that you understand and meet those requirements if you want to grow these flowering plants successfully. Remember that Jacqueline Kennedy and Aristotle Onassis signed an agreement of terms before they got married? Well, if you want to make a success of caring for any beautiful woman—and that includes Little Orchid Annie—it's not a bad idea to have some sort of agreement of terms and conditions under which the two of you live together. You see, Annie is one of those beauties who demands that someone pay constant attention to her needs.

Orchids need a tropical temperature, most of them preferring 70 degrees by day and 65 degrees at night. (However, a daytime temperature up to 90 degrees can be tolerated by these plants; but the nighttime temperature must be kept above 60 degrees.) They also need ample humidity. Most of the cattleyas will take kindly to this, though epidendrum and cymbidium like things a little cooler. They prefer a minimum temperature in winter of 45 degrees and 60 degrees at other times of the year. Temperatures must be kept as constant as possible. Never let your orchids touch a cool window glass at night.

The principal difference between orchids and other house plants is their root system. The orchid root consists of a fine, wire-like center covered with a spongy jacket. The root system serves two functions: first to secure the plant to its tree or rock support; and second, to gather moisture and food. It is the outer cover, which is very absorbent, that soaks up available water. This must be done very rapidly, because the roots are not in contact with moist soil and when it rains, the moisture must be assimilated with all possible speed. To get a drink by this method the plant must have a large surface area.

You can provide the best possible environment for your house-grown orchids by breaking up some fir bark into small pieces and placing these into a large pot with some osmunda fiber (chopped portions of the matted roots of the osmunda fern) and some peat moss. These materials hold moisture and humus and will prevent the roots from drying out too quickly, and therefore it will not be necessary to water so often. Just like your other pot-grown plants, orchids of this type should have plenty of drainage material (shards, crumbled brick, or gravel) placed in the bottom of the pot.

For best results I like an 8-inch pot for an average-sized plant. This will allow a good root system to form.

When planting orchids, try to determine what type of growth they have *before* placing them in the pot. Those that grow upright (monopodial) may be centered in the pot. However, other orchids (sympodial) have a horizontal characteristic of growth and do best when their roots are placed against one side of the pot rim, thus allowing their new-growth stems to expand toward the center. It's a good idea to give the leaves an upright support by inserting one or more coat-hanger wire masts and securing the leaves to them with nylon ribbon or a soft yarn.

Orchids need a humid environment, but excess watering may cause the plant to rot, so reduce watering in order to keep the soil composition moist but not soggy. It will take a little trial-and-error testing until you find the proper watering program for these plants in your home. Once you find the correct balance, try to maintain it.

With no terrestrial roots, orchids must have some means of storing water to enable them to live through dry periods. This is done by enlarged sections of the stem called pseudobulbs. Because of these built-in water-storage tanks, orchids can go quite a long time without moisture, especially during the inactive season. This gives them an advantage over other house plants, which may die if left unwatered for several weeks. Orchids just rest and then start growing again when water becomes available to them.

As the plant uses the stored water, the pseudobulbs will shrink in size, but they will rapidly return to normal as soon as moisture is obtainable. In caring for your plants, learn to watch these pseudobulbs, as they are excellent indicators of the plant's watering needs. If they are plump, *don't water*. If they are shriveled, *investigate*. You may find that the plant doesn't need water but that the roots have rotted and the plants can't absorb any more water. If the roots seem okay, water as necessary.

The accepted practice is to pour sufficient water through the pot to completely soak all the fiber. Do not water again until the bark is reasonably dry. After a little practice this can usually be determined by lifting the pot. You will get to know by the weight whether more water is needed or not. When you water, always use dechlorinated water at room temperature. Pots should always be allowed to drain after watering. Spray your orchids with a mister every day to supply the humid conditions these plants love. A pebble tray filled with water will also help provide humidity.

Orchids are light feeders, but during growing periods they need a weekly feeding, and you may occasionally give them weak manure tea or compost water as a pick-me-up. Another good idea is to give them a snack by adding a small amount of leaf mold to the bark from time to time. Just be careful not to interfere with the air circulation in the pot or you will destroy the plant's health.

If you want your orchids to bloom, you will have to see that they get long periods of light at a high intensity. Most orchids like at least five or six hours of sunlight a day. Some will enjoy full sun all day. But use caution—orchids can get sunburned just like you and me! Give your plants time to adjust to the sun by putting them out in it for short periods at a time. Just as with people, this gives the pigmentation in their skin a chance to adjust to the increased light conditions. What I am saying is, don't take a plant that has been grown indoors and has not seen sunlight all winter and place it outside in full sunlight in the spring (or in a window bathed in sunlight), because it will burn. Instead, take it from shade to semishade for a week or two, moving it up to a brighter spot each time. It will gradually adapt itself to its spring and summer place.

You can, if you like, use artificial light to grow your orchids, but the intensity must be a lot stronger than that sufficient to display the plants. At least 5,000 footcandles are needed to induce them to bloom. A good way to tell if your plants are getting enough light is to check the color of the leaves—if they are dark green, the orchids are not getting the light they need. Increase the intensity of the light until the leaves turn yellow-green or reddish (depending on the variety you are growing). The intensity must be increased gradually or burn spots will appear. If this happens, reduce the light. As you can see, orchids are a mite finicky where light is concerned. If the light is not exactly right they will not bloom.

Like many of your indoor plants, orchids often benefit from a summer outdoors. But with one exception—*Bletilla hyacinthus*— do not treat an orchid like any other house plant vacationer and bury its pot in the earth. Instead, take a wire and hang the pot from the branch of a tree. Choose a place where the sunlight will be filtered and the air circulation good.

The best time to repot an orchid is just as the new roots appear. This usually coincides with the appearance of new growth. Take the plant from the pot and cut the rhizome into several sections, each to have three or four of the back bulbs. Place each section into an individual pot. The one with the new growth will probably bloom first; the other portions of the rhizome will also form new leads, though they may not bloom for a year or so.

The potting medium should be a mixture of fir-bark pieces and osmunda fiber or peat moss. Pack loosely enough to guarantee proper circulation of air. Good drainage is as important with these beauties as it is with your other potted plants.

It is also possible to grow orchids in hanging baskets of a certain type. These are made of strips of hardwood, such as teak, redwood, or cypress. Potsherds, rather large and flat, are placed in the bottom of the basket to retain the compost. The advantage of such baskets is the ease with which the compost may be renewed. When this is necessary, prick it out with a sharp pointed stick and put in the new material, being careful not to disturb the roots of the plant.

Your best chance of success with orchids will be in the more easily controlled atmosphere and environment of a greenhouse. An orchid greenhouse should be shaded. I will describe these greenhouses and how to shade them in a later chapter.

Here are a few of the 25,000 or more orchid species. These are some of the most popular types grown indoors by American orchid fanciers.

Cattleya trianaei is one of the most tolerant species. This is a short-day plant during the winter months. It may be grown on pebble-filled trays if you will pay special attention to its needs.

Phalaenopsis, the "moth orchid," is among those that you see most often in bridal bouquets. This beauty comes in white, pink, and yellow as well as in other colors.

These plants may be grown with the cattleyas but should have more water and less light. Unlike the cattleyas, most kinds—particularly the ones from Burma—have no pseudobulbs. The flower stalks are usually long, arching, branched, and hold many flowers. The leaves are large and leathery.

Phalaenopsis requires a warm, moist atmosphere free from drafts and is best grown in a well-heated greenhouse. The potting compost should be two parts sphagnum moss and two parts osmunda fiber, well mixed. Repotting should take place in late February or early March. Occasionally some of the old compost should be removed and fresh added.

Miltonias grow wild in Central and South America, chiefly in Brazil. They are epiphytal and have small, smooth pseudobulbs. These orchids have rather large, flat flowers which resemble huge pansies, and they vary in color from white to deep crimson.

Compost for growing miltonias is prepared from two and a half parts of cut osmunda fiber and one and a half parts of sphagnum moss sifted, to which a little sand has been added. If available, a few well-decomposed oak or beech leaves are also good to add. All orchids of this species like well-drained pots.

There are many hybrids of miltonia, all beautiful and interesting. Most need a winter temperature of not less than 55–60 degrees, but those with hard pseudobulbs, such as *M. cuneata* and *M. candida,* will safely withstand a slightly lower temperature.

VANDAS

My friend Afton Keeton, who is an orchid grower of repute in the Orlando, Florida, area, says that vandas are among the most easily grown orchids and suggests that you begin the hobby of orchid culture with vandas, cattleyas, and laelias. Vandas are also epiphytal, but they are without pseudobulbs. Some vandas have flowers that are deliciously fragrant. One of the loveliest vandas is *V. coerulea,* which bears flowers in delightful tones of blue or lavender-blue. It has evergreen foliage, and the roots are thick and fleshy.

Vandas prefer a potting mixture of three parts of osmunda fiber and two parts of sphagnum moss, along with plenty of drainage material and some small pieces of charcoal. Many kinds are strong-rooting, with the roots clinging tightly to the pots, making it difficult to repot without injuring them. If you find this happening, remove as much of the old compost as you can and put in new.

All vandas need warmth and moisture. Those that need intense sun are not recommended for indoor culture, but many will grow well under approximately the same conditions as cattleyas. An excellent miniature vanda, Ascocendas, is good for growing in a limited space.

CYMBIDIUMS

Cymbidiums are noted for their long-lasting flowers and are great favorites for corsages. They need bright light, high humidity, and cool nights in summer. They grow best in gardens where the climate is right for them, such as in southern California. Les Baxter, the famous composer, has quite a collection of these plants growing in his incredible garden. By the way, Les says orchids grow better to music—as long as it's *his* music!

Most cymbidiums are not successful as house plants unless grown in a greenhouse under carefully controlled conditions. They will take more kindly to a lower temperature than most orchids but prefer 50–55 degrees at night and a few more degrees in the daytime. Although, as I've said, these plants like light, strong sunlight is to be avoided, so your greenhouse should be shaded during the summer months.

Cymbidiums have strong roots and need a potting mixture

of fibrous loam mixed with osmunda fiber and crushed potsherds, broken brick, or gravel, well blended, to keep the mixture open and aerated. Repotting should be done in the spring after the plant has flowered. Take care to cut away all dead or decaying roots.

CYPRIPEDIUMS

These are the popular members of the orchid family called "lady's slipper." They get this name from the shape of the lip, or slipperlike pouch. Cypripediums are mostly small plants. You may have either warm-growing types or cool-growing types; both need moist conditions and considerable shade.

Hardy cypripediums may be grown outdoors in the garden, but they vary in ease of cultivation, some being difficult and others easy. A lot depends on the conditions under which they are grown. If you simulate their native conditions as nearly as possible, they may be used in rock gardens, woodlands, or even bogs.

Inside, in a greenhouse, certain cypripediums—the paphiopedilums—are easy to grow and care for. These very popular flowers are both long-lasting and useful. There are more than fifty types that have been adapted to this culture. They come from as far away as India and Hong Kong. Several thousand hybrid types have been produced, and some of these are winter-flowering.

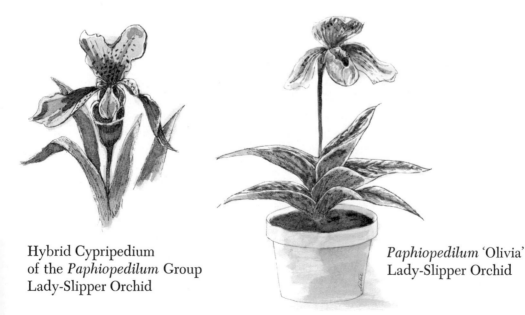

Hybrid Cypripedium
of the *Paphiopedilum* Group
Lady-Slipper Orchid

Paphiopedilum 'Olivia'
Lady-Slipper Orchid

Temperature requirements depend on the particular type you wish to grow, but most of the hybrids now grown will settle for a minimum of 60 degrees. Potting soil varies according to the various kinds. Some require more osmunda fiber, sphagnum moss, or fibrous loam than others, some need crushed limestone added to the mix.

ODONTOGLOSSUMS

These are very graceful orchids that grow on long, arching stems. Size, shape, and coloring are extremely varied—some are large, some small, but all are attractive. Most orchids of this type are hill plants that grow in the wild at fairly high altitudes and don't like high temperatures. So a greenhouse with a cool temperature and good ventilation is necessary for their cultivation.

Light is also necessary, but strong sunlight should be avoided, particularly with young, tender growth. However, they will need good light during the fall and winter months. A slight reddish tint in the mature foliage at this time will tell you that their light requirements have been met. Pot these orchids in a mixture of osmunda fiber and sphagnum moss, along with a little sand. Provide plenty of drainage material.

ONCIDIUMS

These are close cousins of the odontoglossums and are also epiphytal and evergreen. *Oncidium papilio*, one of the loveliest, is called the butterfly orchid.

A great number of oncidiums come from high altitudes, and many have hard pseudobulbs that mature in autumn. They will winter in a greenhouse at the same temperatures that are suitable for odontoglossums, requiring 50–55 degrees at night.

The flower stems may be many-flowered and branching and need support, or they may be erect, with the flowers in dense clusters. Compost should be a mixture of osmunda fiber and sphagnum moss, with more moss used for the smaller types.

Sometimes it's more convenient to grow these orchids in flower pans than in pots so that they may be suspended in autumn, where they will receive more light. Whether you choose pots or pans, make ample provision for drainage.

Many people I know grow orchids and feel they are no more trouble than other house plants. But if you would like to grow several types in the same environment, try to plan for congenial friends who like the same temperature and humidity. Then they will be easier to care for and your chances of success will be good. When you bring your orchids to successful bloom, you'll know without a doubt that it was worth all the trouble.

13

The Carnivores:
Plants That Ambush Their Lunch

When I say that plants are like people I don't mean that all of them are just like you and me. There are people—and then there are people. The plants we'll be looking at in this chapter most resemble those primitive peoples in the world who hunt for and kill their own food. These insectivorous, or flesh-eating, plants are strange and foreign to us but completely fascinating. Some of them even have a strange beauty. A few of these on your windowsill will probably attract more attention than all your other plant people put together. Oldsters and youngsters alike will be fascinated by them. Perhaps it's because their method of obtaining food makes them seem more savage than they really are.

Carnivorous plants take many physical forms in nature. Some lurk on the ground, others are tree-climbing vines, some even live under water. They grow in many shapes and are found in out-of-the-way areas from tropical swamps to upland marshes and rain-drenched mountainsides. All of them sprout in wet, acid soil lacking the nutrients and foods that ordinary plants need to survive and thrive.

The carnivores have one thing in common—the special ability developed by their leaves to attract and capture small flying or crawling insects, which they digest, or absorb, to supply the missing nutrients necessary for their growth that their roots cannot draw from the ground. The foliage traps and devours crawling and flying life. The word "carnivorous" comes from the Latin words meaning "flesh-devouring."

These meat-eaters spring three different but equally lethal types of traps—well-like pitchers, steel traps, and flypapers, the last a sticky substance that entangles the feet of its victims. All three of these types are found in eastern North America from Canada to Florida. One species, the hooded cobra plant (or cobra orchid), stands three feet tall and is found in the region where California and Oregon meet.

If all of this sounds a little like the product of some mad scientist's brain, relax. These are not botanical monsters—they aren't even gluttons—and many can live for months on a single kill. Furthermore, despite what novelists and sci-fi movie-makers have been telling us for years, there are no huge man-eating versions of these plants ready to ambush unwary and unclad females as they wander through some backwater bayou. None, none at all.

Another old wives' tale about these plants has recently caused considerable discussion and disagreement among experts. It was once thought that when insect life was not available, small pieces of meat would aid in the plant's growth. It has been learned, however, that this is unnecessary and may even be harmful. Apparently insectivorous plants consume large volumes of insects when they are available, but are capable of healthy growth for long periods without them. So you need not be too concerned if insects do not seem to be present. I usually send the kids out to find some ants (there are plenty of these around most homes). If these are unavailable because of all the ant-eaters in your neighborhood, then—and only then—give your plants the tiniest piece of liver you can obtain. Not hamburger—liver.

SARRACENIA, OR PITCHER PLANT

This group of perennials—the pitcher plants—is native to the boglands of eastern North America and includes those called pitcher plants, huntsman's horn, and others. They are easily adapted to pot culture and make interesting additions to your window garden. Their curiously shaped leaves are open funnellike tubes forming pitchers, or vase-shaped receptacles, in which the plant entraps and devours the insects it catches. While they seem to flower freely in the wild, they usually are not dependable bloomers under cultivation.

The pitchered leaves attract insects by their bright colors and nectar-secreting glands around the mouth of the orifice. Beneath the sweet bait the inner surfaces are lined with slippery hairs pointed downward and so arranged that once an insect starts down it is virtually impossible for it to return. The victims eventually fall helplessly into the digestive fluids at the base, where they are dissolved and absorbed into the tissues of the plant.

Active growth commences in early spring and continues through the summer, each plant producing three to eight pitchered leaves. As the older pitchers die, others are produced to replace them. They stay inactive or dormant during the winter months or when exposed to cold weather but can survive temperatures that approach the freezing point in winter.

Huntsman's Horn (S. flava)

This small "trumpet of doom" is native to southeastern states, and the pitchers are erect and horn-shaped. Their color is an astonishing bright yellow-green with reddish, longitudinal veins. In nature it may grow to two feet, but in pots it usually only grows a foot. This type probably has the greatest capacity for absorbing insects of all the pitcher plants.

Pitcher Plant (S. purpurea)

This plant, on the other hand, is the most modest in its requirements and needs far less insect life to maintain itself. It is the most common of the sarracenias, and is found in native boglands from the Gulf States north to Labrador and Minnesota. It is also the hardiest and easiest to grow of all the pitchers. The inflated pitcher-shaped leaves vary from bright green in shade to dark reddish-purple in full sun.

The needs of these plants (huntsman's horn and the pitcher plant) are so similar that we can discuss them together. They are best planted in 5- or 6-inch clay pots in pure sphagnum moss. Presoak the moss until it is saturated and then wring it out. If the material won't accept water, let it soak for some time or pour boiling water over it. When planting sarracenias, their extensive roots, or rhizomes, should extend downward, with the base of the plant set even with the moss at the surface.

The roots should be immersed in water at all times, so the pot should stand in a separate container in which about an inch of water is maintained. When sufficient moisture is available the plants will drink enough to maintain a constant internal supply. Rainwater or refrigerator drippings are the best source for watering. Alkaline waters are always detrimental, and if your water has a high degree of alkalinity, use bottled water. Pitcher plants thrive best in full sun, but will tolerate partial shade. Under no circumstances should you use any form of fertilizer, and do not expose these plants to insect spray.

Hooded Cobra Plant

Darlingtonia (cobra plant) is a real dilly neatly calculated to outsmart any insect that comes upon it suddenly in the wild. It's a perennial bog plant native to the Sierra Mountains. Each leaf is a hollow funnel-shaped stalk, or pipe, the mouth of which is covered with a rounded hood at the top suggesting the hooded cobra of India. This hood is beautifully colored and mottled and bears many honey glands which attract ants, flies, and other insects toward the mouth and lure them inside the funnellike stem. The upper portion is very smooth, affording the insects very little foothold. The lower portion is lined with innumerable hairs pointing downward, making it easy for the victim to descend but impossible to return. The trapped insects are absorbed in the digestive fluid at the bottom of the tube.

Darlingtonias will do well under cultivation. To succeed you

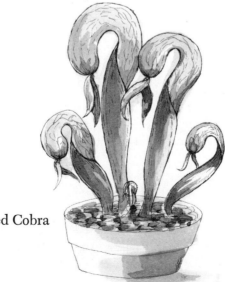

Hooded Cobra

will have to provide them with a cool temperature in a shaded location. They will do best if planted in 5–6-inch clay pots in pure sphagnum moss. Their extensive roots, or rhizomes, should point downward, with the base of the plant set even with the surface of the moss. The roots should be immersed in water like those of the pitcher plants, so provide a separate container with water in the bottom. Use rainwater or bottled water (or even refrigerator or dehumidifier drippings) if the normal water supply is high in mineral content or has been chemically treated. Never give fertilizer in any form, and do not expose the plants to insect spray.

During the winter, or where there are no insects for it to trap, drop a piece of liver the size of a grain of wheat into each funnel every ten days to two weeks. Always keep the plant out of direct sunlight. As with other carnivorous plants, the pipes mature and die as their replacements develop.

Darlingtonia (named after Dr. William Darlington, an American botanist, and not because of its endearing qualities) is propagated by side shoots, which may be detached in summer and set in small pots. Keep them under a bell jar or plastic bag until well established. Seeds may also be sown in pots on the surface of finely chopped compost.

Venus Flytrap

The Venus flytrap (*Dionaea muscipula*) has the ability to catch and actually digest its prey in the traps it produces in place of normal leaves. The leafy structure consists of two blades, hinged in the center, with interlocking teeth along the margins. Trigger hairs are located on the surface of each blade and they operate the hinged mechanism. When the trigger hairs are disturbed by a walking or crawling insect, the jaws snap shut like a steel trap to form a tight pouch, or miniature stomach. Continued irritation by the struggling, entrapped insect causes the leaf glands to exude the digestive fluids that disintegrate the soft tissues of the insect's body.

After several days—or even weeks, with a large insect—the nutrients will be absorbed into the plant tissues and the trap will reopen to release the skeleton of the insect. If the trap is purposely or accidently stimulated, it will snap shut. But when it finds itself without a real meal it will automatically reopen in a few days.

Plant your Venus flytrap in a shallow dish without any drain-

Venus Flytrap

age, and set the roots in fairly loose, live sphagnum moss. Water frequently and pour off the surplus water, retaining whatever amount has been absorbed by the moss. The roots must be kept moist at all times, and high humidity is also essential for these plants. In homes with dry heat, use a pebble tray filled with water, or a terrarium. Under no circumstances should plant foods or insect sprays be used on this plant.

Venus will grow best in full sunshine but will tolerate shade if given plenty of artificial light. When the plant is kept in the sun the leaf traps take on a reddish color, but when grown in the shade they are always green. Regardless of their color, all mature traps are capable of catching insects.

The entire plant seldom grows over five or six inches high, with about the same spread. The most active growing season is from March until October, when new traps continue to appear and replace the older ones as they mature and die out. Traps reach maturity in about a month after they first appear, and during this time they may grow to the size of a half dollar, but are usually much smaller. A single plant may have as many as six active traps at one time. Stems bearing small white flowers appear in May or June, and these should be removed, as they are unattractive and tend to weaken the plant.

Venus' roots are quite hardy and may survive winter temperatures as low as 10 degrees above zero. However, if it is exposed to extreme cold or allowed to become too dry, the top may die, but under proper growing conditions a new growth cycle will start from the perennial bulblike root after a few weeks' rest and the plant will produce a new top the next spring. Propagation is by division at potting time.

BLADDERWORT (UTRICULARIA)

This one is somewhat different from those we've already seen. It catches its prey under water. These plants are sometimes grown in indoor aquariums or submerged gardens for the interesting look of their feathery foliage and their insect-catching valves. The bladderworts are very versatile, being of hardy and tender types, terrestrial as well as aquatic. The name "Utricularia" refers to the little bottlelike bladders on the leaves.

The aquatic kinds, native to tropical America and Europe, have submerged leaves that are finely divided. The small bladder-like structures are fitted with valves that only open inward. Once the small insects enter, they are unable to escape. As soon as the prey is captured, the plants emit a fluid containing enzymes that decompose their bodies into nutrients; these are absorbed into the plant's tissues.

The terrestrial bladderworts are very different from the aquatic plants. They have lancelike leaves six inches long, and produce slender, wiry flower stalks. Toward the tip these bear a raceme (a simple inflorescence in which the elongated axis bears flowers on short stems in succession toward the apex, as in the lily of the valley) of yellow, blue, or purple flowers.

These bladderworts require a minimum winter temperature of 55 degrees and a soil compost made up of equal parts of fibrous peat, sphagnum moss, and broken bricks or shards. Set the plants in well-drained pots and keep these in saucers of water. They can be placed in a terrarium or, more correctly, a bell jar, and kept in a shady location. Ventilate daily by tipping the jar a few inches each morning.

The plants should be watered freely during the summer months, but in winter they only need watering when the soil shows signs of becoming dry. Repotting is done in March. Remove the old compost from the roots and place the plant in a slightly larger pot if necessary. New plants may be obtained by sowing seeds on the surface of damp peat moss and sand in a seed pan. Cover with a bell jar or plastic bag until they are large enough to pot separately, starting with 3-inch pots and gradually shifting to larger ones as the plants grow.

14

Growing with Artificial Lights: A Bright Idea

Let us assume that you have become a confirmed indoor green-thumber and have a pretty good idea of the pitfalls and rewards that can be yours when you grow house plants. But now that you've learned the rules and have gained enough experience to experiment on your own, what if I were to tell you how all the rules can easily be changed so that you can grow pot plants and bring them to flower even in the darkest city apartment?

Just picture a situation in which every day is a sunny day. In which you can have windows any place in the house, and it rains only when you want it to. In which there needn't be any winter or summer seasons. In which you don't have to give your plants that daily "walk," the quarter turn toward the light, that they must have when grown on a windowsill. No, I'm not describing house plant heaven, I'm just telling you what it's like to grow your indoor plants under artificial lights!

The use of artificial lighting as a means of growing plants, or as a supplement for growing them more satisfactorily (plants brought in from the greenhouse will last longer and do better), is becoming more popular each year with amateur growers. Professional growers have known most of the secrets of growing under lights for a long time. They use this knowledge to bring plants to bloom for holidays and special occasions. You can do the same thing.

When I mentioned room dividers in an earlier chapter, I suggested that the plants you use in them be shade lovers, but with artificial light placed above them, you can grow just about any type of plant you want. Flowering plants in dramatic colors and shapes to harmonize or contrast with the rest of your decor will be the biggest bonus of all.

What's So Important About Light?

Back in the 1920s two government scientists, W. W. Garner and H. A. Allard, discovered that the ability of a plant to flower had a great deal to do with the length of the daylight hours it was exposed to. Their experiments showed that the *length* of time that plants are lighted is more important than the *intensity* of the light.

All plants will grow much more sturdily with increased intensity, but only up to a certain point. Your own common sense will tell you that continued intensity can be as dangerous for plant leaves as overexposure to the sun can be for people with delicate skins. When experimenting with light on your plants, be careful not to burn them.

There are four classes of plants that you will want to know about before you plug in the light bulbs. They are: (1) the long-day plants; (2) the short-day plants; (3) plants indifferent to the length of light periods; (4) plants that prefer an intermediate-day length. These four classes of plants relate to your ability to control blooming periods with the help of artificial light.

Other characteristics of plant growth can also be speeded up or delayed, augmented or restricted, by varying the length of daylight with lights. For example, runner production in strawberries and bulbing in onions require a long day, while tuber formation in tuberous begonias requires a short day. The height of many plants may also be limited or extended by changing the day length.

Light Needs and How to Meet Them

The summer-blooming plants are the ones that most need a long period of daylight. They require about fourteen hours of sunlight. If you provide them with this under artificial lights, they will blossom for you during the winter too.

At the opposite extreme are the short-day plants. These want about ten hours of daylight. By completely darkening chrysanthemums early in the afternoon, you can force them to blossom early in the summer. You may have already discovered that these are short-day plants when they set buds during a two- or three-day period of cloudy weather.

Poinsettias are also short-day plants. And the reason that these and many other similar flowering plants fail to blossom the second year is that they are growing in your living room with light on them throughout the evening. Set them in a dark room, but be sure that it also has the same temperature as the lighted room—and not less than 60 degrees at night.

By studying the natural preferences of your plants for the length of daylight hours where they grow in nature, you will know to which one of the four groups above they belong. After you have learned this, you can trick your plants into blooming when you want them to by experimenting with varying periods and intensities of light.

Plants have become so important to interior decorators that they use them in even the darkest part of a room to add life and color. However, even when placed next to a window, plants grown in the average house receive much less light than they do when they live outside. Thus decorator plants, though they may be chosen from varieties that require less light than the average flowering house plant, will improve in growth and appearance if some provision is made for giving them illumination. Four to six hours of extra light a day, or throughout the evening hours, will probably be sufficient.

Extremely ornamental and dramatic effects can be achieved by placing a floodlight in exactly the right position to shine on one of your plants. Since this will bring beauty to your room and to your plant, you should consider the placement of the lamp and the plant very carefully before making any kind of permanent installation. Experiment a little with distance and slant so that highlights and shadows may show up at their best.

For most indoor gardening with artificial lights, fluorescent light tubes are more satisfactory than the ordinary filament-type bulbs, because fluorescent tubes don't give off as much heat and can be placed closer to the plants. You can now buy bulbs that give off light in the blue daylight spectrum and are available in both fluorescent and filament types. Regardless of the type of light, be sure to use a good reflector that will direct the light where it will be of the most value.

As I have mentioned in my recent book *Talk to Your Plants,* my Grandmother Putt was an extraordinary gardener who had great success with both indoor and outdoor plants. She wasn't able to enjoy all the advances in gardening that are available to you and me, but I'd be willing to bet she'd be the first to take advantage of any new tool or idea that seems to have possibilities. Don't be afraid to experiment with gardening under lights. But whether you use artificial light or not, why not buy an inexpensive light meter at your garden center and check the light intensity where you have placed your plants. Be sure you buy a light meter that measures intensity in terms of footcandles. Some meters available at camera shops are not suitable for this purpose.

Pick a day when it is sunny outdoors. Adjust your curtains to their usual daytime position. (Drawn curtains, whether sheer or opaque, greatly alter the light level.) Hold the light meter level to the ground and take several readings in the area where you intend to place plants. Use an average of these readings to measure the light. After finding out the light level from natural sources, you can determine how much artificial light to add.

Most plants should have a minimum of 50 footcandles (page 63) for twelve hours a day, but 500 footcandles is the required amount for a flowering plant. This is only about a tenth of what your flowering plants receive out of doors. Some plants will not do well indoors. These plants are sun lovers, and even though the lamps in the indoor garden are bright, they still are pale compared to the sun. The midday summer sun produces 7,000 to 12,000 footcandles of light, which is very bright compared to indoor light.

Indoor light levels of only 1,000 footcandles can be irritating to the eyes of some people. Screening the lights with foliage will reduce glare. Direct glare can be avoided if you will locate the lights carefully.

Here is a list showing the minimum and preferred number of footcandles you should use to light selected plants when they are illuminated twelve to sixteen hours daily. The following plants require low light—a minimum of 50 footcandles and a preferred intensity of 100–500 footcandles.

> Aglaonema (Chinese evergreen)
> Aspidistra (cast-iron plant)
> Dieffenbachia (dumb cane)
> Dracaena
> *Monstera deliciosa*
> Nephthytis (Syngonium)
> *Pandanus veitchii* (screw pine)
> *Philodendron oxycardium*

The following plants require medium light—a minimum of 500 footcandles and a preferred intensity of 1,000 footcandles:

Aglaonema roebelinii (Chinese evergreen)
Anthurium hybrids
Begonia metallica
Begonia rex
Bromeliads
Cissus (grape ivy)
Ficus (rubber plant)
Kentia forsteriana (Kentia palm)
Peperomia
Philodendrons, other than oxycardium
Pilea cadierei (aluminum plant)
Schefflera
Scindapsus aureus

The following plants require high light—a minimum of 1,000 footcandles and a preferred intensity of 1,000 footcandles or above.

Aloe variegata
Begonias, other than metallica and rex
Codiaeum
Coleus
Crassula
Episcia
Fatshedera lizei
Hedera (ivy)
Hoya carnosa
Impatiens
Kalanchoe tomentosa
Pelargonium species (geranium)
Petunia hybrids (cascade type)
Saintpaulia species (African violets)
Salvia splendens (scarlet sage)
Sinningia species
Tagetes species (marigold)

Of course this is not an all-inclusive list, but the plants mentioned are those generally available through the usual supply sources and have been grown successfully by indoor gardeners for many years. Do not necessarily limit yourself to these plants. As you become more experienced, you will very probably enjoy growing many others and may even want to try some of the more unusual species.

You should replace the fluorescent or day-glo lamps when the light output falls below the minimum required for your garden. The normal life of a fluorescent lamp is about one year when operated fourteen hours a day.

Foliage plants should be lighted from the top only. So for these use only fixtures that are parallel to the planter and mounted over it. Flowering plants should be lighted from the top and back of the indoor garden. If you are willing to mount lighting fixtures on the standards so the lamps shine forward onto the plants, you will find they are perfect for flowering plants.

It is now possible to get cabinets and racks with built-in lights, or you can construct your own to fit your location. Be sure to provide means of controlling the humidity and temperatures in a completely closed cabinet, and you will be rewarded with prize plants. Books, pamphlets and brochures that give directions on how to build these cabinets and built-in planters are available from state and federal agricultural agencies. Automatic timers are available at electrical supply houses and hardware stores which assure that the lighting system in built-in planters and cabinets will turn on and off at the proper time every day.

Experience Is the Best You-Know-What!

Since the most important factors governing a plant's growth— such as light, temperature, humidity, aeration, and even nutrition —vary from one household to another, it is difficult to give any hard-and-fast rules for cultivating plants indoors under artificial light. So you will have to experiment and observe your plants and develop rules that apply to your own conditions. This isn't as tough as you might think—it can be a lot of fun.

Watch the reactions of a particular plant. It will tell you in its own way whether it is content with the conditions and the amount of light you are providing. If your observation tells you that the plant is *not* happy, be cautious. It's not necessarily a good idea to make sudden changes. Plants, like people, are often shocked by being subjected to sudden intensities of light, heat, or cold. Whatever change you decide to make, do it gradually. Give your plants a chance to adjust, and you will quite possibly begin to notice their reaction to improved conditions. Reactions to poor or harmful conditions are more quickly noticeable but take longer to overcome. Try not to let them happen in the first place.

Some General Tips

For greatest success, a nice balance must be kept between the various growing factors. Plants growing in decreased light need a lower temperature and less water than those growing in strong light. Most homes in winter are warmer than your plants like (I know I've said this many times before), and the humidity is too low. Most plants prefer temperatures between 60 and 75 degrees, with not more than a 15-degree variation between day and night—too much either way will shock them. Remember, too, that a plant can use the available food only when there is enough light for it to carry on the process of photosynthesis. Additional light results in a shorter, stockier plant, while too little light causes plants to become leggy.

If your plants are not growing well in their present location, check the light before you force more food on them, which will cause indigestion. The small cost of giving them some artificial light will do them much more good and may even make it unnecessary to be constantly replacing those you keep in shady spots, in room dividers, and in dark corners.

The most desirable place to put an indoor garden is where the temperature during the day is about 70–75 degrees and the nighttime temperature is about 65 degrees. Avoid locations near heating ducts, exhaust fans, refrigerators, or outside doorways. Air from heating ducts heats and dries your plants, and drafts from exhaust fans, refrigerators, or outside doorways will chill them. It's also a good idea to avoid placing planters in heavy-traffic areas in your home. Not only does the planter get in the way of passing traffic but the plants sometimes get damaged.

Bear in mind that the planter will light the ceiling and walls as well as the plants. This extra light may be welcome and even serve as the primary source of room illumination. On the other hand, it may cause glare rather than brightness. You may want to diffuse this by putting fiber glass diffusers on the backs of the panel lamps, on the side away from the plants. You can also use patterned, rigid, and heat-resistant diffusers, but don't place the diffusers between the lamps and the lights or they will screen out the light rays in the growing spectrum.

Selecting Your Plants

Maybe you don't want to grow conventional house plants. Perhaps you would enjoy a collection of ivies, mosses, or even orchids or bonsai. Go ahead, dare to be different! Here are some tips. If you use the garden for orchids, surround it with a clear plastic-sheet material to hold in moisture and keep the humidity high.

If you intend to use the garden exclusively for the display of florist plants, you might have a metal pan made to fit over the opening in the planter. Have the pan three to four inches deep and paint it to match the planter. Fill the pan with pea gravel or marble chips and set the plants on the gravel-filled pan. When you water, let some of the water drain into the pan. Evaporation from the gravel or marble chips will increase the humidity of the air around the plants.

You may also want to change your plants according to the different holiday seasons—poinsettias or Christmas cactus at Christmastime, azaleas for the period around St. Valentine's Day, lilies or tulips at Easter, hydrangeas for Mother's Day, potted annuals during the summer months, and chrysanthemums in the fall. A changing scene will keep your garden interesting at all seasons of the year.

Almost any plant can be helped by artificial light. My mother grows many members of the Gesneriad family, including gloxinias and achimenes, in this way. We have a Crossandra that, under normal circumstances would get by on four or more hours of sunlight a day. However, this plant has grown well over the foot in height promised by the nurseryman when Ilene bought it. Because it looked uncomfortable on the counter near the kitchen window, I moved it to a small table where it gets eight hours of artificial light from a high-intensity daylight (incandescent) bulb mounted in the ceiling. You can also use a pole light for this purpose.

The pleasure that your lighted indoor garden will give you may depend in a large measure on your life style. Ask yourself how much time you are willing to devote to its care, how often you may be away, and consider any other factor that may apply.

Try to select plants that are both attractive and adaptable to growing indoors. The skill you develop in arranging and caring for them will add to your enjoyment of your indoor garden.

Caring For Your Indoor Light Garden

Of all the steps in the care of an indoor garden under lights watering is the most important. You should water the plants thoroughly but infrequently. If they get too much water, they drown or rot. If they get too little, they will wilt and may never return to their former health and beauty.

As soon as you place your friends in the light garden, begin adjusting them to their new indoor environment. Water the soil ball, clay pot, and surrounding sphagnum moss to saturation, but don't flood it. Allow the whole garden to dry until the plants are near wilting. This can be detected by watching the leaves; they change from green to gray-green and begin to droop. But never let them wilt completely. When you notice the telltale signs, water them thoroughly again.

You can be sure of watering exactly the right amount if you will use a plastic or metal funnel. Here is how to use it. Insert the neck of the funnel into the soil of the pot. Fill the funnel with water. When it empties, fill it again. When the water no longer drains from the funnel, stick your finger in the neck so the water will not run out, then remove the funnel. Only the amount of water that the soil can hold will leave the funnel—never too much. Plants watered in this way usually will not need water again for several weeks. Flowering plants require more frequent watering than foliage plants.

Wet moss or a newspaper mulch on the surface of the planter tends to raise the relative humidity of the air around the plants as moisture evaporates from it. This high humidity is beneficial to your plants. When you are watering, turn the lights off if possible. Don't get water on the lamps, fixtures, or planter.

Careful and regular feeding is even more important for pot plants than for those grown out of doors, because your indoor plant pals can't spread their roots and reach out for food. What is in the pot soil is all that's available to them. For this reason you should set up a regular feeding program. In our busy schedule we sometimes forget when was the last time we fed our plants.

It's a good idea to keep a little notebook in which to record the dates when your plants got their rations and vitamins. This will ensure that your plants are well nourished and will keep you from worrying about whether you are neglecting them.

Here's a good feeding plan. Every two to four weeks treat the plants in your garden with a solution of water-soluble fertilizer used at half the strength recommended on the label. Fertilize only when plants are actively growing. Do not use any dry fertilizers for plants growing under lights indoors. Such fertilizers don't dissolve completely and may build up over a period of time to a strength that will kill the roots. Even when you use a soluble fertilizer, you may notice an accumulation of the fertilizer on the surface of the soil. It will be a white crusty deposit. This deposit should be removed along with a little of the surface soil and replaced with new soil.

Plants will adjust better to an indoor garden if they are not planted directly into it. If possible, pot them first, and then set the pots in the planter, cabinet, garden, or lighted area. This will also allow you to arrange and replace them from time to time as their blooming period wanes or you want to try something new. While plants are adjusting to the indoors, some of the oldest leaves may yellow. If so, remove them, wash the remaining leaves with warm soapy water, rinse with clear water, and stake the plants. They should now be ready for a long life in your indoor garden.

Even in a planter box or illuminated cabinet your plants will need some regular exercise. It's a good idea to turn each of the pots in the planter about once a week. This will encourage more even development and will keep them from rooting into the surrounding sphagnum moss through the drain hole of the pot. Sometimes these old friends become sick or get so oversized that even pruning will not help. When this happens, steel yourself— even plants have got to go sometime. Take them out of the planter and replace them with new, healthy, moderate-sized plants.

One question I'm asked all the time is: How much light do indoor plants need? While it's tough to have to generalize, most plants need light for about 12 to 16 hours a day. But they need darkness too, sometimes more than light, so if you're going to be away it is better to have the plants in continual darkness than in continual light. If they receive some sunlight during the day, give them four to six hours of supplemental lighting. But if there is no sunlight, give them anywhere from eight to 16 hours. Use an automatic timer for best results. Don't depend on your memory.

Summer Vacation or a Weekend Trip

Up to now I've kept mentioning the necessity of considering the times when you will not be at home. But I haven't told you what to do about it. That two-week vacation doesn't have to be a period of agony for either you or your plants if you will just do a little look-ahead planning. Obviously, if you can get someone to look in on the plant pals at your house while you're gone, that's the best answer. You might make a trade arrangement with a gardener friend who will be going on vacation later on.

If you can't get someone to care for your plants, cover them with a large polyethylene sheet and tie it to the pot or box to prevent loss of moisture. Keep the lighting on the automatic timer but reduce the artificial-daylight period to eight hours every day. If you have time before leaving, you can train the plants to get along with less water (many will adjust better than you think). If not, just give them a good drink, using the funnel method, before you leave.

My friend Mary Kibbie takes her pot plants outside when she is planning a weekend in the mountains with her family. She uses her son Matt's sandbox and, after thoroughly wetting the sand, buries the pots in it. Then she covers the entire sandbox with the least expensive plastic painter's dropcloth. This creates a rather large but practical microenvironment, or terrarium. She says it seems to serve the purpose and keeps her plants healthy until she and the family return to free them. Plants cared for in this way can get along satisfactorily by themselves for about two weeks. If you must be away for more than two weeks you can expect to lose some of your plants, especially the flowering ones.

Moving or Mobile-Homing with Plants

Many a cherished house plant made a long journey back in pioneer days coming across country in a covered wagon. Today it takes less time to move, but if you will plan a little in advance for the comfort of your friends, there is no reason why they should not arrive in good condition. Secure a sturdy cardboard box, large enough to set the pots in and tall enough so they won't have their tops broken. If the trip will take several days, water your plants well and put one of the large plastic bags that cleaners use over each one. Roll up the excess and make a sort of collar around the pot. Stuff additional bags in between the pots so they won't rock around or turn over.

Statistics, as usual, are as clear as mud to me so I don't know whether there are 6.5 million campers and mobile homes (*Time*, July 2, 1973) or if there are 14 million of them, as suggested by various camper magazines. I do know, though, that there are one hell of a lot of them on the road whenever I go to visit my mother in northern Michigan. And I'm sure that all these camper folks, like my friends Tom and Holly Azzari, like to travel with their house plants. One of the Azzaris' favorite trips is to take their potted cactus plants to visit their cacti cousins in the desert!

If you are going to do a lot of traveling in your mobile home during the next few months, I suggest you check ahead to where you are going, to see if there are any legal restrictions that prohibit your "importing" agricultural products. Such laws—especially in California—are designed to keep certain crop-destroying insects, bacteria, and organisms out of certain states. The authorities have no special interest in your house plants, but only in the "concealed weapons" they may be carrying.

Also, see that you are not breaking a law if you decide to carry off plants growing along roadsides or from campgrounds in state or national parks. Such plants are often protected by conservation laws. If you find plants that are not on such restricted lists, have fun—take them along with you, and if they survive, bring them back to your home. They will serve as constant reminders of the places you have been and the good times you had there.

Light measurements in trailers and mobile homes are normally quite low in terms of footcandles and intensity. I suggest therefore that you make your prized house plants only temporary visitors to your mobile home. If you are traveling, move sun-loving house plants to the rear window ledge of your car or to any sunny window in the trailer. Watch them carefully to see that they don't get sunburned.

One of the reasons you go camping is to get outside in the fresh air. If you are parked in a campground, your plants will enjoy being placed outdoors for four to six hours every day. Again, watch out for sunburn damage. Place the plants where they'll get filtered sunlight in the hottest hours of the day.

The current craze in terrarium culture dovetails nicely with the trailer and mobile-home boom. These self-contained microclimates (discussed in Chapter 8, Terrariums) are very good travelers and are usually unaffected by their surroundings of the moment, be it Alaska or Death Valley. Follow the instructions given previously and they should flourish while you discover America.

New portable fluorescent lights, which are both plug-in and battery-operated, now make it possible to grow many plants (including African violets) that were previously unable to survive in trailers. Whenever possible, give these artificially lighted plants a breath of fresh air. You may be surprised to find that plants like to travel as much as people!

15

Fun Gardening Under Those Lights

Using artificial light will definitely increase your chances for success with even the most popular and traditional plants found in most American homes. Assuming that you have read the previous chapter carefully and want to proceed, let's discuss some of these plants in detail.

African Violets

Most experts will agree that growing African violets is a good way to separate the gardeners from the *gardeners!* These are the most popular house plants *sold* in America, but that doesn't necessarily mean that they will ever be the most popular plants *grown* in America. These are among the most fussy house plants you will want to bring into your family circle.

Knowing the basic rules for growing saintpaulias, the correct botanical name for African violets, is rather like having a knowledge of good manners. You should know what's correct before you add your own personal touches. There are a few things that everybody seems to agree on. After that you're on your own. Here in the most simple terms I can manage are the "pleases" and "thank yous" of their culture.

To begin with, use a 3-inch pot to set the new plants. This may be either the common red clay unglazed flowerpot or the glazed containers offered. They can be used with or without a wick for continuous feeding. If the unglazed pots are used, protection must be provided along the rim so that the leaf stems don't

Saintpaulia
African Violet

come into direct contact with the pot, as this will result in development of leaf or stem rot. Sometimes the rim is coated with paraffin, or it may be covered with metal foil. Either is satisfactory. If a glazed pot is used, be sure that drainage is provided at the bottom.

African violets like loose, fertile soil. You can purchase a commercial African-violet potting soil at your garden center or you can use my Mix #5, suggested earlier. My mother gives me this additional soil recipe:

> 1 part sharp medium-fine sand
> 1 tablespoon bone meal per quart
> 2 parts garden loam
> 2 parts leaf mold or peat moss
> 1 part well-rotted manure

Sift this soil mixture through a ¼-inch screen to remove any coarse particles. All of these mixes will work, so take your pick.

Use a broken crock over the drainage hole in the bottom of the pot to keep it open. This is one of the most important success factors with African violets. Place the plant in the pot so that the crown is just above the surface. Press soil about the roots and thump the pot on the table to further settle the soil. Stand the pot in water until the soil soaks up all it will hold, then set it out to drain.

The following precautions seem to be agreed upon by all growers:

1. Don't keep plants in direct sunlight, especially in summer. Diffused light from the east or north is best, although insufficient light means few flowers.

With artificial light your African violets don't have to be limited to your windowsill—they can grow anywhere. Their light requirements aren't excessive. Two 40-watt fluorescent tubes, turned on for twelve hours a day, will serve nine to twelve standard-size plants. You can grow many more miniatures in the same space if you want.

African violets aren't really very fussy about light. They are what is called "neutral day-length plants." This means that they don't require a specific number of hours of light or darkness in order to bloom. They will do well under a wide range of day lengths.

2. Water used should be of room temperature. Always water from the bottom, setting the pot in a saucer. *Do not* get water on the foliage.

3. Don't allow the soil to become soggy. Good drainage is important. Check the pot occasionally to see that the drainage hole isn't plugged.

4. For healthy foliage and numerous flowers, maintain a regular feeding program. Many commercial fertilizers especially recommended for African violets are available. Follow the directions on the container.

5. Watch plants for any indication of insect attack. If you detect mealy bugs—small cottony white spots—touch them with a small swab dipped in alcohol. Most other insects can be controlled by dusting with a complete insecticide, especially in the heart of the plant.

There you have it. Points that are often hotly disputed include required temperature, humidity, and whether or not the foliage should be washed off gently with water or a soft, dry brush. I believe that after the plants get adjusted to your home, they'll stand any medium temperature range between 60 and 75 degrees, provided they aren't subjected to sudden changes, drafts or chills at night.

These plants require constant care, but they are easy to propagate and have no resting period. If cared for properly they should bloom continuously. New flower buds form in the axil of each new leaf, so the more new leaves a plant has, the more flowers it will produce. This is one of the best reasons for growing African

African Violet Leaf

violets under artificial lights—the lights will keep the plants growing continuously, putting out new leaves and consequently more flowers. Artificial lighting also eliminates all the tedium of having to exercise your plants—giving them that quarter turn every day to keep them symmetrical. They will grow upright and uniform, with sturdy, healthy, and rich-colored foliage.

There are several hundred varieties of African violets, and new ones are constantly being introduced. The differences between many of these varieties are so very slight that it's difficult to tell some of them apart. Yet if you want to become a collector, there are enough variations in flower size, color, leaf shape, leaf color, leaf margin, and leaf markings to give you a wide range to choose from.

The flower color range is blue, violet, lavender, pink, red-violet, blue-violet, lavender-pink, and white. The flowers are either single or double. Double varieties seem to bloom better for me. In some varieties the upper two petals are darker than the other three. Or the center may be darker than the rest of the flower. In the variety "Lady Geneva" the petals have a distinctive white edge. The "Fringette" varieties have ruffled petals. The "Amazon" and "Dupont" varieties produce quite large, heavy-textured flowers. There are even "girl" varieties, such as "Blue Girl" and "Red Girl", and these have foliage that is deeply scalloped, with a white spot at the base of each leaf blade.

Here is a list of popular varieties representative of each color group:

SINGLES: Blue: Sailor Girl, Blue Boy, Blue Heiress
Purple: Ruffled Queen, Emperor Wilhelm, Purple Knight
Orchid: Painted Girl, Sunrise, Lavender Beauty

White: Snow Prince, Innocence, Snow Girl
Pink: Pink Cheer, Pink Delight, Pink Wonder
Reddish: California Dark Plum, Red King, Velvet Girl
Bicolor: Bicolor, Dupont, Lavender Pink
DOUBLES: Blue: Azure Beauty, Double Neptune
Orchid: Double Rose, Snowline
Purple: Double Margaret
White: White Madonna, Purity
Reddish: Fire Chief

Propagation of African violets sometimes happens by accident. A clump gets too large and you pull off a crown or two and then you just can't bear to throw the thing away. So you plant it in a small pot, pat the soil down, water, and—presto!—you have another plant! This *root-division* method is the easiest and usually the most successful. Leaf cuttings also work well, and this is a good way to get a new plant from the collection of a friend.

Insect Pests

The insect that most commonly preys on African violets is the *cyclamen mite*. Injured plants are dwarfed; leaves are reduced in size, cupped upward, and have a white swelling on the upper surfaces, especially on young leaves; flowers don't open properly, and new flower formation soon stops. If one of your plants has a very serious infestation, it isn't practical to try to save it. To avoid such trouble, sodium selenate should be used in the soil. This material—available in small capsule form for house plant use—must always be used carefully and according to the manufacturer's directions. *It is a deadly poison.* Malathion is also effective against cyclamen mite and spider mite.

African violets may also be attacked by *crown rot*, a disease that causes the plant to become injured at the soil level and wilt. Careful watering and good drainage help to prevent this damage. Don't plant African violets too deeply. A plant that has rotted off may sometimes be saved if you cut off the diseased portion and a few of the older leaves and then reroot the plant in sand or water. When new roots develop, the plant should be repotted up into sterilized soil.

Nematodes, another hazard, cause the leaves to appear dull and the flower stalks to become aborted. An examination of the roots will reveal small knots. Control the spread of nematodes by destroying infested plants and disposing of the soil. Use only sterilized soil for potting.

Ring spot is recognized by the yellowish or white rings or irregular spots on the upper surface of the leaf. One cause of this is too much strong light. Another is applying water that is either decidedly warmer or cooler than the plant. Water that's 10 or more degrees cooler than the leaf will cause ring spot. Use tepid water on these plants.

Petioles of the leaves sometimes become soft or discolored when they come into contact with the rim of the pot. This injury is due to an accumulation of soluble salts that are deposited on the rim of the pot by evaporation of water from the soil. Cover the rim with waxed paper or aluminum foil or repot into a clean, sterilized pot. Nonporous types of pots generally don't absorb such salts, and injury of this kind is not likely where they are used.

BEGONIAS, BOTH BLOSSOMING AND REX

Begonias are slowly but surely creeping up the ladder of popularity toward first place as a choice among house plants. Don't let their delicate beauty put you off—they're not nearly as complicated as the gardening books would have us believe. If you plan to grow these beauties in a home greenhouse, you've got it made. And, with a little more care, you can grow them anywhere indoors under fluorescent lights.

TUBEROUS-ROOTED BEGONIAS

For the tuberous-rooted begonias, which are the frilled and fancy ones, the soil should be plentifully enriched with compost, leaf mold, decayed manure, humus, or peat moss. It should be coarse, rather than fine, well drained but always moist. Tuberous begonias may be planted any time from February until spring. They are ready to plant when the buds commence to swell at the crown, and should be planted so that the pink swellings remain aboveground.

Good drainage is a must, so see to it that the bottom of the pot contains plenty of broken crockery. Water sparingly until growth starts, increasing the amount of the moisture as the plants develop. These plants grow best if they're kept at a temperature range between 65 and 70 degrees, and in partial shade. In the late fall, after the tops die down, allow the plants to dry, then store them in a warmish place, between 50 and 55 degrees.

Here are the principal things to be careful of with tuberous begonias. Don't plant them until the pink swelling appears, and don't cover the top of the bulb with soil. Too early or too deep planting is liable to cause the bulb to rot.

If you live in a climate in which summers are mild, you can even plant tuberous begonias outdoors in your flower beds. After the weather has warmed and settled—about two weeks after it's safe to put out tomatoes—begonias may be planted, twelve inches apart, in beds. Choose a partially shaded location.

Hanging-basket types. There are many varieties of tuberous begonias that have a drooping habit of growth. These are ideal for cultivation in hanging baskets. Their long shoots hang gracefully over the sides and produce masses of blossoms. Start the tubers as already explained. Line your wire basket with premoistened moss and fill with the compost described earlier. Plant the sprouting tubers about six inches apart and just barely cover the tops with soil.

Hang the basket in a moist, warm atmosphere. A temperature of 55 to 60 degrees is ideal, but I have grown them successfully at 80 degrees or more. Sprinkle the basket often to prevent the soil from drying. Pick off the flower buds until the plants are well rooted and growing freely. Feed them a liquid fertilizer twice a week when they are in full flower. At this time they should be given cooler conditions. After flowering, treat them just as advised for pot-grown plants.

THE FIBROUS-ROOTED BEGONIAS

This branch of the begonia family includes a lot of beauties too, and they are, if anything, easier to grow than their larger flowering brothers and sisters. But if their blossoms aren't too big, they more than make up for this in their abundance. These are often called wax begonias and, like the tuberous types, may be used either for pot culture or as bedding plants.

Most begonias of this type grow an average of twelve inches high, although one—the angel-wing begonia—grows twelve feet tall! Angel-wing has evergreen leaves and great bunches of cerise-colored flowers. It is a climber and looks very nice growing on wires fixed to a home greenhouse roof. It can be kept within bounds by taking cuttings from it each spring. The leaves resemble wings. The smaller wax begonias also have evergreen leaves, but they are roundish, and the plants bear clusters of pink, white, red, or dark-crimson flowers. They bloom almost continuously, but the greatest profusion of flowers appears during the summer months.

Fibrous begonias can be grown from seeds or cuttings. If cuttings are taken, do this in the spring or early summer. Insert the young shoots, three to six inches long, in sand and place them in a warm propagating case. Keep this closed until they are rooted. Pot up separately in 3-inch pots and move them progressively into larger ones.

Christmas begonias are a popular kind that were developed by hybridizing. Florists plan very carefully to bring them into bloom during the winter holiday season.

All the begonias just described are what I like to think of as the frilly, girl types. There is another, a boy type, just as handsome, grown principally for the marvelously marked and colored leaves. This, of course, is the rex begonia.

Begonia Rex

Begonia rex is even more practical for working folks and apartment dwellers than any of the others. These have short rhizomes, or rootstocks, from which arise the long-stalked, ovate, wrinkled leaves averaging about six inches in diameter. These plants, like many human males, have hairy chests! The leafstalks, veins, and, in some varieties, the upper surfaces of the leaves are covered with fine hairs. The beautifully marked leaves may be silver and green, light and dark green, red and green, purple and green, and on and on. One of the most striking, *Begonia masoniana* ("Iron Cross"), has leaves distinctly marked with radiating bands of chocolate-brown. It's terrific!

While rex does need warmth (a minimum temperature of 55–60 degrees) and moisture, he is very accommodating in the matter of shade. He is a fine house plant, and out in California he goes inside and out with equal ease. His soil requirements are much the same as those of other types. The best potting mixture is loam and leaf mold in equal parts, along with coarse sand and

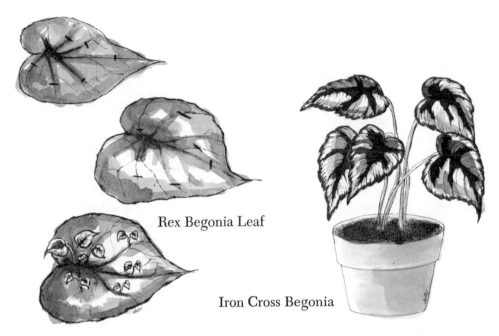

Rex Begonia Leaf

Iron Cross Begonia

rotted manure. Add some charcoal to keep the mixture "sweet." Water well in summer, but only when the soil becomes dry during the winter months. Propagation is easily accomplished by division or by leaf cuttings, as described in the "Family Planning" chapter (Chapter 21). Rex can be safely left for a week or so if you will provide for his comfort as suggested in Chapter 14.

OTHER TYPES OF BEGONIAS

While these three types of begonias comprise the principal and best-known families, there are a number of others that you may want to know about if you become a begonia freak. The following partial list may be helpful.

B. fuchsioides: Has small, dark-green leaves and pendulous bunches of tiny pink flowers. They really do resemble fuchsias.

B. scharffii (Haageana): Another boy type that has large, hairy leaves. But he must have a little peacock in him, because he insists on blooming immense trusses of white flowers, faintly tinged with pink. He grows about four feet tall.

B. manicata: Has large leaves and bears large panicles of pink flowers in late winter. The odd stalks are covered with red, scalelike hairs.

B. metallica: Growing to a height of four feet, this one bears blue-white flowers. The leaves have a metallic coloring.

B. nitida: Is a dainty plant with glossy green leaves and pink flowers. About three feet tall.

B. heracleicotyle: An excellent window plant, bearing very dainty flowers on long stems. This one grows from creeping rhizomes.

B. argenteo-guttata (the trout begonia): Has silver-spotted leaves, bears bluish flowers, and grows four feet tall.

With all this wealth of beauty in blossoms and foliage spread out before us to choose from, becoming a begonia addict can be easy.

ANTHURIUMS

There is a large family of these lovely, long-lasting, and easy-to-grow tropicals.

A. andraeanum: Has an exotic, waxy "flower" in pink, red, orange, salmon, or coral. The flowers will last for a month or more.

A. scherzerianum: Another beauty, with blossoms in white, pink, red, and spotted. The flower is said to look like a graceful, wind-filled boat sail. But I am reminded of Pinocchio's nose!

Anthurium

Anthuriums should have a minimum temperature of 65 degrees, and A. *scherzerianum*, especially, makes a fine potting plant for indoor culture, as it grows only about a foot tall and is very tolerant of house conditions. Anthuriums are ideal for growing under lights, but they don't need strong light. Place them some distance away from the light source.

Pots for this plant should have good drainage, and the soil should be a mixture of orchid peat (osmunda fiber), sphagnum moss, charcoal, and sand. The medium should be kept very moist. Potting should be done early in the spring, just as soon as new roots begin to develop from the rootstock. Fill the pots, which should be 6 to 7 inches in diameter, about half full of crocks. The roots must be kept high in the pots. This means that when the potting is completed, the top of the soil will be in the form of a little mound, slightly above the rim of the pot.

As the rootstock elongates, it will produce roots at a higher level each year. The plants will eventually become raised above the rim of the pots. Pack a layer of moss around the bare stems, and young roots will penetrate this. You can then cut the plants off just level with the rim and repot in smaller pots. Anthuriums are propagated by dividing the rootstocks in February. These will grow best if kept in a propagating case for a few weeks until roots are well formed.

Bulbs Are the Breath of Spring

Bulbs are just the thing for the impatient gardener who just can't wait for spring. After the long, cold days of winter, most of us are so anxious for something green and growing, fresh and pretty, that it amounts almost to a physical hunger. Forcing bulbs indoors for early bloom can give you just as much pleasure in the doing as in the results. Approached in the right way it isn't difficult or messy. As with most other things, getting it all together before you start will make the whole procedure go more smoothly.

Before discussing the cultivation of various spring- and summer-flowering bulbs, we should define the three related terms "bulbs," "corms," and "tubers." Although bulbs, corms, and tubers are all referred to as "bulbs," they do differ in appearance. A true *bulb* is composed of layers of flesh, or scales, that overlap each other like the layers of an onion. A complete flowering plant develops inside the bulb. Each year the growing plant replaces the bulb either partially or entirely. A *corm* is a swollen underground stem that grows upright. Each year the growing plant produces a new corm on top of the old one. The plant grows from the top of the corm. A *tuber* is the swollen end of an underground side shoot that has eyes, or growing points. Each eye produces a separate plant. Tubers multiply from year to year and may be cut apart, or divided, to increase the number of plants you can have in your garden. When tubers are divided for replanting, each division must have eyes on it. Tubers without eyes will not grow.

All bulbs will bloom, but the larger the bulb, the more buds you will have. It is possible now to buy precooled bulbs, which are shipped at the right date for immediate forcing. If, when they arrive, you find you cannot plant them immediately, they can be stored at 34 to 40 degrees for a time (in your refrigerator) until planting is convenient. If you plant several every few weeks, you will have a long period of bloom.

SPRING-FLOWERING BULBS

The spring-flowering bulbs—paper-whites, crocuses, grape hyacinths, scillas, chionodoxas, daffodils, hyacinths, snowdrops, and the early single and double tulips—can all be forced into flower with complete success. Speaking of tulips, did you know that at the height of the tulipmania (tulip madness) that swept over Holland between 1634 and 1637, 2 loads of wheat, 4 loads of rye, 4 fat oxen, 8 fat pigs, 12 fat sheep, 2 hogsheads of wine, 4 barrels of 8-florin beer, 2 barrels of butter, 1,000 pounds of cheese, a complete bed, a suit of clothes, and a silver beaker was the price paid for just *one* tulip bulb? The ones you will buy are far more modest in price, and the equipment you will need is neither expensive nor elaborate.

The best containers to use are spoken of as bulb pans. They are not really pans as we think of them but clay pots that are wide at the top and shallower (in proportion to the diameter) than ordinary standard pots. There are all sorts of variations on the theme, depending on what you plan to grow and individual preference. Azalea pots, for instance, are deeper than bulb pans but not as deep as standard pots.

The bulb itself contains enough stored-up food to bring forth a good flower. A good general potting mixture consists of equal parts of top soil, humus, and sand to which you may add a little plant food or well-decayed manure. It is very important to mix all the ingredients very thoroughly in a large container of some sort, such as a tub or a bushel basket, and get them well pulverized. Few things are more frustrating than running out of soil mix and having to start all over again. It is better to have a little too much—*you can always store it in a polyethylene bag and use it next time*. And if you plan to start several pots, you will have a succession of blooms.

In choosing your bulbs for indoor forcing, select only those indicated by your catalogues as suitable for this purpose. Remember—ten days to three weeks is the longest you can reasonably expect your bulbs to stay in flower. To have continuous bloom you

Bulb Pan

must plan to keep bringing new pots into the house. And here's something else to remember. Hardy bulbs bloom outside naturally during the cool and even frosty days of late winter and early spring. Forcing them indoors does not mean using a high temperature to obtain flowers ahead of the normal flowering season outdoors.

I hate to say this again, but I must: Provide drainage in the bottom of the pot with pieces of broken crock. You can use either clay or plastic containers if you will remember what I told you about the properties of each. Fill the pot about halfway and place the bulbs on top of the soil. Plant several to a container and space them so that they almost touch each other. Fill in around the bulbs, but leave the tips uncovered. They should be just seen above the surface of the soil. The soil itself should be an inch below the rim of the pot to allow for watering.

Have your labeling sticks ready, and after potting the bulbs, mark them as to color and variety. You may want to wait until they bloom to give them each a personal nickname. They should now be given a thorough watering. The best way to do this is to stand the pots in a pan of water, letting it seep upward until the surface soil is completely moistened. After this, set them where they can drain.

Now the potted bulbs are ready for that period of cold, without which they will not grow. All the hardy bulbs need this time of cold and darkness to enable them to develop a strong root system before their top growth starts. Right here is where we start to separate the men from the boys—the experienced growers from the amateurs. Many people succumb to the present desire for instant everything and bring the bulbs into the house far too soon. Don't. Most bulbs need *a minimum of ten to twelve weeks of the cold-and-dark* treatment before they can safely be brought in.

Practice the first "P"—*patience.* Where will you put the bulbs in the meantime? Most home gardeners dig a trench twelve to fifteen inches deep, eighteen inches wide, and long enough to hold the number of pots they plan to put in it. The trench should be dug in a well-drained part of the garden where there is no danger of water collecting in the bottom. You may place a four-inch layer of cinders or coarse gravel at the bottom. This will help the drainage.

Set pots and pans in the trench with the rims touching. You can pack damp compost or peat moss around the pots and three inches deep over them. Just before freezing, place a heavy layer of old hay or straw over the peat moss. Weight this down with boards or evergreen branches. This is to prevent the pots from being frozen too solidly in the peat moss, which will make it difficult to remove them.

An alternative to this method is to use Styrofoam chips on top of the pots. This material will provide excellent insulation during the cold treatment, it will not absorb water or freeze, and it will give protection to the young shoots. If you cannot obtain the chips, use shredded or pulverized Styrofoam over the bulbs. (Building-supply stores usually carry this type.) If you use the shredded Styrofoam, keep it in place with wide wire mesh weighted with boards or stones. Rain will go through the Styrofoam and prevent the bulbs from drying out, much as if they were in the ground.

While the bulbs are out of doors you need not worry about them, as they will go on developing a strong root system without producing a great deal of top growth. Leave them in the trench for a minimum of ten weeks—twelve is often better. When this cold period is about over, examine some of the pots. If you see roots growing out of the drainage holes in the bottom, it's time to take a few of them inside. Put these where they can acclimate themselves for several days. This should be a cool and light, but not sunny, place. It may be a cellar or a north room. Check the moisture of the pot soil. Watering from now on will be very important, and the soil must never be allowed to dry out completely. If watering is needed, set the pots in a partially filled basin of water as before, and let the soil soak it up from the bottom.

Keep an eye on the bulb tips, because once the leaf growth is well up, you will need to place the pots in a moderately warm, sunny window. The night temperature should never be higher than 60 degrees—50 degrees is preferable.

When they are in the flower and bud stage, all bulbs need daily watering. The cooler the room, the longer bulb flowers may be expected to last on potted plants. Therefore they should be moved away from direct sunlight once the flowers start to open. Placing the pots for the night in a room where the temperature ranges between 40 and 50 degrees will also prolong the life of the flowers.

After bloom is over, remove the faded flowers, but do not reduce water. Wait until the foliage shows signs of maturing. Store the pots somewhere temporarily, and as soon as the ground can be dug, you can put the hardy sorts out in the garden to grow on for a year and have a chance to recover their vitality. When the foliage dies down on the half-hardy and tender bulbs, they should be rested completely. Either allow the bulbs and corms to remain in their pots or remove and dry them completely. If they remain in their pots, they should have a small amount of moisture, best provided by setting the pots in a cool, damp place.

Hyacinth

There are tall glasses made expressly for the purpose of growing hyacinth bulbs in water. If possible, use rainwater and fill the glass almost to the base of the bulb. A few pieces of charcoal put in each glass will help keep the water "sweet." Place the glasses in a cool, dark room until the growth is about three inches high. I would recommend that for best results you select only the larger bulbs when using this method.

Paper-White Narcissus

Paper-white narcissus is one of the easiest bulbs to force, and the snowy flowers are delightfully fragrant. Start the bulbs around October 1 if you would have them bloom in early December. If they are planted in succession, every ten days to two weeks, they will keep coming on and you can enjoy them all through the holiday season.

Paper-whites are easy to grow, because they need not be planted in soil and they do not need a resting period in the dark. Select shallow containers just deep enough to hold enough pebbles or small stones so that the bulbs, when set in place on top of these, will have at least two inches of space below for the roots. After placing the stones in the container, set the paper-whites on them, three or four inches apart. Add water at room temperature, bring-

Paperwhite Narcissus

ing the level up to within one-half inch above the bottom of the bulbs. As the water level drops from evaporation, continue adding enough water to keep it constant at the base of the bulbs. The container should be kept in a sunny window.

As with other flowering bulbs, remove the pan from the sun as soon as the buds start to open. It is difficult to get paper-whites to bloom successfully for another season. The best thing to do is to discard them completely after blossoming.

SUMMER-FLOWERING BULBS

Many summer-flowering bulbs can be grown as pot plants, useful indoors or pretty to brighten up the patio. Here are a few suggestions for their selection. Bulbs are sold in nurseries, drug and variety stores, garden shops, florist shops, and through nursery catalogues. Buy from a reputable dealer. Make sure bulbs are not diseased. Diseased bulbs may be moldy or discolored, or they may be soft and rotted. Bulbs should be firm and have an unblemished complexion.

For those who do not know what Rembrandts, or "broken" tulips, are, I would like to explain. Some dealers sell these bulbs, which are infected with a virus disease that gives the flowers a "broken" appearance—striped, blotched, or mottled. Do not buy any bulbs so advertised. They are diseased and will infect healthy tulips and lilies that are planted near them. Diseased plants get smaller every year and die in three to five years. If you want to grow these bulbs, which are usually cheaper in price than others, keep them in a separate place away from your healthy bulbs.

Buy bulbs of varieties that flower together and grow to about the same height. Be sure to buy enough of each color and type for a good display. If you buy bulbs before planting time, keep them in a cool, dry place. A temperature of 60 to 65 degrees is cool enough to prevent most bulbs from drying out until you plant them. Some kinds of summer-flowering bulbs are grown in the garden outdoors and others in pots indoors. The ones we are concerned with here are those that will do well indoors.

ACHIMENES

Achimenes (nut orchid) grows eight to twelve inches high and blooms in summer. The abundantly produced flowers are almost every color and include both singles and doubles. Plant the tubers in 4-inch pots in early spring. Use a mixture of equal parts of peat moss, sand, and garden soil. Grow the plants in a lightly shaded area away from direct sunlight. Water and fertilize the plants at monthly intervals throughout the growing season. Use a mixture of one teaspoonful of 20-20-20 soluble fertilizer per gallon of water.

The tubers will die down in the fall. Take them up, allow them to dry, and with the soil still clinging to them, store them in a cool, dry area at a minimum of 50 degrees. In the spring, wash the soil from the tubers and start the growing cycle again.

I have grown achimenes, sometimes called the "magic flower," for many years, and while they are easy to grow, I have the best results with "Purple King." They should receive the north light, but no direct sunshine. They bloom continuously all summer long.

CALADIUMS

Caladiums, like rex begonias, are grown for their colorful leaves. These natives of Brazil are heat-loving, tender bulbs and, if grown out of doors, will need to be lifted in the fall and stored like gladioli and cannas. They have heart-, or arrow-shaped, leaves in almost limitless variations of pink and red. These, which may be light or dark, are accented with green or red veinings in intricate

Caladium bicolor
Caladium

patterns. Some, called Candidum, are green and white, an excellent contrast for the warmer hues.

Ordinary tall varieties will grow up to eighteen inches, but there are dwarf varieties that will attain a height of only nine inches. Colocasia, or elephant's ear, is also a caladium. The leaves of this species are huge, the heart-shaped blades measuring up to two feet in length, smooth and green, with prominent midribs and purple or violet leafstalks. Colocasia, sometimes grown in tubs, will grow to six feet or more.

Despite their delicate appearance, rainbow-hued caladiums are easy to grow. Bulbs can be started indoors any time from late February through April. They need six to eight weeks to develop clumps or several strong leaves. The potting mix should be half-and-half peat moss and coarse sand. Cover the planted tubers with a one-inch layer of peat moss. Water the tubers often enough to keep the soil mixture damp. Roots grow from the top of the tubers; they must be kept moist and covered with peat moss. Keep the room temperature no lower than 70 degrees. Tubers often rot in cool soil.

As soon as roots develop, replant the tubers, putting them in 6-inch pots. Use a mixture of equal parts of garden soil and peat moss. Grow the plants in a lightly shaded area, never in direct sunlight, as the leaves burn easily. Try to balance the light and shade to get the most color in the leaves. When plants are grown in deep shade, the leaves will have more green coloring and less pink or red. Water and fertilize caladiums at least once every week. Don't allow the soil to become dry. Fertilize with a mixture of one teaspoonful of 20-20-20 soluble fertilizer to a gallon of water.

Caladium varieties include:

FRIEDA HEMPLE: Solid red leaves with a green border.
IDA RED: Deep Christmas red or blood-red with small, prominent, sharp deep-green veins and margin.
JUNE BRIDE: The whitest of the white caladiums with lacy green veining.
PINK CLOUD: Large crinkly leaves in a lovely pink shade with green border and mottling.
POSTMAN JOYNER: Dark-red leaves with deeper ribs set off by a forest-green border.

CANNAS

Canna is a large plant and may grow four to five feet tall. It's a surpriser, because it blooms almost anytime. Flowers may be white, red, pink, or yellow. It makes a dramatic accent in any room, where it may be used as a focal point. Plant the tubers in 6-inch clay pots in October. Use a mixture of equal parts of garden soil, peat moss, and sand. Barely cover the tubers with the mixture. Grow the plants in a temperature of 50 to 60 degrees. Water heavily every day during the growing season. Reduce watering gradually in the spring and let the tubers dry. Fertilize canna every other week. Use a mixture of one teaspoonful of 20-20-20 soluble fertilizer to a gallon of water. Store the potted tubers in a cool, dry area in summer. Leave in the same pots for many years.

ISMENE

Ismene is a lovely Peruvian daffodil that grows two feet high and produces large, funnel-shaped, white flowers that have green stripes running down the funnel. Plant the tubers close together in a flat from January to mid-May. Use a mixture of peat moss and coarse sand. Cover the planted tubers with a one-inch layer of peat moss.

Water the tubers often enough to keep the soil mixture damp. *Roots grow from the top of the tubers.* Because of this they must be kept moist and covered with peat moss. Keep the room temperature no lower than 70 degrees. As soon as roots develop, replant the tubers in 6-inch pots. Use a potting mixture of equal parts of garden soil and peat moss. Grow the plants in a lightly shaded area, never in direct sunlight. They may also be grown outdoors. Water and fertilize Ismene at two-week intervals. Do not allow the soil to become dry. Fertilize as for canna.

When the leaves turn yellow in the fall, dig the tubers from the garden and store with dirt around them. Store potted tubers in the pots. Keep the storage area dry and at no less than 60 degrees. Start the growing cycle again the next year.

AMARYLLIS

Amaryllis (Hippeastrum) grows about two and a half feet tall. The handsome flowers, large and funnel-shaped, are rose, blush, or white, and are borne on thick, fleshy stems.

Amaryllis

Amaryllis

Amaryllis Bulb

Plant the bulbs in May, with the upper third of the bulb exposed. Blooms will be bigger and better if the bulb is pot-bound, so place in a container that will encourage crowding of the roots. Amaryllis does not like to be disturbed once it has become established, so repot only when absolutely necessary. From the time the bulb is potted until growth begins, give very little water. Place the pot in a dim light and leave until new growth appears. Now is the time to increase the moisture and bring the pot to full light.

When the flower scape becomes apparent, give weekly feedings of manure water or liquid fertilizer until the buds start to show color. After blooming, cut off the flower scape and gradually reduce watering until the foliage dries off. Bulbs should then be rested in their pots, which are turned on their sides and may be placed under a greenhouse bench or in a damp, frostproof cellar.

Have You Ever Seen a Potted Lily?

Of course you have—most likely an Easter lily. But these are by no means the only possibilities. Either for forcing into bloom in the spring or for other seasons of the year, the Mid-Century hybrids should be better known. These lilies have a wide and beautiful color range. There is "Destiny," a lemon-yellow, "Croesus," golden-orange, "Joan Evans" and "Harmony," rich orange, "Cinnabar" and "Tabasco," deep maroon-red, "Enchantment," blazing orange, and an outward-facing type, "Prosperity," which is a lemon-yellow.

The proper planting soil should be loose and porous and an inch of gravel should be placed in the bottom of the pot. Use a soil mix of two parts sandy loam, two parts leaf mold or peat, and one part sand. Place an inch or two of soil in the pot, plant the bulb, and then continue filling the pot with soil. Water thoroughly.

Place all varieties (except "Prosperity") in a temperature of 60 degrees by day and 55 degrees by night. "Prosperity" should have a temperature of 40–50 degrees until roots are established, and then it should be moved to a location with a higher temperature. When growth has been established and roots are forming, feed the plants with nitrogen. Ten days later feed again. Wait another ten days and feed with a complete fertilizer; continue until buds appear. Moisture is important and should be uniform. Too much water will cause root rot.

LYCORIS

This lovely plant has the undeserved name "spider lily." I much prefer "Lycoris," though I don't know exactly why the name was given. (Lycoris was a Roman actress and the mistress of Mark Antony.) The beautiful, delicate flowers come in several colors. I have grown the deep-red ones, squamigera, which blooms from early July to August. The foliage, produced in early spring, dies in early summer. The flower stalk arises in the late summer. Radiata blooms from late July to October. The foliage, produced in the fall, remains green all winter and dies in the spring. Lycoris grows fifteen to eighteen inches tall, depending on season and variety. It may be used as a pot plant in areas where the ground freezes in winter.

Plant the bulbs in 5–6-inch pots in a mixture of equal parts of garden soil, peat moss, and sand. Water and fertilize the plants at weekly intervals. Use a light ring of 5-10-5 or 10-6-4 fertilizer around each plant.

TUBEROSE

Tuberose (Polianthes) grows two feet high and blooms in late fall. The waxy, white, double flowers are very fragrant. Plant the tubers in 5–6-inch pots in a mixture of equal parts of garden soil, peat moss, and sand. Water plants every day; fertilize every other week, as for canna. The tubers should be taken from the pots in the fall and stored; they will not overwinter in temperatures as low as 40 degrees.

THE SEA ONION, AN UNUSUAL PLANT

Most people grow only the "popular" plants. Of course, they are generally the most beautiful and easiest to take care of—or there may be some other good reason for walking down the well-trodden path. But I'm strongly inclined to believe that there is a spirit of adventure lurking somewhere in the consciousness of all gardeners, an urge to experiment and to travel on uncharted seas. It's also nice to be able to show your gardening friends that you have been successful with a plant they've never even thought of growing! Here is one—the sea onion.

Sea Onion

The sea onion is a member of the lily family. She is called *Urginea maritima* and is a half-hardy perennial found wild on semitropical seacoasts of Africa and India. Her interesting generic name seems to come from the Arabian tribe Ben Urgin, in Algeria. She is closely related to Scilla and Ornithogalum. One of her names is *Scilla vivipara*, which means "life bearer"—and in a minute I'll tell you why.

This interesting, intensely maternal lady is a lovely light green all the way through, and she sits like a queen on top of the soil, which should consist of equal parts of loam, leaf mold, and sand. She grows fairly fast, and when her roots begin to crowd the pot they must be changed into the next larger size. Bulbs live a long time and may attain a foot in diameter. The long, straplike leaves may run to five feet or more, and the flowers, which are rather small, assume the shape of white stars, and are borne in short racemes on the ends of slender stalks in summer. This slender stalk may be as tall as eight feet in older plants!

What is most noteworthy, however, about Mother Onion is her method of propagation. Seeds will follow the florets in neat three-part saclike structures, and she sends up shoots around her base from the roots. Her third method is what makes her almost unique. Bulblets may develop at any point on the surface of the "mother," and it is for this reason that she came to be called "vivipara." Mother Onion gets pregnant. You may suspect that this is occurring at any time that her sides begin to swell and bulge. Watch carefully and you will see a split appear and one or more bulblets will pop into view. You can pick these off or let them drop as they mature. In her natural environment she drops these and they start new plants because environmental conditions are right. You will probably be more successful if you will plant them in small pots, to be gradually shifted as they grow to flowering size.

If you do not fancy the long leaves which your plant pet sprouts naturally, you may cut them back, for she is a strong, healthy lady and more will constantly grow. The papery fiber (similar to household onions) of the large bulb will slough off after the bulblets are born and each time she grows successively larger.

The sea onion, like the aloes, is a medicinal plant. The thick juice from the leaves makes an excellent healing ointment for burns. The bulbs also have a high sugar content and are sometimes employed in the manufacture of a type of whiskey in Eastern countries. Learning to enjoy this grand lady is easy, and finding adoptive parents for her "children" is never a problem.

17

Herbs, Fruits and Vegetables
Have Your Houseplants
and Eat Them Too!

Mini-gardening with vegetables, fruit trees, and herbs can be fascinating fun. And you can mix or match—all vegetables or vegetables and flowers. You can grow them in greenhouses, under fluorescent lights, or in a sunny window. Although the type and kind are somewhat more limited than outdoor culture permits, the satisfaction may be just as great. And the hybridists are on our side. They've been busy for a long time creating new types of the old favorites—just as delicious but requiring smaller space in which to grow. Perhaps now, with the prices of fresh vegetables competing with those of meats and dairy products, this is more than ever an important aspect of indoor gardening. But entirely aside from the economic dividends, there is the pleasure of enjoying a truly fresh product, one you grew yourself from plant to plate.

Maybe you'd like to have a vegetable garden, but you live in a room, an apartment, a townhouse, or a mobile home, and you think there is no place at all for such activity. But if you have a doorstep, a balcony, or even just a windowsill, you have space enough for a mini-garden. Suppose that even the windowsill is inadequate, shaded most of the day by the tall building next door. Cheer up—now many vegetables grow and prosper under fluorescent lights.

The basic materials you will need for mini-gardens are some containers, soil (either garden loam or synthetic), and seeds. To start a mini-garden of vegetables, you will need containers large enough to hold the plants when they are fully grown. You can use plastic or clay pots (remember the good and bad features of each), an old pail or tub, a plastic bucket, a bushel basket, a wire basket, a cheese box, or a planter tray. Just about any container is satisfactory, from tiny pots for your kitchen windowsill to large wooden boxes for your patio. The size and number of the containers can vary with the space you have and the number of plants you want to grow. Six-inch pots are satisfactory for chives; radishes, onions, and a variety of miniature tomatoes ("Patio" and "Tiny Tim") will do well in 10-inch pots. If you have patio space, five-gallon plastic trash cans may be used. Half-bushel baskets also work well if you have the room.

Ready-made containers of plastic, metal, and wood are so widely available that it is not necessary to build your own. Many are designed especially for growing plants, but others can be easily modified, particularly pails, tubs, baskets, and trash containers. Plastic laundry baskets can be adapted to use by lining them with plastic sheeting. If you use solid plastic containers, allow for drainage. Drill four or more ¼-inch holes, spaced evenly along the sides near the bottom. Then, to further help drainage, put about one-half inch of coarse gravel in the bottom of each container. Wood containers, such as bushel baskets, will last three to five years if painted both inside and out with a safe wood preservative.

Soils: A Fertile Field

As with house plants grown for flowers or foliage, vegetables have preferences in soil, but that good old garden loam we keep talking about will grow most things. Nevertheless consider it carefully. If your soil has either too much sand or clay for potting use, you can improve it by sifting in an equal amount of screened compost or leaf mold, granulated peat, shredded sphagnum, or some other material with a high humus content. Also mix in plenty of organic material so the potting soil will have that spongy feeling that tells the experienced gardener it will have good water-holding capacity, aeration, and drainage.

If you are an apartment or mobile-home dweller, you may not have the opportunity to obtain this type of soil—so what do you do? You can buy a soil substitute, or synthetic soil, prepared from a mixture of horticultural vermiculite, peat moss, and fertilizer. This mixture, sold by seed dealers and garden supply centers, comes ready to use, and for mini-gardening it has several advantages over soil. It is free of plant-disease organisms and weed seeds, it holds moisture and plant nutrients well, and it is very *lightweight* and portable.

You can prepare your own soil substitute from horticultural-grade vermiculite, peat moss, limestone, superphosphate, and 5-10-5 fertilizer. To one bushel each of vermiculite and shredded peat moss add 14 ounces of ground limestone (preferably dolomitic), 4 ounces of 25-percent superphosphate, and 8 ounces of 5-10-5 fertilizer. This material should be thoroughly mixed. If the material is very dry, add a little water to it to reduce the dust during mixing.

Seeds

Your success in mini-gardening will depend partly on the quality of the seed you plant. Vegetable seed envelopes are stamped with the year in which they should be planted. So check the seed to see that it is not old. Old seed often germinates poorly and does not grow vigorously.

Seeds of many varieties of each plant are available. Miniature vegetable varieties are best for mini-gardens. Miniature varieties of vegetables now available include cabbage, cantaloupe, carrot, cucumber, eggplant, tomato, onion, sweet corn, head lettuce, peas, watermelon—and, if you are quite adventurous, you might try mushroom spawn. Any type of standard-size vegetables, such as lettuce, can be grown indoors, and there are many varieties of ornamental peppers, suitable for seasoning, that also make pretty house plants—the Christmas pepper in particular.

Light, Watering, and Cultivating

Vegetable plants grow better in full sunlight than in the shade. Some vegetables need more light than others. Leafy vegetables (lettuce, cabbage, mustard greens) can stand more shade than root vegetables (beets, radishes, turnips). Root vegetables can stand more shade than vegetable fruit plants (cucumbers, peppers, tomatoes), which do very poorly in the shade. Plant your vegetable fruit plants where they will get the most sun, and your leafy vegetables and root vegetables in the shadier areas.

Vegetables need a water supply equal to about one inch of

Vegetable Power

rain every week during the growing season. Since you are gardening in containers instead of a garden plot, you can easily control moisture. Fill the bottom of your plant containers with gravel or similar material to allow for good drainage. Water each time the soil becomes dry down to a depth of one-eighth of an inch. During hot, dry weather you may need to water three times a week. But be careful not to overwater. If your soil becomes waterlogged, the plants will die from lack of oxygen. If you use a sprinkler can, do not water too late in the evening or the leaves will stay wet during the night. Wet leaves encourage plant diseases.

Weeds rob plants of water, nutrients, space, and light. If weeds come up in your mini-garden, pull them by hand or use a small hand weeder to loosen the soil and remove the weeds while they are still small. Be careful not to injure the plant roots.

Insects and Diseases

Vegetables grown in mini-gardens are as susceptible to attack by these troublemakers as those grown in a garden plot. This is especially true if they are grown near other plants. But, remember, these plants are going to be eaten, so you will not want to use anything on them that could prove harmful to you later on. Try some of the organic remedies suggested, and do it before the problem gets a stranglehold. You can also write to the Superintendent of Documents, Government Printing Office, Washington, D.C. 20402, for a copy of pamphlet HG 46, "Insects and Diseases of Vegetables in the Home Garden." (There is a small charge.) This will tell you what you can safely apply on specific plants.

LETTUCE

Lettuce, so expensive to buy during the winter months, is one of the very best vegetables to grow indoors and will do particularly well under fluorescent lights. For this I would recommend four tubes, two cool-white and two Gro-Lux. As with flowering plants, you will be better off if you use a small electric timer. This will ensure that the plants get the seventeen hours of light each day that they need to keep growing. Have several containers for a constant supply and plant them progressively (about three weeks apart). As lettuce develops many fine hairlike roots, the containers should be at least five inches deep.

Do not plant too thickly, for practically every seed will germinate and soon begin crowding. Thin if necessary. If you have used a good potting-soil mix, well supplied with nutrients, you will not need to do much extra fertilizing. If you want some extra zip, use a "compost tea." You can make this by draining off the water in which you have soaked some manure, leaf mold, or fish fertilizer. Fish emulsion (the directions for diluting are on the bottle) can be purchased at garden centers and is probably the best bet for those who do not have access to other materials.

You will need to keep your plants well moistened. Water in the morning, using lukewarm water. If the plants seem to be wilting at any time of the day, give them water, as they can dry out quickly under the lights. All plants need a temperature fluctuation on schedule, and lettuce prefers 65–70 degrees during the day and 60 degrees or a little lower at night.

If you like, you can grow midget lettuce, "Tom Thumb," that makes tennis-ball-size heads at maturity. This will also grow well in a sunny window box. But for a large and constant crop, leaf lettuces are the most practical. Just keep cutting the outer leaves for salads (using scissors) until the plants are spent.

TOMATOES

There are about as many different ideas for growing tomatoes as there are gardeners to advocate them. There are several miniature varieties of tomatoes that differ little in flavor and content from the larger ones but grow on smaller bushes. Of these "Tiny Tim" seems to be the favorite. The little tomatoes, just about bite-size, are very pretty in salads. "Patio," which bears medium-size red fruit of excellent quality, is also suitable for container culture. And then there is "Small Fry," which produces miniature tomatoes but on a larger plant. This one is suitable for tub culture. Any of these tomatoes may be grown from seeds, started in soil or in one of the peat pellets now available for starting plants. The compressed pellets are moistened and the seed is put in place and covered with peat soil. After the seedling begins to grow, it is transplanted to a larger container, in which it will grow to maturity and bear fruit.

If you have a garden, you can cut off a branch from a bearing tomato plant, place it in a container of water, and leave it until roots appear. This should take about a week. Pot up the rooted branch. Or you can try layering. In the fall, after you have picked all the fruit, lay down a branch of one of your garden plants without removing it, cover it with soil, and, if necessary, place a small weight on it so it will stay down. Be careful not to bruise or break the branch, which can sometimes be brittle, especially if the plant contains much moisture. After the roots begin to grow, cut the branch loose and place it in a pot. It is a good idea to leave the potted tomatoes in the garden for a few days to become established before bringing them indoors. Another idea for growing tomatoes indoors is to put the plant in a large pot in the spring of the year, fastening to the pot a trellis of wood or wire. Plunge the pot in soil outdoors during the summer, excavate it in the late fall, and bring it indoors.

Try to bring plants in before it is necessary to start heating the house, and keep them away from gas stoves and out of drafts. Where you will put your plants depends, of course, on your facilities. They will often do well if placed in a south or southeast window, blossoming and bearing fruit all during the winter months. If you do not have such a window available, remember that tomato plants handle with ease under lights.

Eggplants

For a change of pace to your palate, try "Modern Midget" eggplant. Eggplant is pretty enough for anybody's flower garden, with its purple, jewellike blossoms and its glossy, deep-purple fruit. Eggplant takes practically the same culture as tomatoes, growing well from seed, and is especially well suited to indoor culture. Harvest the fruits when the color is deepest and before the sheen on the skin is lost. "Modern Midget" is the earliest of all eggplants and makes small, sturdy, bushy plants. The fruits are of very good quality and may be used as the larger types.

PEPPERS

Peppers are another vegetable both pretty and practical that do well inside. We've already mentioned the Christmas peppers, sometimes called Christmas cherries (but only because they are similar to cherries in appearance), and these may be round, or elongated and pointed. "Christmas Cherry Jubilee" is very showy, with white berries changing to orange. The spreading plants will grow nicely in 8-inch pots. Cornuliculum, another Christmas cherry, has large yellow fruit which it produces on plants one to two feet tall.

Other ornamental peppers, also good for seasoning, include "Fiesta," bright red; "Fips," whose tiny one-inch rockets change from green to yellow to orange to red; "Variegata," with pods of black, green, or purple; and "Black Prince," which has black leaves even in the young stages and bears black, candlelike fruits that mature to a bright red. These are only a few possibilities. There are many more. But you don't have to settle for growing the small, ornamental peppers only. Ordinary bell peppers will grow well as house plants if placed in 8- to 10-inch pots. Give them a good soil, well mixed with organic matter, and they will stay healthy and bear flowers and fruit for a long period.

Dwarf Italian sweet peppers or the hot Mexican types also perform well indoors. You can start all of these from seed or you can dig up a couple of plants in the autumn, place them in a pot, and grow peppers on your windowsill. Follow the same directions as given for tomatoes. Leave the peppers out of doors in their pots for a week or ten days, depending on weather, but be sure to bring them in if it turns cold. Peppers are somewhat more susceptible to cold injury than tomatoes.

PARSLEY

Another vegetable easily grown indoors is parsley, and this one is so pretty that it will be very attractive mixed in with your flowering plants, especially if you choose the moss-curled variety. Grow it under lights or on that sunny windowsill. Use 6-inch clay pots and fill them with garden loam and compost, about half-and-half. Sow the seed in the fall and keep the pots in the shade. Don't let the soil dry out, for parsley is slow to germinate and needs constant moisture. Old folks used to say, "It goes ten times to the devil and back before it decides to grow"—and sometimes I think this is true. So be patient. A trick you might like to try is sinking the pots in a cool, moist, shady spot in your garden until the little plants decide to show up.

If you are lucky enough to have most of the seeds sprout, thin them to two or three in each pot before you bring them inside. For succession, you can start other plants indoors all during the fall and winter months. They will thrive best in a cool room where they get plenty of sunshine. Sprinkle them weekly with room-temperature water and take advantage of any warm winter rain by setting the pots outside. Parsley is very hardy and can stand considerable cold. Save your raw eggshells and soak them in water for a day or two. Use this water for your parsley. Or water with liquid fish fertilizer every two weeks.

CURLY CRESS

Curly cress is another delicious salad green pretty enough to grow right in with the flowers. It can be used for salads or for garnishing meat dishes. If grown under lights, both cress and parsley should be spaced about eight inches from the flowers. Unlike parsley, however, you should sow the cress rather thickly. It grows very fast and will be ready for use in about a month or six weeks. As with parsley, you can have more by making succession sowings.

Cress will do well in a mixture of about two-thirds good garden soil and one-third fine compost, well mixed together. If you want a larger crop than pot culture affords, try sowing it in wash basins—small, square plastic tubs about 10 by 14 by 5 inches deep. Tubs, like other plastic containers, should have drainage holes and some gravel should be placed in the bottom before putting in the soil.

Chives

Chives are another plant exceedingly useful for indoor culture. If plants are well grown, you can keep snipping the tops for salads and dressings almost indefinitely. Shallots may also be grown indoors and the tops snipped off for use in the same manner.

Garlic

Garlic is as wonderful to grow among your flowers indoors for protective purposes against pests as it is outdoors in the vegetable garden, where it acts as an insect repellent. For successful growth garlic should have about fourteen hours of light. A handy way to grow it is to place the bulbs in pots, providing good soil and adequate drainage material, then placing the pots in a square plastic container to prevent any damage that might occur from water runoff. Snip the shoots as you would for parsley—they will gradually "run down" as the bulb spends itself. An easy way to replace the bulbs is simply to buy them at your local supermarket. Be sure to select heads that have large cloves and look at them carefully to see that they are not dried out.

Garlic brought in from your own garden in the fall of the year may be stored in polyethylene bags and placed in a cool room or in your refrigerator. In the bag they will gradually begin to form roots. Remove a few of these at a time and plant them for your indoor garden. Garlic grown near tomatoes—or even in the same container—has a beneficial effect. Garlic plants will get a lift if watered with liquid fish emulsion about every two weeks. A little bone meal in the soil also helps. To use liquid fish emulsion, add one teaspoonful of the emulsion to one quart of water and mix thoroughly. This fertilizer is very good for many house plants as well as vegetables.

How About Mushrooms?

Growing your own mushrooms all winter isn't at all a big deal. All you need is a dark corner somewhere. A basement or a spare closet will do, or put them in that space under the sink.

Mushrooms

For indoor growing of mushrooms your best bet is to buy one of the prepared trays or planters offered by seedsmen. These contain composted soil already impregnated with mushroom spawn. You will find them less trouble to take care of than a bowl of goldfish and almost as ornamental. All you need do is keep them moist —but never soggy—in a dark, well-ventilated place. They should also be kept cool, with a temperature below 70 degrees—50–60 degrees is better—for this will give you a longer growing period and a larger crop. You can "amaze your family and friends" by picking several crops before the spawn is spent. If you become really mushroom-conscious, you can buy the mushroom spawn and grow them on a large scale either in a handy cave or down in your basement.

RHUBARB

Perhaps not many people will want to grow rhubarb indoors, but it is not at all impossible. For this you should have a redwood tub, and no more than one crown should be planted in the tub. Crowns should be taken from the field after summering for two years; the best ones are those that have never been harvested (cut). Crowns that are either older or younger will not produce as well indoors. Crowns ready for digging should be in the field for at least six weeks after their tops have died and should have been exposed to near-freezing temperatures.

Start digging off to the side and gradually work in, digging deeply under the crowns to avoid as much injury as possible to the storage roots. The tub should have ample drainage material placed in the bottom and since rhubarb is a heavy feeder, the growing mixture should contain plenty of organic nutrients. A good soil is made up of five parts compost, one part well-decomposed manure, and five parts of sandy loam. Mix well. Allow at least one to two square feet of growing space for each crown you bring in.

After planting, place the crowns where there is mild warmth but not excessive heat. If you prepare more than one tub, let some of the crowns remain dormant so you will have them available later. Expose the others to temperatures of about 60 degrees. Keep the soil moist to maintain quality. You can start harvesting about a month after beginning exposure to additional heat, and the stalks should be cut when they attain a length of about sixteen to twenty inches.

CUCUMBERS

The English are especially adept at growing cucumbers in greenhouses. A heated greenhouse having a minimum temperature of 60 degrees is best. Cukes like a soil rich in compost and ample moisture, but a three-inch layer of coarse fibrous loam should be placed on the bottom of the container to assure good drainage. Because they are natural viners, a trellis of some sort should be provided for them to climb on. Or you can attach each plant to a cane, which is in turn attached to a wire, and allow it to grow toward and around the greenhouse roof. One advantage of growing cucumbers on supports is that they have a better form. They are more likely to grow quite straight than if they are allowed to ramble over the ground.

Cucumbers may be picked at any stage of growth, and the smaller they are picked the more they produce. So enjoy. Never allow them to ripen on the vine, because the strength of the plant will be wasted on seed production. The "Burpless" is a particularly desirable variety. There is also a midget cuke ("Shumway"), four inches long, whose vines grow only two feet.

NASTURTIUMS

Nasturtiums may be either bush-type or climbers. They grow rapidly and will often come into bloom in about six or eight weeks after planting. The nasturtium is not only a pretty flower but also most parts of it are edible. The young flower buds and unripe seeds have a pleasantly pungent flavor. The seeds are the source of those expensive capers that many people consider a delicacy. The round leaves also have a peppery flavor and may be used in salads, mixed with other greens, or in sandwiches like lettuce.

If you have a greenhouse, or even if you don't, you might like to try an experiment in companion planting. Many plants are beneficial to each other; in the garden, marigolds protect against the bean beetle as well as other insects. Indoors, nasturtiums, which also tend to repel insects from their immediate vicinity, are useful to plant among vegetables and also near indoor fruit trees. An excellent combination is tomatoes and nasturtiums or cucumbers and nasturtiums. Or you may plant all three in the same container if it's large enough.

RADISHES

As in the outdoor garden, radishes are one of the quickest and easiest crops to grow indoors. They may be grown in pots or boxes. If you like this crispy addition to your salad bowl, plan for succession crops.

MIDGET CORN

While midget corn is available and is an excellent choice for the gardener whose outdoor space is small, I do not recommend it for indoor culture, as even the small stalks take up considerable space. But don't let me stop you if you want to try it. Go right ahead—there's no law that says you can't!

SOME ORNAMENTAL VEGETABLES

"Salad Bowl" lettuce produces many curled, wavy, bright-green leaves. If you want color in your lettuce, grow the "Ruby" variety. This is a beautiful, nonheading salad lettuce with fancy, frilled leaves that are bright red. Another bright-red vegetable is a Swiss chard variety called "Rhubarb." It looks like rhubarb and is easy to grow, but is cooked like other leafy vegetables and is not suitable for pies. A kale variety called "Flowering Kale" or "Flowering Cabbage" is also very pretty. The colorful heads of red, green, and white grow close to the ground, and the little heads spread their ruffled skirts in small circles.

FRUIT TREES

Indoor gardeners are just as adventurous as outdoor gardeners, and the variety and types of fruits that can be grown indoors are amazing. Gardeners everywhere have discovered that it is not only possible but often easy to grow warm-climate plants in the North. Of course the answer is tub culture. While vegetables may be grown in substitute soil, I do not recommend this for small trees. Grow these in soil that is rich in humus, and while they may be placed outdoors in the summer, you should provide a suitable environment for them to thrive in during the winter months.

Of course, growing fruit trees indoors is nothing new. In fact, it was quite the thing a century or two ago, when just about every wealthy estate in Europe boasted an orangery. Here not only oranges (which were not nearly as tasty as the ones we have now) were grown but many other tropical plants as well. These, often huge in size, were taken outdoors in summer and used as ornamentals in the estate gardens. They were stored and displayed in winter in ornate glass structures. It often required considerable skill on the part of the keeper of the orangery to maintain a temperature in winter just above freezing.

Today interest in tub culture is again reviving in such plants, especially citrus trees. They're exceptionally beautiful and often very fragrant as well. These plants open up many new avenues, offering almost unlimited possibilities for their use as decorative accents, creating striking effects both indoors and out.

The best tubs for these trees are wooden—whether you buy them or make them yourself—and the best woods are cedar, cypress, oak, and redwood. With good provision for drainage, you can reasonably expect to have such a planter last at least ten years, and some woods will last even longer. If the tubs are put together with removable bolts, disassembling them for root-pruning will be a fairly simple matter. They should also have wood or metal handles for easy movability.

Be sure to place drainage material in the bottom of the tub before putting in the soil. Since most of the plants you will grow will be tropicals, the soil should be well enriched with good humusy material that is loose, porous, and well balanced in plant nutrients. If you are in any doubt, you can have this soil tested, just as you would for an outdoor garden. You may find that the addition of phosphate rock, finely ground potash, or bone meal may be indicated when you make up the potting mixture.

Remember that fruit trees, like other potted plants, cannot reach out with their roots; you must bring what they need to them. Manure tea, compost-water tea, and diluted fish emulsion are all good to use as liquid fertilizers. Used periodically, they will keep the plants healthy and stimulate growth.

When it becomes necessary to repot tub-grown plants you should incorporate generous amounts of organic material in the soil. As with other plants, you can sometimes delay repotting by removing the top layers of soil and replacing them with new material, thereby causing little disturbance to the roots.

Next to soil the most important factor is light. Fruiting plants need all they can get. You will get some fruit in a fairly sunny location, but trees will bear far more heavily in full sun. Temperature is also important, and the best growing climate ranges from 65 to 75 degrees, with cooler temperatures at night—down to about 55 or 60 degrees. I stress this, because trees, like other plants, need to rest at night and this enables them to mature the growth they have made during the day.

Do your watering with care. No house plant should be allowed to suffer from lack of moisture, but overwatering can be just as bad as underwatering. Many a house plant has been killed with kindness. When you water, water deeply, and then let the plant remain dry for a while until more water becomes necessary. As I have mentioned before, giving the plants a soap-and-water bath occasionally will keep the leaves clean and free from dust and will also discourage insects. Try to do this in the morning so the leaves will dry out well before night, and always allow the foliage to dry before placing the plants in direct sunlight.

CITRUS-FRUIT TREES

Of course, citrus plants for indoor culture have a long history and are general favorites. They are beautiful with their glossy leaves and fragrant blossoms, and of special interest because their fruits may ripen at any season. One of these treasures is the Meyer lemon. This is a naturally small, hardy variety that produces thin-skinned, yellow to golden-orange fruit the year round. The sturdy little tree will even thrive outdoors if winter weather does not go below 10 or 15 degrees. When winter temperatures do go below freezing and remain there, the trees can be placed in a greenhouse.

One of the nicest things about the Meyer lemon is that you do not have to wait a long time for it to bear fruit. In nurseries you can buy blossoming and fruiting specimens in one- to five-gallon cans which are suitable for window growing. This particular lemon will enjoy having a little lime and blood meal worked into the soil, which eventually reaches the roots through watering.

The trees may have drops of blossoms, small to large green fruit, and fruit in all stages of ripeness on them at the same time. The quality of the fruit is as good as that of standard lemons, and many think it is superior. The ripened fruit, left on the bushes, will hold its quality for several weeks and may be picked as needed. Little pruning is necessary—usually the occasional removal of a dead branch is all that is needed. Branches that bear fruit and rest on the ground should be cut back. Growing bushes should be kept in direct sunlight.

Aphids may bother this tree, but they can be easily dislodged with a needle-sharp hose spray. This is not likely to happen unless the tree is placed out of doors in the summer where the blossoms may attract ants, which plant colonies of aphids on buds, flowers, and branch tips.

The Ponderosa lemon is another indoor citrus that is both beautiful and easily grown. The lemons are enormous, measuring five inches across and weighing up to three pounds. You can make from three to five pies with just one lemon.

In the Tahiti orange the fruit is miniature as well as the trees. The oranges grow from one to two inches in diameter, and the tree often bears when it is only six to eight inches tall. The blossoms have the heavenly scent of the full-size orange tree, and the little fruits, about the size of a half dollar, will make excellent preserves and marmalade, as well as a refreshing drink. Lemon and lime trees must be somewhat larger and older than the orange tree before they will bear fruit.

Other types of oranges are the Chinotto, King, and Sweet Orange. The dwarf tangerine, *Citrus nobilis deliciosa,* has handsome foliage, aromatic flowers, and bright-colored delicious fruit. There are also dwarf kumquats and grapefruit and a Persian lime that grows full-sized bright-green juicy limes on a miniature tree.

All of these trees will grow well in the following recipe for potting soil. It should be passed through a half-inch screen before being used.

1 part sand
1 part leaf mold or other humus
1 tablespoon bone meal per quart of the mixture
(a 5-inch potful per bushel)
2 parts garden loam
½ part well-rotted or dried cow manure

Place the plants where they will receive as much sunlight as possible. The soil should not be allowed to dry out completely, nor should it be kept wet to the point of being soggy. Good drainage, therefore, is important and can be provided by placing a few pieces of coarse gravel on the bottom of the pot. Avoid a dry atmosphere. Citrus plants prefer humid conditions for best results, and even indoors these conditions can be provided by placing the pot in a container half-filled with coarse sand or fine gravel that is kept wet at all times. The evaporation of the water from the sand or gravel will humidify the plants.

Place the plants outdoors during the summer months if you live in a cold climate. The plants benefit from this treatment, and when they bloom outdoors, bees and other insects aid in pollinating the blossoms. Plants that are grown indoors exclusively should be lightly shaken each day they are in bloom so as to distribute the pollen and ensure a set of fruit. There are very rarely any bees or other insects indoors to do this job for you. Improper pollination and too dry an atmosphere are often the causes of fruit not setting on plants that bloom indoors. However, overfertilization, like overwatering, can cause a failure of the plants to bear fruit.

FIGS

Ficus diversifolia, the mistletoe fig, is a smooth shrub commonly used as a house plant. Its leaves are short-stalked, or sessile. As they mature, the color changes from a dark green to a dull yellow or reddish, and they fall off naturally. The fruit, which is edible but not much larger than a pea, goes through the same color transformation as the leaves. An epiphyte in nature, deriving its moisture from the air like an orchid, this plant originated in

Ficus lyrata
Fiddle-Leaf Fig

India and on the Malay Peninsula. Strange though it may seem, it belongs to the mulberry family, Moraceae.

The suggested planting medium is a soil having equal parts of loam, sand and peat. The pH should be slightly acid. The light requirements are partial shade to shade, and the noon sun should be avoided. An average temperature of 70 degrees, with 30 percent humidity, is best for growth. Washing the leaves twice a week or spraying with a mister is suggested. Every two weeks, or a little more often, apply diluted liquid fertilizer in the proportion of one level teaspoonful of liquid fertilizer to two quarts of water.

Pigmy Date Palm

The pigmy date palm, *Phoenix roebelenii*, with its soft-textured bright-green leaves, is considered to excel all other small palms in grace, elegance, and beauty. It is a native of Laos. This plant is sometimes also called the pigmy Phoenix, and specimens twenty to thirty years old have been observed with stems not over two feet in height. It is by far the smallest member of the many kinds of known Phoenix plants. This Peter Pan of palms is especially good for low-light areas indoors.

Here are the "bear facts." The plants of the entire Phoenix family are either male or female—that is, both types of flowers do not occur on the same plant. You will need more than one tree for this palm to produce edible fruit. Pigmy date suckers easily and in the wild state grows in clumps. In the South, where it is hardy, it can be grown outdoors and should have a rich, moist soil and at least a half day of shade for best results. When growing it as a house plant, prepare the following potting soil:

> 2 parts good garden loam
> 1 part sand
> 1 part leaf mold or peat moss
> ½ part pulverized cow manure, if available
>   (This ingredient is not absolutely necessary.)

Add one tablespoon of bone meal for each quart of the mixture. In larger quantities, use one 5-inch potful of bone meal per bushel of the mixture.

The pigmy date palm requires a good deal of water, so keep the soil moist at all times, but not soggy. Keep the plant out of direct sunlight, and, if possible, create a somewhat humid environment by placing a pan of water near it. Do not overpot a palm, as it likes having its roots somewhat crowded. Crowding the roots will also aid in forcing the plant into growth. Naturally, the plant shouldn't be neglected, but it will thrive much better than most tropicals with only a moderate amount of care.

TREE TOMATOES

Have you ever heard of a tree tomato? This is *Cyphomandra betacea*, which is a native of South America. The soft wooded tree, or bush, belongs to the potato family, Solanaceae. It is a very pretty house plant that will produce edible fruit sweeter than ordinary tomatoes which may be used for dessert or jam. The tree has heart-shaped leaves and fragrant purple flowers, followed by pendulous red or red-orange oval fruits about two or three inches long by one and a half to two inches wide.

This little tree will grow outdoors in the far South, but in the North should be placed in a greenhouse during the winter months. It may be expected to bear fruit when it is about two years old, and will continue to bear over a long period of time. The trees reach four to eight feet at maturity, but can be pruned back to just about any height and width. Under normal growing conditions one tree may yield as much as thirty or forty pounds of fruit a year.

PINEAPPLE

For an indoor touch of Hawaii you might like to try a pineapple plant. The pineapple plant (*Ananas comosus*) will thrive best in a greenhouse with a minimum winter temperature of 65 degrees. It may be grown in a loamy soil in large pots, and during the summer months hot, moist conditions are required. The temperature may then rise to 80 degrees or more. The fragrant, snowy white blossoms are followed by edible fruit, usually smaller than field-grown pineapples.

Plants may be propagated in the spring by detaching suckers, or side shoots, and placing them in small pots of sandy, loamy soil. Repot as needed. You may cut the leafy top from a store-bought pineapple, set it in a pot of sandy soil and keep it in a warm propagating case, and it will form roots.

Miniature Pineapple

TOMATOES AND POTATOES IN THE SAME POT

There is an amusing hybrid plant available (Lakeland Nurseries) that will enable you to grow tomatoes and potatoes in the same area. Since both are members of the same family, Solana-ceae, they are compatible, and both grow on one planting in the same space. As the tomatoes ripen above, the potatoes are grow-ing on their own roots below!

PEACHES

There are few things more delicious than a tree-ripened peach. Many people have never tasted one. Peaches are not the best keepers or shippers, and most of those found in the super-markets are picked slightly green so they will not spoil before they reach their destination. Now even indoor gardeners can have a perfectly peachy miniature tree. "Bonanza" (Lakeland Nurseries) is a true genetic dwarf and never grows taller than four to five feet, but will produce full-size freestone peaches.

This miniature peach should be grown in a large tub or wooden planter box, and if you would have the tree bear well, should receive full sun during the time it is blossoming (bees or other insects should be present), and fruiting. This tree will bear young, possibly even the first spring after planting, and very likely in the second year. It is a most attractive little tree, with long, bright-green, lancelike leaves and blossoms of a delicate rose-pink.

ROSE HIPS

Have you been listening with envy to all that talk about the wonderful vitamin C contained in rose hips and wished you could grow a plant like this? Well, you can. *Rosa pomifera* bears spec-tacular brilliant orange, golf-ball-size fruits containing ample quantities of nature's richest source of natural vitamin C. These hips will make delicious jellies, jams, nectars, and teas. The plants grow five to six feet tall but may be pruned back to form a bushy plant for container culture. The lovely single rose-pink blossoms with their delicate golden centers are reminiscent of the wild rose of song and story. The nursery company (Farmer's) that offers this rose will send along a free leaflet of rose hip recipes when you receive your plant.

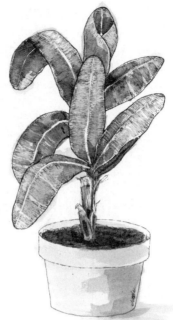

Musa cavendishii
Ladyfinger Banana

Bananas

Did you ever consider the possibility of growing a dwarf banana? *Musa cavendishii* is the type most generally cultivated in the United States. For indoor or greenhouse culture, the plants are grown in large tubs, which must be two feet or more in diameter.

Bananas require rich soil, which must be perfectly drained, and they need full exposure to sunlight. The minimum temperature must not drop below 65 degrees. If you will give them plenty of moisture, feed them often and well with liquid fertilizer, and topdress them with fresh loam and decomposed manure, you will probably succeed in getting them to produce a "hand" or even several. A friend of mine succeeded in growing banana trees quite triumphantly in the climate of Oklahoma City. He kept the trees indoors in the winter, but plunged the pots in the ground during the summer months. He used to astonish his friends by telling them to go out in the garden and pick themselves a ripe banana. Their amazement was a source of constant delight.

Mangoes

Mango (Mangifera) trees when young are very attractive house plants and may be easily raised from seeds. The seeds should be planted in sterilized soil and may be expected to germinate in about three weeks. A shoot will develop from the top of the seed and roots will grow from the bottom. The foliage is a beautiful, glossy, deep green as it matures. New leaves will unfold to a rich brownish-red and retain this color over a long period of time.

The soil for mango trees must be kept moist, well fed, and occasionally topdressed. They will grow well in a temperature of 60–70 degrees. They need not be given direct sun but do require good light. Mango, like Elsa the lioness, was born free and in her native Burma will grow to 120 feet or more. When she becomes too large for indoors, free her and start over with a new plant.

Avocados

Growing an avocado (Persea) from seed is a bit of fun no indoor gardener should miss. You can buy your avocado for this purpose at the supermarket and it will grow. All you need to do is to remove the single large seed from the center of the fruit and plant it. The seed may be planted either vertically, with its pointed end up, or horizontally in a well-drained 4- or 5-inch pot. Use good rich soil and place the seed so that the top shows just above the soil surface.

Keep the pot in a temperature of 60–70 degrees. The soil should be moist but not soggy. A young stem will soon emerge from the seed, and the resulting plant will last for several years, making a most attractive accent for any room. In time it will grow large and need to be replaced or placed elsewhere. The plant will need good light but not direct sun. When it grows too large for its first container, repot in the spring.

Others!

The sea grape (Coccolobis) is another tropical whose young trees are sometimes grown as house plants. Its natural environment is a sandy seashore, and it may be found growing wild in Florida. The fruit is used for making jelly.

Eugenia jambos, the rose apple, is an evergreen tree belonging to the myrtle family. It is a very attractive plant and is easily grown in pots for indoor use. The cloves of commerce are the unopened flower buds of its close relative *Eugenia aromatica.*

Grow strawberries indoors under lights? Yes—and here's a trick. Let the runners root in small pots, and when the plant is well established, detach it. It will flower indoors and even produce a small crop of berries—though usually not as large as those that mature in the garden. Use a small paint brush to flick pollen from one blossom to another.

And speaking of strawberries, have you ever heard of the strawberry guava, *P. cattleianum?* This member of the Psidium family is hardier than the common guava and grows more slowly, making it ideal for pot culture. Guava plants require a minimum winter temperature of 55 degrees and should be planted in soil composed of two parts fibrous loam, one part leaf mold, and one part well-decomposed manure, mixed with some sand.

The plant will need a large tub or pot, or it may be planted directly into a bed or prepared soil in the greenhouse. The experienced grower of guavas prepares the pots by placing potsherds (or crocks) in the bottom of the tub to a depth of three or four inches, covering these with a layer of rough, fibrous compost. Soil is added over this and should be worked well around the roots of the plant and then firmed down. Leave a two-inch space below the rim of the tub for watering.

Water the plant when it becomes moderately dry, and then water thoroughly, repeating this procedure as it becomes necessary. Plants that are bearing fruit should receive liquid fertilizer twice a week when the fruit is forming. The flowers of strawberry guava are white and the fruits are reddish. They are used for making a particularly delicious jelly. There is also a pineapple-flavored guava.

Herbs

There is nothing in the rules that says a strawberry jar may be used only for strawberries. It is an almost perfect container for a large variety of herbs, and you can have a small kitchen garden in one of these pretty pots. What you will plant in it is entirely up to you, as it may be used for either annuals or perennials or both.

As with many other things, there's a trick to filling a strawberry jar correctly. Secure a length of plastic pipe, about one inch smaller than the jar's opening and long enough to be inserted the full depth of the jar. Using a sharp instrument (a nail will do), pierce holes in the pipe at intervals, staggering them the entire length about two or three inches apart, so that water can seep out at all levels into the soil. Keep the opening covered with a bit of masking tape until the soil is put in place.

Herbs do not like a soil that's too rich, so fill the jar with a mixture of sandy loam. Start filling the plants in from the bottom, setting each one in place as you go and continue up the sides. Tamp the soil down carefully and be sure the roots are well covered. When you reach the top with the soil it may be seeded or planted as well, but leave an inch or so of the pipe uncovered so soil will not fall into it. Take off the masking tape and water the jar thoroughly so there will be no air pockets around the roots of any of the plants.

Suggestions for planting the jar include parsley, garden thyme, chives, winter savory, apple mint, orange mint, lemon thyme, burnet, sweet marjoram, bush basil, and rosemary. Rose geranium is particularly pretty for setting at the top of the jar and so is moss-curled parsley. You may even want to plant such a jar entirely with scented geraniums, which include rose, nutmeg, lemon, peppermint, and apple. Other possibilities are annuals, such as dill, basil, chervil, anise, and summer savory.

If you plant the jar with annuals, be sure to keep the soil moist until germination takes place. Slipping a large plastic bag over the jar for a day or two will prevent drying out and convert the jar into a miniature greenhouse. Sometimes herb seeds are slow to germinate, so be patient. Parsley, especially, takes time. If you do secure a good stand, thin the plants to just a few in each opening; crowded plants will be spindly.

Herbs need sunshine, so you must provide them with adequate light. A sunny window will be just fine, but you must remember to turn the jar at regular intervals so all the plants will receive the sun in turn. Window boxes planted with herbs and set on a sunny kitchen windowsill are both practical and attractive. These, like other containers, should have provision for drainage. Place a layer of small stones or broken brick at the bottom before filling in with the soil.

You may seed the box or bring in plants from the garden. If you bring them in from outside they should be given a chance to adjust and have protection from extremes of temperature. French tarragon is nice for a window box, growing bushy and attractive as it is clipped for use. Chives should be clipped regularly whether you use the clippings or not. Moss-curled parsley, grown around the outside edge, is both pretty and practical. Sometimes you never seem to have enough parsley, and the bunches sold at the grocery are so often dry and wilted. Many times you can't even find it at all.

Something else you should consider about herbs grown indoors is their height. Actually, this is not as much of a problem as you might think. They do not seem to grow as tall as they do in the garden if you pot them young. Then, too, you will use your kitchen herbs, cutting them regularly for soups, salads, and other seasonings. This will help to control their height.

Pot culture for any of the herbs that you particularly like is entirely feasible, and lots of them are pretty enough to be grown right in with your flowers. If you live in a climate in which you have lots of dull, dark winter days, you may find that growing herbs under lights will give you success not otherwise possible. For culture under lights you can bring in already started plants from the garden or greenhouse or plant seeds in pots or flats. When seedlings are large enough, transplant into 2-inch pots of sandy loam. Place these about four inches from the lights (parsley should be placed about eight inches away), and, as they grow, gradually move them farther away from the tubes.

Just one more word about herbs: *Use them.* Sweet basil is a fragrant herb, delicious in sauces or tossed salads. Be sure to pick the leaves from the center of the plant—this will keep it bushy. Garden cress is another tasty addition to salads, and it shoots up rapidly. Add a few finely chopped rosemary leaves to your recipe for baking-powder biscuits. Sweet marjoram leaves will add zest to meat loafs, meat balls, or tomato sauce, and it's not bad over sizzling steak or broiled fish. Dill seeds will add a whole new dimension to apple pie. Mint tastes great with lamb, and parsley is good for you (my friend Richie Victor calls it "nature's little vacuum cleaner"). Ways for using snippings from the growing tops of shallots, chives, and garlic are almost endless. Herbs have long been the secret of gourmet cooking, lifting ordinary dishes from mediocrity into sparkling drama.

Sweet Violets

Sweet violets (*Viola odorata*) were a great favorite with everybody long before African violets came on the scene and took the center of the stage. The plant comes in a wider range of colors than most of us realize—deep violet, rose, violet-blue, lavender, and white. The "new" violets are just as sweet, but no longer shy. They bloom much longer and are far larger and very fragrant. Violets may be grown in cold frames or in cool greenhouses. They do well in partly shady locations. The soil for violets should be rich, cool and moist; they may suffer from attacks of red spider mites if the soil is allowed to become too dry.

Violets tend to grow vigorously, and the clumps should be separated often or the plants will become weakened and will not bloom well. If you have a violet bed outdoors, you can peg down some of the runners, pot them up, and bring them indoors. A potting mixture of one part well-rotted manure to four parts garden soil is good. If the soil is acid you may need to add a small amount of lime or bone meal. Do not use any artificial fertilizers for violets.

Cool growing conditions are necessary for sweet violet success. They need a temperature between 40 and 45 degrees at night and about 10 degrees higher in the daytime. They should have good ventilation and be protected from strong sunshine. Pick off spent blossoms and dead or drying leaves.

Violets are edible. The blossoms can be made up into violet syrup, and the syrup may be used in a variety of other delicacies, such as violet sherbet and violet candy. The violet blossoms may also be used in salads, where they are both pretty and tasty. Young violet leaves, which have a high vitamin C content, may also be used in salads—just be sure they are tender and of a good bright-green color. Wash thoroughly and snip them into shreds. They also may be cooked and eaten with a lemon-butter sauce.

ROSES

We have already spoken of roses for indoor culture in Chapter 10, but here I would like to tell you that roses are edible also. The miniatures are just as delicious as their larger sisters and may be prepared in exactly the same way.

Snip away the white bases of the petals, which are bitter, and measure one cup of the petals. Put these in a blender with ¾ cup of water and the strained juice of one lemon. Blend until smooth and gradually add 2¼ cups sugar, keeping the blender running as you slowly pour this in. Place the mixture in a saucepan and add one package of Pen-Jel and another ¾ cup of water.

Bring to a rolling boil and cook hard for one minute, stirring constantly. Pour into sterilized jars and seal. Allow to cool and store in the refrigerator. If you prefer, it may be frozen for later use.

Rose petals may be candied. Snip off the petal bases. (To do this easily, pluck the petals from the rose in bunches.) Mix the white of an egg with a tablespoon of water and dip each petal in the liquid. Place the petals, concave side down, on a paper towel to drain. When the liquid has drained off, but petals are still evenly damp, sprinkle both sides with finely granulated sugar. Shake off the excess sugar and place the petals on wax paper to dry. Place the petals in polyethylene bags and store them in the refrigerator. They will keep for about a month. Pink or red petals are prettiest.

House plants for decoration or for food are available in almost limitless profusion. Some are permanent residents, others are temporary but honored guests. Vegetables will be used, herbs will be snipped, flowering plants retired, and trees may eventually grow too large. Thus the scene is continually changing, full of endless variety and a source of constant interest.

18

Greenhouse Gardening

As you become more and more interested in growing plants indoors—and under lights—you may find that you want to extend your activities to a home greenhouse. Today greenhouses come in many sizes and shapes and are well within the reach of most middle-income families. But before you go into greenhouse growing whole-hog, I suggest you try a solar plantarium. This is really little more than a fancy large terrarium. It is 48 inches long by 22 inches tall, including the legs. Solar plantariums have hinged, removable tops and sliding front panels that permit easy plant care and control of ventilation and temperature. A gravel pan is included, which may be filled with gravel chips or moist sand to maintain humidity. There is also a hygrometer-thermometer for reading humidity and temperature.

Of course, unless you provide your solar plantarium with a light fixture, you must locate it in an area where it will capture enough light for the particular plants you plan to grow. A sunny window is recommended for flowering varieties, and a darker spot for shade varieties and foliage plants. Exposure to morning sun is most desirable. An eastern or southeastern exposure is best.

Maximum exposure to light, especially in winter, is essential to almost all flowering plants. Only a few flowering plants, such as African violets, gesneriads, ferns, and orchids, will grow well in winter without direct sunlight. If these are what you plan to grow, a western or even northern exposure will do.

Humidity Is a Key Factor in Greenhouse Success

Whether you start with a solar plantarium or invest in a larger, more elaborate type of greenhouse, providing proper relative humidity—a high moisture content in the air—is important to your success. Moist sand, pebbles, gravel, vermiculite, peat moss, or soil in the benches will help maintain sufficient humidity. Or you can invest in an automatic humidifier.

Good humidity will enable you to grow many of the plants we have been discussing that are difficult to care for in the drier atmosphere of your home. These can be grown in the greenhouse and brought into your living room to be enjoyed. They can sleep in the greenhouse at night and occasionally go back there for a resting period to keep them looking attractive longer.

Ventilation

Greenhouse plants, especially the flowering ones, thrive best with lots of sunshine combined with good circulation of fresh, cooling air provided by an adequate ventilating system. The prefabricated greenhouses of today are designed to capture and retain the heat of the sun. Because of this your greenhouse can sometimes become too hot, causing the plants to wilt, unless the greenhouse has adequate, easy-to-use ventilation. Plants can suffer from too much heat even on a cold but sunny winter day.

An accessory that you may want to purchase at a later date is a soil-heating cable. This is a little wonder-worker when it comes to starting cuttings and seedlings in a bench of the greenhouse or in the soil for an under-bench growing area. The standard electric soil heaters will provide even bottom heat, automatically controlled, for a propagation area of thirty-six square feet. Soil-heating cables are also valuable additions to cold frames and a necessity for today's hotbeds.

Cold Frames and Hotbeds

Cold frames and hotbeds, as we use them today, almost have to be discussed together. This is because your hotbed is quite likely to be a cold frame with a heating cable.

The cold frame without the cable is used for *summering* special plants that will be moved into the greenhouse before cold weather, for *bulb-forcing* in autumn and early winter, and for *wintering-over* plants of doubtful hardiness that would find your greenhouse too warm. It may also be used for *hardening off* seedlings and bedding plants in the spring. Sizes vary, but a standard model is 36 inches by 42 inches by 12 inches high at the back, sloping to 8 inches in the front. Cold frames are most often situated to face south, and several may even be grouped in a row along the south foundation wall of a home or greenhouse.

The hotbed, as used today, is practically the same as a cold frame. Originally they were dug deeply into the earth, and layers of fresh manure were used to heat them. This heat in a sense turned the cold frame into a hotbed for plants. It is now completely practical to install an electric soil-heating cable, complete with thermostat, and eliminate the manure. The extra growing space in your hotbed will be very handy in late winter and early spring for germinating seedlings, growing seedlings, and forcing spring-flowering plants and vegetables into an early start before the ground warms up outside.

Greenhouse Tools and Equipment

Of course you will need some tools. The most essential are: trowel, hand shears or pruners, gloves, stakes, plant-tying material, labels, and a waterproof marking pencil. For pest control you'll need a small hand-operated mister or hose-end sprayer. You may also find a hose with a pistol-type spray attachment useful.

If you build a larger greenhouse, think carefully before you install benching all around. You may have some tall-tubbed specimens that will need to be placed directly on the greenhouse floor. An area left open for this purpose will come in handy later. Choose a rot-resistant material such as redwood for these benches.

You can use your greenhouse to grow orchids, which need high humidity, or such tall crops as hybrid tea roses, tree ferns, bananas, tropical trees, or even vegetables. But, if you use your greenhouse, as most gardeners do, for propagating and growing young plants, there are certain things you will need to plan for and stock in good supply.

Among these things are wooden or plastic boxlike containers, called flats, in which large quantities of small plants can be started. These shallow trays, usually two or three inches deep, are fine for starting seeds. Sixteen by twenty-two inches is the standard size for a wooden seed flat, but there are others on the market in fiberboard and plastic in just about every conceivable size. The 6-by-9 size is the most convenient to use on shelves. A nice size for bench use is 12 by 18 inches—large enough to contain a number of small plants but not too heavy to lift. If you plan to grow cut flowers or force bulbs in a flat, use one that is about six inches deep.

Pots are also needed in good supply. These can be of clay or plastic. The good and bad properties of each have already been discussed, and the use of either kind is really a matter of personal taste. Pots come in sizes of 2½, 3, 4, 5, 6, 8, and 10 inches. You should lay in an adequate supply of each, with many more of the smaller sizes than the larger ones.

If you plan to force spring-flowering bulbs such as tulips and daffodils, you will want a bulb pan. This is a pot approximately half the height of a standard clay pot. These pots are also excellent for fibrous-rooted begonias, because these plants have very shallow root systems that like to spread out instead of down.

In the category of "nice to have but not absolutely necessary" are azalea pots. These are sometimes referred to as three-quarter pots because they are about three-fourths as deep as standard clay pots having the same top diameter. They are about one-fourth deeper than the bulb pans described above.

In addition to the pots, stock up on some hanging baskets. Your best chance of success with a hanging basket is in the humid atmosphere of a greenhouse, and begonias are among the most satisfying plants you will grow. Culture is as described earlier.

Artificial Lighting

When you plan for your greenhouse lighting, be aware that there are two types possible—fluorescent and incandescent. Each of these has its own peculiar function.

Fluorescents may be used in order to make available more growing space. You can install them underneath the benches or in a dark area of the greenhouse. This may be next to a house wall or where trees have grown so large that they block necessary light, particularly in winter. Here is a rule of thumb. Allow one commercial fluorescent unit with reflector, and two or three 40-watt tubes, for a growing area approximately two feet wide by four feet long. If these are the only source of light, they should be used fourteen to sixteen hours out of every twenty-four. If they are only supplemental, burn them from about 4 P.M. to 10 P.M. daily. This can be particularly useful in the short days of fall and winter as a way to extend the daylight hours. It will bring annual flowers —which need lots of light—into earlier bloom.

Incandescent lights may also be used for extending daylight in fall and winter. This will help the plants you wish to bring to bud and flower on long days. For best results, install one reflector with a 60-watt incandescent bulb over every four to five feet of bench space. Plug this into an automatic timer that has been set to turn the lights on at 5 P.M. and off at 10 P.M. daily. You will be most likely to use this supplementary light from the time seedlings on young plants are making vigorous active growth until flower buds are beginning to open.

Plants Suitable for Greenhouse Culture

Acacia
Acalypha hispida
Achimenes
Aeschynanthus
Agapanthus
Ageratum
Allamanda
Alyssum maritimum
Amarcrinum
Amaryllis
Anemone
Anthurium
Antirrhinum
Aphelandra
Ardisia crispa
Asparagus fern
Astilbe japonica
Azalea
Begonia, fibrous-rooted
Begonia, semituberous
Begonia, tuberous

Beloperone
Bessera elegans
Boston Daisy Marguerita
Bougainvillea
Bouvardia
Bromeliads
Browallia
Brunsvigia
Buddleja, or Buddleia
Cacti and other succulents
Calceolaria
Calendula officinalis
Callistephus chinensis
Camelia
Capsicum
Centaurea cyanus
Centropogon
Choisya
Chrysanthemum carinatum
   (annual)
Chrysanthemum morifolium
Chrysanthemum parthenium

Citrus
Clarkia elegans
Clematis
Clerodendrum
Clivia
Codiaeum
Coleus
Columnea
Crassula
Crocus
Crossandra
Cyclamen
Cytisus
Daphne cneorum
Delphinium ajacis
Dianthus caryophyllus
Episcia
Erica
Eucharis grandiflora
Eucomis
Eupatorium
Euphorbia fulgens
Exacum
Felicia amelloides
Freesia
Fuchsia
Gardenia
Gazania
Geranium
Gerbera jamesonii
Gladiolus
Gloriosa
Godetia
Gypsophila
Haemanthus
Heliotrope
Hibiscus rosa-sinensis
Hoya carnosa
Hyacinthus
Hydrangea
Iberis amara and *I. umbellata*
Impatiens

Incarvillea
Iris, Dutch
Ixia
Ixora
Jacobinia
Jasminum
Kaempferia
Kalanchoe
Lachenalia
Lantana
Lathyrus odoratus
Lilium
Lobelia
Mathiola incana
Milla biflora
Myosotis
Narcissus
Nemesia
Nephrolepis bostoniensis
Nerine philodendron
Piqueria trinervia
Plumbago
Primula malacoides
Primula obconica
Primula sinensis
Ranunculus
Rechsteineria
Reinwardtia
Roses
Saintpaulia
Salpiglossis
Schizanthus
Sedum
Senecio cruentus
Sinningia speciosa
Smithiantha
Solanum
Sparmannia
Spathiphyllum
Stephanotis floribunda
Strelitzia
Swainsona

Tagetes erecta	Veltheimia
Tecomaria capensis	*Viola tricolor*
Trachymene caerulea	Zantedeschia
Tropaeolum	Zephyranthes
Tulip	*Zinnia elegans*
Vallota	Zygopanthus

General Suggestions

If you and your plants want to share an enjoyable pastime, why don't you have a radio in your greenhouse? Plants are music lovers too, and as I said before and will say again, it appears they grow better to music. . . .

When you have a greenhouse you may be considered to have a plant hospital in your home. You can take plants out, to be placed in other rooms in your home, when you feel they are growing or blooming at their best. As I have mentioned before, if they begin to look unhappy—dry or droopy—you can return them to your hospital until their health and appearance perk up. For certain plants it may be a good idea to return them to the greenhouse every evening for a comfortable night's sleep. . . .

Many of the plants suggested for greenhouse culture in this chapter vary in their requirements from cool temperatures to higher ones. You can grow both types in the same greenhouse if you will place the "cool" plants nearer to the glass and the "warm" plants nearer the heater. As time goes on and you become more and more interested and enthusiastic, you will probably want to try to grow some of each.

19

Soils:
It's a Treat to Beat Your Feet
in the Mississippi Mud

I knew that sooner or later I'd have to get around to this chapter. The reason I've been putting off writing it is that I'm afraid too many of you will put off reading it. And I suppose you are right—reading about the soil requirements of your plants may tend to get a little muddy and bog you down. However, the information contained in the next few pages is one of the most vital keys to growing success.

Too many beginning gardeners—and some intermediate gardeners—fail to provide the proper fertile foundation for their plants. Then they work overtime showering them with tender loving care and all the other cultural requirements, only to watch with dismay as one or more of their best-loved beauties goes into a decline and finally dies. Next to overwatering I'd have to say that planting in the wrong type of soil mixture is the biggest single mistake made by amateur growers of house plants. As my Grandma Putt used to say, "If you want things to grow, put some common sense into the pot along with the plants." So starting with this rarest of all ingredients, let's look at what else we should put into those pots.

No matter where you go in this great country of ours, from the Alaskan tundra, to the deserts of New Mexico, to the bogs and bayous of Louisiana, you will find plants growing in an endless variety of soils. Sometimes the ability of a plant to survive against all odds in an alien soil environment—like that famous tree in Brooklyn—taxes our credibility or gives us a new will to survive. Over the course of many thousands of years and countless generations, plants have learned how to adapt themselves and adjust to

217

growing in the soil that's available to them. Now, because of those special adaptations, house plant gardeners must try to duplicate the composition of the soils that our foliage, flowering, cacti, and bulbous friends found in nature. In order to do this you will need to know enough about the structure and texture of several basic soils so that you can at least purchase the correct potting mix for any particular plant. And if you want to get fancy (or save money), you can even make up proper mixtures from the soil in your own backyard or garden.

Soil Structure and Texture

The structure and texture of any soil is determined by the percentage of sand, silt, and clays that make it up. These three types of soil particles can be identified through the sense of touch by rubbing a handful of moist soil between your fingers. Sand is the gritty material you feel; silt is the floury-feeling material; clay is the sticky material. A combination of sand, silt, and clay is called loam. If the soil is what it should be, *good sandy loam*, it will break down as two-fifths sand, two-fifths silt, and one-fifth clay. Of course, all soils are not good sandy loam.

The various combinations of sand, silt, and clay you will find in natural soils are usually described as: fine texture—the clay soils; medium texture—the silty or loamy soils; coarse texture— the very sandy soils. Clay soils are also called *heavy soils*. Sandy soils are often called *light soils*. Because of the special adaptations I have mentioned, some plants need soil that will become saturated and hold a great deal of moisture (clay). Others need fast-draining, almost dry soil (sandy). Most plants need soil that's somewhere between these two extremes. Almost *all* plants need soil that contains *humus*.

Humus and Nutrients

I can hear the new gardener asking, "What's humus?" Humus is the decayed or decaying organic matter contained in soil which is so important to almost all plant life (less so for cacti and succulents), and particularly important to indoor pot plants. Humus is a loose, spongy material that works to benefit the soil in a mysterious and wonderful manner.

Humus—which is really compost in its final form (more about that later)—serves to buffer overdoses of plant nutrients, whether spread by the gardener or resulting from driving rains which dissolve nutrients already in the soil. These are absorbed into the complex humus particles, to be gradually released as these particles decay.

Humus becomes home to bacteria, those most useful microscopic bits of life that feed on the particles and help the decaying process. As they slowly feed, their wastes release the valuable nutrients back into the soil in soluble form. Your plants need these nutrients to carry on the vital processes of life. As an important source of slowly available nutrition, the humus in your soil may provide proper amounts of plant food for several growing seasons.

Actually, in the strictest sense, nutrients in the soil are not plant food. They are the minerals and chemicals the plants need to manufacture their own food. In order to grow house plants, certain chemicals must be present in the soil. The most important of these are nitrogen, phosphorus, and potash (a potassium compound). Outdoors, these chemicals are supplied by rain and snow. Old Jupiter Pluvius, the rain god, mixes a mighty brew that's 78–21–1 (78 parts nitrogen, 21 parts phosphorus, 1 part potash). Indoors these elements will have to be supplied by you.

Nitrogen encourages leafy growth and succulence.

Phosphorus promotes the development of the root system of your plants. It also helps the plant mature quickly. Most pot plants require large amounts of phosphorus, as this material tends to leach out of the soil with constant waterings.

Potash helps build fibrous tissues. It is also an important ingredient in the manufacture of starches and sugars. If your soil is sandy, the plant will need a higher amount of potash in its fertilizer.

Trace elements, such as boron, calcium, chlorine, copper, iron, manganese, sodium, sulphur, and zinc are also indispensable soil ingredients. Your house plants need these elements in order to successfully carry on the processes of reproduction and growth.

The trace elements occur in the soil in extremely minute quantities, but if they are not present, your plants will suffer. Old-timers in the gardening game knew this and devised all sorts of home remedies to replace them. A friend of my Grandma Putt used to boil old newspapers and pour the water over her plants. The boiling dissolved the zinc in the newsprint and released it in a form her plants could drink. She called it her zinc toddy.

Grandma didn't boil newspapers, but she did use tiny bits of moist newspaper as a mulch for her plants. I do this on a larger scale in the vegetable garden and Ilene does it on her house plants. It's one of the best mulches around, being inexpensive and containing zinc.

Another timeworn trick is to sprinkle a handful of Epsom salts on top of your house plants' toes and then water the salts in thoroughly. This will supply magnesium sulfate, which deepens color, thickens petals, and increases resistance to disease. To supply iron, old-timers would stick an old rusty nail into the soil or just plain old rust scrapings. If you want, you can dissolve a few drops of tonic containing iron into the watering solution. Old-fashioned garden gypsum provides sulphur and calcium and is an excellent soil conditioner to boot.

You don't have to do any of these things—but doing one or another may make both you and your plants feel better.

The "Acid Test" for Your Soil

It isn't enough that all the elements mentioned above be present in your soil. In order that they can be used properly by your plants, they will have to be available on demand. Sometimes the plant roots are unable to tap the nutrients because of too much acidity or alkalinity in the soil. It's important that planting soils have a proper balance between acidity and alkalinity for this reason. You can check the balance by a very simple test that measures the pH factor. The term "pH" means "potential of hydrogen." It's measured on a scale of 0 to 14. The balanced soil has a pH factor of 7. So the closer your soil is kept to that magic number 7 the happier your plants will be. Seldom, except perhaps in the Western part of the country, will the soil be over 7 on the pH scale. You can determine this pH factor in your soil with the help of an inexpensive soil-testing kit sold commercially or by taking a soil sample to the local Ag station, where it will be checked for a minimal charge.

Soil that is on the acid side is aften called "sour" soil. You can sweeten it by adding a tiny amount of agricultural lime. Soil on the "sweet," or alkaline, side can be corrected by adding coffee grounds or one of any number of acid plant foods. Remember— in nature, plants have learned to adapt to the soil as they find it. So some of your house plants will want soil that is on one side of this scale or the other. I will try to remind you of these special plant preferences as we discuss specific plants or types of plants.

Generally, plants purchased from a reliable source are already potted in a soil mixture that's just right for them and contains all the necessary nutrients to keep them fat and sassy for a while. They will not require the immediate addition of fertilizer. You can make it a rule of thumb *not* to fertilize for at least the first three months after you bring a plant home. Later, when the nutrients in the soil become exhausted, you may feed every two or three months while the plant is growing and not at all during dormant periods. Dormant plants are catching up on their sleep; they won't wake up and eat no matter how nice a Sunday dinner you prepare.

Don't Give Your Plants Heartburn!

To feed your plants, obtain fertilizers in concentrated form, and instead of using them according to the directions on the package, play it safe and use the Baker dosage. The Baker dosage is half the dosage prescribed on the fertilizer container. Too many well-meaning folks shove too much food down their plants' throats and give them heartburn. How would you like someone to stuff a whole jar of hot chili peppers down your gullet? Use common sense—be moderate.

Commercial Fertilizers for House Plants

There are many fertilizers on the market designed especially for house plants. They are of two main types, fast-acting or slow-dissolving. They are either dry and granular or liquids. I recommend the liquid types, at half dosage unless you really know what you are doing. Of the dry types, bone meal is safest. To apply it properly, remove the plant from the pot and put some bone meal on top of the drainage materials in the bottom. Then replace the plant and water thoroughly. Remember that when you use a slow-acting type of fertilizer such as bone meal you will not need to fertilize every month on schedule, because the slowly dissolving fertilizer is feeding constantly. *Important*: No matter what form or formula of fertilizer you select, *be sure that the soil is moist before feeding. Water plant before you sprinkle dry fertilizer on the soil surface. Never feed a dry plant!*

A complete plant food will contain a balanced ration of the three main elements—nitrogen, phosphorus, and potassium—that are most necessary for plant growth. Theoretically these three elements should be present in a 1–1–1 ratio. However, since phosphorus is so easily leached-out by waterings, many house plant fertilizers are sold in a 5–10–5 or 4–12–4 ratio. This basic formula is good for any plant that produces flowers, fruits, or vegetables. If you want to give certain plants more nitrogen or more potassium, select your fertilizer accordingly.

Commercial Soil Mixtures

If you are a beginner at raising house plants, and your need for potting soil hasn't grown to enormous proportions, I suggest you save time and energy and spend a few extra cents on a commercially prepared soil mix. Prepackaged and sterilized mix is especially convenient for the apartment dweller, who doesn't have the time or a place to prepare potting soils and lacks a good source of ingredients. Commercial soil mixtures come in one or two general or basic types and also in special mixtures for particular plants or types of plants.

The *sowing mix* is a special formula designed as a growing medium for seeds. It contains the correct amount of nutrients to get the seedlings off to a good start without burning them. The *growing mix* has a higher nutrient content than the sowing mixture. It is a heavier, firmer mixture, with more clay and enough nutrients to assure a balanced diet for fast-growing plants for a period of up to eight weeks. Plants will grow successfully with this mix in any size pot, basket, tub, or greenhouse bench flat. It is a good general mix that largely eliminates the need to have a special soil recipe for each plant.

Most of the other prepared mixes on the market are based on what is commonly called the Cornell Mix. This was developed by plant researchers at Cornell University and is sold under any number of brand names. Most of these mixes are sterile, weed-free, and prove to be reasonably acceptable as a substitute for the real thing (good weed-free garden compost). However, these mixes do have a few disadvantages. The material is usually ground up so fine and is so powdery that it tends to pack and has little capacity to absorb or hold water. It lacks the springiness of natural compost and may in time become so hard that air is excluded.

If you decide to work with these store-bought mixes, at planting time try adding some other easily obtainable materials and a half teaspoonful of a complete plant food to a 6-inch pot of soil. These supermixtures of your own will help adjust the soil to proper conditions for the type of plants you want to pot and will make certain that the final mixture has the necessary nutrients to give your newly potted plant a healthy start.

Here are four basic soil mixes you can put together from a basic commercial mixture and materials you can buy at any garden center. If you haven't got a good source of supply for your sand, you might want to consider using horticultural perlite, which makes a very good substitute. Vermiculite, in place of leaf mold or compost, will lighten and condition heavy, sticky soil and make it acceptable to plants that need well-aerated soil. And one good thing about these inexpensive substitutes is that they are already sterilized.

Baker's Basic Mix #1. This mix is good for most flowering, fruiting, and vegetable-type house plants from chrysanthemums to zebra plants. I suggest you make enough so that you can use some later. This will save you making a big mess every time you pot. (You always have to make a little mess.)

> 1 quart Cornell Mix or African-violet soil
> 1 quart perlite or sand and finely broken eggshells
> 1 quart brown peat moss (moistened in warm water and wrung out until damp)
> 3 tablespoons bone meal
> 1 tablespoon agricultural lime

Mix thoroughly.

Baker's Basic Mix #2. This is a drier mixture than Mix #1 and is fast-draining. It is especially good for cacti and members of the succulent family.

> 1 pint Cornell Mix or African-violet soil
> 1 quart perlite or sand and eggshells

Mix thoroughly.

Baker's Basic Mix #3. This is a heavy mixture that is particularly good for such large, leafy plants as elephant's ear and the India rubber plant.

> 1½ quarts Cornell Mix
> 1 quart peat moss (moistened in warm water and wrung out until damp)
> 1 quart perlite or sand and broken eggshells
> 4 tablespoons bone meal or other slow-action fertilizer for house plants

Moisten and mix thoroughly. The final mix should be moist but not soggy.

Baker's Basic Mix #4. This is actually not a mixture, although the materials may be mixed if you want. They are the growing medium for most orchids and bromeliads.

> 1 part osmunda fiber, unshredded sphagnum moss, or redwood bark (chipped)

Compost

If you are a gardener who wants to keep time with Mother Nature's basic rhythms and you have access to a place to make compost, remember—nothing takes its place. Even if you have only a small area this is possible with a compost kit that's sold commercially by Burpee. The kit includes a heavy-duty plastic-mesh compost bin that can withstand temperatures from 30 degrees below zero to 150 degrees above zero. It is 28 inches high and 4 feet in diameter and is completely corrosion-resistant. With it you get a supply of Compost Maker tablets, 6 Twist-Lok fasteners, and a booklet on scientific compost-making. The tablets speed up the decomposition of organic waste materials. The compost produced will be ample for your indoor plant needs. If you have a larger area, you will possibly want to make a larger compost heap to furnish potting soil for your indoor plants and your garden as well.

Things to Do and Know Before Making a Compost Heap

Before starting your compost heap, there are two things you should do. First, check your local ordinances to find out whether there are any rules or restrictions in regard to composting. Then, if you find out you are free to go ahead, find out the exact makeup of the soil in your garden. I like to do this every year, because I am constantly adding nutrients to the soil. You may find that every two or three years it's a good idea to go through the steps to recheck the composition of your soil.

How to Take a Soil Sample

Collect soil samples properly. Remember, if the sample is not representative of the whole area you will be using for gardening or potting house plants, the test will be misleading and the Ag station's recommendations will be of little value.

Take your soil samples with a probe, spade, garden trowel or soil auger. You will also need a bucket or other container for mixing samples, and a box or paper bag to hold one pint of the mixed soil. Study your land and determine the number of composite soil samples you will want to take for a comprehensive test. Be sure to clear away any trash on top of the soil before sampling. Sample light and dark colors of clayey and sandy soils separately. Keep in mind that soil texture is determined by the percentage of sand, silt and clays that make up the soil. The soil takes most of its character of workability from the *total* structure and texture of the topsoil.

The larger the area you plan to use for your gardening the more important it is to collect a composite sample. This composite soil sample means the *composite* of several borings or spade slices from one sampled area. Obtain a composite sample by gathering soil from ten to fifteen or more spots in your yard or area to be sampled. Place these plugs, taken with the soil probe or shovel, in a clean bucket and mix them thoroughly. Supply one pint of soil for each area you want tested. If you have more than one, label each sample plainly so you will know the exact area to which your recommendations apply. For the home gardener with a small plot, the testing of one pint of soil (taken from your garden area and mixed as directed) is all that is necessary. Do not take soil samples when the area is wet. Soil should be dry before testing.

Start with a simple test to determine acidity and the availability of nitrogen, phosphorus, and potassium. Make the test yourself with the commercial kit I have previously mentioned or take a soil sample to the local or county Ag station and have this test made for a small fee. Either way, the soil test will take the guesswork out of this initial step in gardening and may mean the difference between failure and success. The soil test measures the relative nutrient levels of the soil. Results of these tests, used together with the soil type and previous crop and fertilizer history, serve as the best guide to the use of fertilizer and lime. Lime should be added to acid soils.

If you are testing the soil yourself, you may do it any time. If you send the sample to your state university or county Ag station, you will probably get faster results if the sample is submitted after September and before March. The results of the test will tell you what to do next.

FIXING UP POOR SOIL

If the soil test shows a substantial lack of soil nutrients, you can use natural minerals and additives to correct the imbalance. Blood meal (purchasable at garden centers) will add nitrogen. But use it sparingly. Add it to your compost or sprinkle it lightly on the soil. Animal manures, which will be discussed in the next few pages, will also aid in building up the nitrogen in your soil. Preferably these should be well rotted before being applied to the soil surface. Since any source of nitrogen will deplete rapidly, it must be resupplied annually.

Another very important soil nutrient, phosphorus, can be added in large amounts by applying bone meal, phosphate rock, or colloidal phosphate. Let me explain right here the difference between phosphate rock and superphosphate. Phosphate rock is a finely pulverized natural material with nothing added. It will give very good results, though perhaps a little more slowly than superphosphate which has been treated with sulfuric acid. This acid treatment causes it to break down more rapidly, but some people think that it leaves undesirable residues. The choice is yours and depends on whether you want to be completely organic in your gardening methods or just a middle-of-the-roader like me.

Phosphate rock has the additional benefit of containing good quantities of trace elements, such as boron, zinc, and nickel. All of these contribute to plant vitality.

These fertilizers should be applied at a general rate of 10 pounds per 100 square feet every three to five years, according to your soil-test results. You may apply phosphate to the surface. It can even be dusted on indoor and outdoor plants as an insect repellent. Potassium may be applied as a topdressing or worked into the soil. It can be purchased in the form of granite dust or greensand. The proper rate of application is about 10 pounds per 100 square feet. Wood ashes or the ashes from your charcoal burner make a good side dressing and soil conditioner when applied several inches from the plant base. These also perform as an excellent insect repellent, particularly against cutworms and slugs. Wood ashes are good for house plants as well as outdoor plants.

Don't forget old-fashioned garden gypsum when reconditioning your soil. If your soil shows too much alkalinity, or sweetness, in the soil tests, apply gypsum in a thin layer at a rate of 3½ pounds per 100 square feet of garden space. As a sweetener, conditioner and provider of trace elements, gypsum can't be beat. If your soil is too acid, add lime at a rate of 5 pounds per 100 square feet.

The best way to work all these nutrients and soil conditioners into your soil is to use a roto-tiller, which you can rent or buy. In addition to mixing in the additives, the roto-tiller aerates the soil. Choose a day when the soil is neither very wet nor very dry for the best results. Late fall is the best season; the nutrients will have time to dissolve into the soil and become available to the plants the following spring.

All of the soil builders and conditioners that we have been discussing will help you bring your soil up to snuff for growing plants outdoors or in the house, but nothing will make it as excellent a growing medium as compost. So bear with me a little longer while I tell you the greatest trick of gardening alchemy—how to turn garbage into "black gold"—humus.

Composting

For someone who has never made compost before, a definite recipe may be of help. Here is one my Grandma Putt passed on to my family. You will find it in another one of my books, *Talk to Your Plants.*

> Locate the spot where you want to build your compost heap.
> Dig up the sod and turn it over. Wet it slightly.
> Build the bottom layer of sod about ten inches high.
> On top of the sod lay on a layer of old newspapers, and wet them down until they're good and soggy.
> Next, a layer of manure or animal waste.
> More wet newspaper.
> Grass clippings or any plant waste.
> More wet newspaper.
> Another layer of topsoil.

Keep alternating topsoil/newspaper/animal waste/newspaper/plant waste/newspaper until you have built your compost heap up to approximately four feet of height. Each of the layers should be no more than a few inches thick. The pile should be wet but not soggy. The size of your composting area depends on how much material you have available for making compost and how much humus you will need for both gardening and house plants.

Finding the Best Location and Setting It Up

Many homeowners do not like the looks of a compost heap, and, admittedly, it can be unsightly if your place is small and there is no really practical spot to put it in. Placing it back of the garage or screening it with attractive shrubs or vines may be a solution, but if neither of these ideas appeals to you there is still another way out—or rather *under.*

If you live on a small lot you may find it desirable to go underground with your composting process. Just be sure that the pit you dig is located on ground that's high enough so the rain will not run into it. A pit can work well during the dry season of the year, because when you wet it down it will hold the moisture longer and with less evaporation. This will speed up the process of decomposition.

The size of the pit will depend on the materials available for composting, a desirable location, and your own inclination and ambition to dig. A four-by-six pit two or three feet deep would be a good size to experiment with to see if you like the pit method. Leave the soil you dig up nearby for gradual use in the layering process. It will be especially useful if you want to use your garbage for composting material. A handy layer of soil will be needed for covering this refuse in order to keep down flies and odors.

Green lawn clippings will give your compost heap a boost. They can be added each time you mow. They will raise the heat of the pile and help the other materials decompose. A well-made compost heap should produce a temperature of 180 degrees. This creates a perfect environment for bacteria to go to work and decompose the fibrous materials.

A good cover made of four-by-eight rippled lucite sheets, plywood, or wood-framed hardware cloth is a *must* for a compost pit. It's not only desirable from a standpoint of safety but it will cut down on the odors. And speaking of odors, check the prevailing winds before settling on any compost area. You won't want those odors to come wafting your way (into the house), nor will you want them in your neighbor's line of smell. You don't want your underground (or even your above-ground) activities to get you on the neighborhood blacklist.

Whether you burrow or heap up is largely a matter of personal preference. Either way, it's obvious that dry vegetable matter needs more wetting than green material. And, of course, the addition of a little fertile soil to each layer does a lot to hasten bacterial action.

It's not desirable to trample the pile or otherwise pack it tight. Some looseness allows oxygen to enter, which stimulates decomposition. I try to turn my compost with a spade every couple of weeks. Also, use moderation when you water your compost. Too heavy watering may interfere with bacterial action and cause loss of nutrients through leaching.

How Long Will It Take?

Of course, one of the first things you will want to know is how long it takes for the composting materials to break down. In this age of instant everything it is hard to accept the fact that you will have to wait. You will know the compost is ready when it resembles dark brown or black earth. It will be spongy, will readily absorb and hold water, and will show little of the original material from which it came.

With easily decomposable materials (and these can be given a good start in the composting process by running them through a shredder), moderate moisture, and warmth, as short a time as six weeks is sometimes sufficient to create humus. But, generally speaking, much longer periods—up to six months or more—may be needed when using coarse materials. Bones, for instance, take longer to break down than other components. If a few of these show up, don't discard them, just be patient. In time they, too, will break down and add their nutrients.

In gathering materials for the compost heap or pit, be as careful as you can to avoid insects and diseases. For example, manure shouldn't contain plant remains that are likely to transmit disease to your garden or house plants.

Where to Get Composting Materials

If you start in the spring and keep your eyes open all year, you will have no trouble in finding an abundance of raw materials for your compost heap. Probably the easiest source of supply for most of us is found in our own yards—namely, grass clippings. Grass clippings are fairly rich in nitrogen and are useful as green manure to be worked into the soil, for adding to your compost heaps, or for mulching. Clippings from most lawns contain more than a pound of nitrogen and 2 pounds of potash for every 100 pounds of grass clippings in the dry stage.

Do you have a local bakery? Find out what they do with discarded eggshells. Maybe you can arrange to pick them up. They will add plant minerals and nutrients to your compost heap. What do the local supermarkets do with lettuce leaves and other refuse they discard from the produce-display counters? Permission to cart this away may be yours for the asking. Is there a large plant near you that has coffee-vending machines? It is possible that hundreds of pounds of used coffee grounds, a valuable soil conditioner, are available for your compost heap. How about some iodine in a nutshell? Yes indeedy, nutshells are an excellent source of iodine. If shelling pecans is a local industry, loads of shells may be obtained free just for hauling away. They will decompose as compost in time, and they make an attractive mulch for flower beds.

Is someone in your vicinity burning packing boxes and shipping-lumber? Wood ashes are also a great soil conditioner.

Any trees being cut down near you, or how about a carpenter shop at your local school? Wood shavings and sawdust are good for mulch and for compost. A lumber mill in your vicinity may prove a valuable source for obtaining sawdust. If you do use much sawdust, always add a little agricultural lime to overcome the acidity.

Don't forget to call your local Sanitation Department and put in a request for at least a couple of truckloads of leaves. Many times the Sanitation Department would rather haul leaves to the home of a property owner than take them out to the landfill where they are normally dumped. You get the leaves and the city saves time and gasoline. If you can be home when the city dumps the leaves, wet them down thoroughly each time a load is delivered. This will keep them from blowing away and will hasten decomposition. Wet leaves are also much easier to load up in a wheelbarrow when you cart them to your compost heap.

Does your city have a riding club? If you can get permission to gather the manure yourself, it will probably be completely free. Or perhaps you can arrange with the man who cleans the stables to haul it to your property. Are there any chicken farms or hatcheries near you? If so, chicken manure or wastes may be had for the asking. Since this is one of the "hot" manures, it should definitely be composted before placing it near any plants. Barber shops and beauty salons may be a source for human hair, which will make good compost. And poodle-clipping services can be found almost everywhere. Paper bags from the grocery store and old newspapers can be shredded and added moist to the compost heap.

There are about as many different ways of using kitchen refuse or garbage as there are people who want to compost it. What you do about it depends largely upon how you feel about it and where you live. I think it's best to keep such stuff in a covered container, separated from cans, bottles, and so on. It can then go directly into the compost pit, where it can be layered in with leaves, soil, sawdust, wood chips, and lawn clippings—whatever reasonably dry material happens to be available.

If you just can't think of any possible sources of compost debris, get out your local phone directory and look through the yellow pages. Some industry near you may produce wastes that will be just great for composting. A friend of mine, searching his directory, stumbled on a local business that was producing leather garments and realized the possibilities. Being of animal origin, all leather will decompose fairly rapidly if left out where nature can break it down. If it is shredded in some manner, decay will begin much more rapidly.

Your Compost Is Like Mother Nature's Own Recipe

The compost that you make yourself most nearly corresponds to the ideal material for house plants—natural leaf mold. Leaf mold is a crumbly, very rich earth that is made by Mother Nature over a long period of time. It is the end product of the natural decomposition of leaves and other vegetable matter in a damp place. For most of us leaf mold is as hard to come by as a bucket of gold. If you were fortunate enough to obtain any, you would find that it is impregnated with gritty particles of rock and sand, which contribute to the desirability of its texture.

Since you will have so many materials to work with, your compost will in some ways be better than Mother Nature's leaf mold. Your compost will have more roughage, which will make it springy and full of air as well as absorbent and friable—a soil characteristic meaning "loose and crumbly." It will not cling together in a sodden mass like a ball of clay and it won't run through your fingers like sand. What you have "made," with the help of Mother Nature, is that superrich substance known by all good gardeners as "good garden loam"!

Compost prepared like this can be used in hotbeds and cold frames. It is fine in flats for starting seeds and growing plants. It's also good for general potting purposes. It is desirable for placing around fruit trees, whether you are growing them outdoors or in the house. Flowering pot plants planted in soil having a generous amount of your compost will be larger and have more blossoms and a better color. They will also have a longer blooming season. Compost is a terrific medium for growing crisp, tender vegetables.

Potting Mixes Made with Your Compost

Now that you've gone to the trouble of producing compost-humus, or good garden loam, you should use it in your potting mixtures. Here are three additional potting mixtures that incorporate this rich life-giving material.

Baker's Basic Mix #5 (with compost)

> 2 quarts garden soil
> 1 quart compost or leaf mold
> 1 quart sand

This will suit plants such as geraniums, amaryllis, dracaenas, oxalis, and palms.

Baker's Basic Mix #6 (with compost)

> 1 quart garden soil
> 1 quart sand
> 1 pint compost
> 1 pint crushed clay flowerpot or brick
> 1 tablespoon bone meal
> 1 tablespoon agricultural limestone

This gritty, lean growing medium is good for cacti and succulents.

Why Mixes Work Best

When you come down to it, you'll have to admit that even though it takes more time and trouble, soil that is specially mixed to duplicate as closely as possible the natural soil environment of a particular house plant will make it easier to grow that plant, whether it's an African violet or a cactus. Needless to say, every good gardener seeks to improve the soil and growing conditions of his plant friends.

There are two reasons why most potted plants don't do as well in ordinary topsoil (loam) as they do when this is mixed with other materials. First, when plants are potted, the soil is usually packed down firmly. Frequent watering tends to make it even more compact. If the soil isn't naturally porous, free passage of water and air will be blocked. The second reason is that the amount of soil available to the roots of a potted plant is necessarily limited by the confines of the pot. Frequent watering causes the nutrients to leach out. When this happens the roots become starved.

This tendency can be counteracted to a large extent by adding compost containing a large amount of decayed organic matter such as I have just described. If this is not available to you, commercial humus—sedge peat, peat moss, or similar material can be gotten at your garden center. Whether homemade or commercial, it is the fibrous organic matter of compost that helps porosity, slows down leaching, and, as it decays, supplies more nutrients. Porosity is usually further assured by the addition of coarse sand, finely broken brick, or coarse cinders. These should never be more than one-fourth to one-third of the bulk of the finished mixture.

Fertilizers added in the mixtures may include small amounts of dried cow manure, bone meal, and wood ashes, but these should be added cautiously in small amounts. Other additions, depending on the type of plant you plan to grow in the medium, may be crushed limestone or lime and chopped charcoal. If you have very young plants, use less of these materials than you would for more mature ones.

"Acupuncture" Really Works

As watering reduces the pores or spaces between the soil particles the air is driven out of the soil. Further waterings will only increase soil compaction and gradually choke the plant to death. Soil in good condition for plant growth should have about 50 percent of pore space. Sometimes soil that is not actually compacted will be so poorly drained that its pore spaces will fill with water at the expense of air, and the plant roots will be starved for oxygen.

If you have a plant in such condition and have time for only stopgap measures, try this. Take a long, large nail and gently work it down into the soil. Easy now—what you are doing is aerating the soil, not trying to stab the plant to death! The number of holes you will need to make depends on the size of the pot you're working with. After the holes are made, water the plant. This "acupuncture" treatment is not intended to cure the situation, but it will give both you and the plant a breather until you find time to take care of the plant properly.

You Too Can Be a Baker

Before you use your home-grown compost mixes in potting, you may want to sterilize the soil by baking it. That's right, you bake out the bugs!

If you have a lot of soil to sterilize, use an old turkey-roasting pan. If you don't have one of these, you can buy very cheaply one made of heavy-duty aluminum foil at any supermarket. Since you will probably use it many times, it's a good investment. Spread the soil in the roaster. If it's a single plant you plan to pot, use a couple of shallow cake tins. Turn the oven dial to 180 degrees and bake your soil for thirty minutes. I usually put a small potato on top; when the potato is baked, the soil is sterilized and all harmful insects and diseases should be baked to death. (If you smell some unusual odors while the soil is baking, don't worry, they'll only be a temporary nuisance.)

While it's not absolutely necessary to bake your soil, it will ensure that your young plants or seedlings won't become victims of damping-off. This is a diseased condition resulting from a fungus that often attacks seedlings, causing them to collapse and fall over, sometimes overnight.

You must be cautious about baking your soil unless your oven is equipped with an accurate thermostat. The heat should never be allowed to go higher than 210 degrees, because plants will not grow in an overbaked soil until untreated soil is mixed with it. The reason for this is that organisms necessary to soil fertility have been killed along with the disease-carrying organisms. The untreated soil will reintroduce these favorable organisms.

20

Allow Your Plants to 'Get Potted' Every Once in a While

Potting can be a lot of fun! So don't start out with the idea that it's a backbreaking chore that should be avoided if at all possible. If you will give some thought to your own personal comfort before you start, the job can be very pleasant, interesting, and relaxing. But if you are miserable, the plants will know. They will feel your resentment—your fingers will be clumsy when you handle them, and you may even break a few.

The Workbench

If there are two or more people in the family who like to putter with pots and plants, see that the workbench either has adjustable legs or is built to suit the height of the taller person. Tuck a platform beneath it for use by the shorter family members when they take their turns. There are times when the potting bench will have to take a great deal of weight, so use lumber that is heavy enough to keep it from wobbling all over the place when you're working. The potting bench should be large enough to hold all the items you will be using and should provide comfortable working space besides. There should be room for several pots, drainage material, adequate soil for whatever job you are doing at the moment, and the actual plants you are working with — whether potting or repotting. Naturally, you will also need space for your tools.

If you cover the top of your bench with Masonite or some other smooth-surfaced material, possibly Formica, it will add to your convenience and speed clean-up operations. Wiping it off after you are through will be a breeze, and you will be doubly pleased with your work when you look back as you close the door and see everything in shipshape condition. A shelf placed above the potting surface will add further convenience. Place your flats on this, plants you have finished potting, or tools you aren't using at the moment.

Even if you are the silent type who prefers to work in a quiet environment, it's not a bad idea to put a radio on that shelf. No question about it, plants respond to the vibrations in the bass speaker and grow better to music, whether it's classical, easy-listening, or hard rock. You don't have to take my word for this— try a little experiment. Place one of your favorite plants close to the hi-fi and play it some of your favorite tunes every day with the bass speaker turned way up. Do this for a period of two months. Place a similar-sized plant of the same species where there is no music, and after the same period, compare the two. I'm willing to bet that the plant that has been listening to music has grown bigger and fuller!

Facing Reality

Now that I've described the ideal setup for potting your plants, let's face reality and admit that most home gardeners don't have the space or inclination to build such a potting bench. But that is no reason to give up. There are any number of compromises that will be good enough to get the job done. If the weather is warm to mild, you can do your potting in the great outdoors. As a matter of fact, your plants will probably appreciate the fresh air and sunshine. And it's a whole lot easier to clean up the excess soil when you're finished with the job outdoors. Be careful, though, that the breeze doesn't dry out the sensitive root system of tender young plants.

There's nothing wrong with using the kitchen-sink counter or the kitchen table if you put down a few layers of newspaper. However, potting requires a certain amount of thumping and bumping and banging, so you'd better not work on a glass-topped kitchen table. A friend of Ilene's lives in a tiny apartment where there is barely enough room to turn around. She has solved her potting-bench problem by using a piece of masonite which she lays on top of her washer and dryer. The Masonite has a one-inch by two-inch lip around three sides which makes it fit snugly. The entire setup couldn't have cost more than a couple of dollars, but it is extremely practical because it is in a well-lighted area and next to a small laundry tub. Who could ask for more? No matter where you live and no matter what your space problems, if you use your ingenuity, you can find a good place to do your potting.

Use Moist Soil

We've already discussed potting soil, so I'll touch on it only briefly here. First, determine the best soil mixture for the plant you are working on. Next, consider the condition of the soil. Don't have it too wet or too dry. Judge it by this test. Pick up a handful of soil and squeeze it. If it falls apart when you release the pressure, it's too dry. If it oozes moisture, it's too wet.

Give Your Plant a Physical

If you buy a plant already potted, you'll probably keep it in that pot until something about the plant indicates it isn't doing as well as it should. It may be that the leaves will turn yellow and begin to drop or that the plant just doesn't seem to be growing at all. Some kind of first aid should be administered but you're not exactly sure what it should be.

The first thing to look at is the drainage hole. If a plant is well potted, it will have a pebble, a small piece of brick, or a shard of clay pot at the bottom covering the drainage hole to prevent the soil from washing out. Sometimes when plants are potted only in soil the soil packs down. It's easy to check to see if this is the case. Just poke a pencil or small stick carefully into the drainage hole. If you don't hit something hard, the pebble or potsherd is missing. The best thing to do is to repot the plant. To remove a plant from its pot, simply turn it over slowly and hit it gently against the edge of a table. Have a piece of newspaper on the floor to catch any loose earth. When you do this properly, the plant, earth and all, will fall out into your hand.

Scrape off some of the overwet soil from the bottom of your plant and put the plant aside for the moment. Thoroughly clean the pot from which you have removed the plant and delve into your box of broken shards. (You know, the one you always have handy for such times as this.) Overlap two or three shards over the drainage hole so that the earth won't get down into it again. Put a thin layer of sharp sand or perlite on top of the shards. Now replace the plant and add as much new soil as may be necessary to bring the potting mix up to the correct level again.

Something that might seem obvious but that is often mis-gauged is the proper soil level for a plant. I usually bring the soil to about one inch from the rim. If the soil comes much higher than this, water will run off over the top before it can be absorbed by the plant. If it is too low, water may stand too long, and re-peated waterings may cause rot to set in. It isn't necessary to use a ruler—the first joint of your index finger should make a good gauge.

Choosing Pots

If plants are like people, young plants are like growing chil-dren—they both grow like weeds! My kids always seem to be growing out of their shoes, and by now many of your plants are doing so well (thanks to your loving care) and their root systems are so dense that their little feet are getting cramped. As soon as you notice this, you'll want to buy them some new shoes in the next-larger size.

Don't let yourself become bewildered by the many kinds of pots and types of planting containers that you will find on display in your market, nursery, or florist's shop. Pots and planters for house plants are currently being made of clay, sandstone, glazed ceramic, wood, plastic, Tufflite, Styrofoam, lava rock, peat, paper, brass, cement, glass, and probably several other materials that I have forgotten or that have come on the market since I began this sentence! All of these materials have their good and bad points, so let's take a closer look.

Clay pots are probably the oldest form sold, and these, in

Container

small sizes, are most often used for "baby shoes"—the first container into which you will pot your seedlings. Clay pots are porous, and this is definitely an advantage. If the temperature is high, soil moisture will evaporate through the pot walls and keep the plant roots cooler. A clay pot is heavier than a plastic one, and this bit of extra weight helps stabilize plants that tend to grow large or top-heavy. Clay pots are suitable for plants of almost any size as well as seedling plants, and always attractive.

As you get deeper and deeper into the gardening game you'll discover that it's peopled by many old-timers who are resistant to any change and reluctant to experiment with any kind of new product. Some of these folks think that potting begins and ends with clay pots. I like clay pots too, and have been using them successfully for years, but new products are flooding the market and commercial growers have been quick to try them out, so why don't you experiment too? In the end you may agree with the old-timers, but it never hurts to find out the good and bad points of a new product. That's part of the fun of gardening.

While clay pots do have a lot going for them, there are also some drawbacks. Clay pots are easily broken, and a sudden shattering may send a particularly sensitive plant into shock. Should this happen, it would take a super effort on your part to bring your plant pal back to good health. However, if you do break a clay pot by accident, save the shards, or pieces. Also, in time clay pots may get mossy unless you buy ones that have been specially treated. (Some manufacturers coat their pots with silicone.) This green scum is a form of algae that grows on unused fertilizer that leaches through the sides of the clay pot, and it is nearly always a sign that you've been overfeeding and perhaps overwatering. While this scum looks unattractive and is undesirable, it is the pot's way of protecting the plant. By disposing of the excess fertilizer and mineral salts in this way the pot prevents the soil from becoming completely overloaded with them to the extent that the root hairs are burned.

This green scum is a warning signal to you. Clean it off and search your conscience—do your gardening habits need reforming? You probably should feed and water this plant less, or eventually this scum will block off air and water and prevent the former from going into and the latter from coming out of the pot. Change your habits and then spray-paint your pots with a silicone substance.

Just recently I read in the paper that many people who live

in the West and Southwest have been buying red clay pots in Mexico. Evidently the clay used in making these pots has a high lead content. Health officials were warning tourists against buying these pots for cooking purposes. Well, plants are like people, and they can get lead poisoning too; be extra cautious about using these pots for your indoor or outdoor plants.

Sandstone Pots

I have noticed in garden centers and nurseries that a lot of sandstone pots are now being offered for sale. These have some of the same advantages as clay pots—for instance, good porosity—and in addition come in a variety of shapes, sizes, and colors. They have thick walls but are lightweight and not as subject to easy breakage as clay pots. One problem, however, is that they usually don't have a drainage hole in the bottom. Be careful not to overwater or you may cause root rot.

Plastic Pots

Plastic pots are inexpensive, lightweight, and easily cleaned at repotting time. And although at one time the color choice was limited, they now come in a great range of colors. They're also easy to stack and store. There's really nothing very disadvantageous about plastic pots, but you will have to bear in mind that the pot walls are not porous, so your plants will need to be given a slightly different cultural treatment. Don't water so often, because these pots hold moisture longer. Actually this is an advantage if, like me, you travel a lot and can't water as often. When you do water, use moderation so that you don't cause root rot.

When you use plastic pots you should cover the entire base with pebbles, bits of brick, or broken clay shards. This base layer should be at least an inch thick. Good drainage is the key to success with these pots. When you buy plastic pots, select those with drainage vents at the lower edge of the walls as well as a drain hole in the bottom center. The older type of plastic pot, many of which are still around in the stores, was very easy to break at the rim. When you lift a large plastic pot full of soil be sure to use both hands and hold it as nearly level as possible. If you grasp the edge with one hand, it may twist slightly and break off.

Tufflite Pots

The newest material for pots on the market is Tufflite. These pots combine the cultural advantages of clay with the lightness of plastic. Their appearance is very attractive and they give excellent results.

Glazed Pots

Decorative glazed pots will dress up your plants. Those that come with drainage holes have the weight of a clay pot; add to this the color advantages of plastic and you have the best features of each. But be sure to check the bottom, as they come with and without drainage holes.

Container

Bonsai (Japanese Black Pine)

Glazed Bonsai Planters

A glazed pot in striking Oriental design makes a terrific-looking container for a bonsai tree. Such containers are usually shallow and should not be more than three inches deep. Generally they are much wider and longer than they are deep, resembling trays or shallow dishes rather than flowerpots. Just as with other types of pots, they should have holes in the bottom for drainage if at all possible. To keep the soil from coming out, cover the drainage hole with fine wire screening, or place a potsherd over it, hollow (concave) side down. Now put a layer of gravel in the bottom of the container and over this a thin layer of sand.

Potting Bonsai Trees

Before placing the bonsai in the container, remove most of the old soil from its roots. Do this gently with a pencil or small stick, working quickly and being careful not to damage the roots. They should not be allowed to dry out—so work in the house or at least out of the wind.

Cut off any roots that may have been damaged or broken, and then put the plant in its new container, spreading out the roots. Make a porous mixture of loam, coarse sand, and peat moss (or compost), and work this new soil between the roots carefully, pressing it firm. After you complete this operation, water the tree with your mister and protect the newly set plant from sun and wind for two or three weeks.

Obviously, the purpose of this type of potting and soil is to prevent the tree from growing too rapidly. Nevertheless in time the tree will grow a little or the soil will become depleted, so that it will become necessary to do this replanting again. Well-cared-for evergreens will need repotting about once every four to five years, deciduous types (leaf-losing) will need it more often.

Jardinieres: The Dress-Up Shoes

Another type of glazed pot—without the drainage hole—is often called a jardiniere. It is really not a flowerpot at all and should not be used for one. What you should do is use these beautiful ceramic pieces as covers, or receptacles for flowerpots. Put a clay or plastic flowerpot inside and the jardiniere will serve as "dress shoes."

If you want to place a potted plant in a jardiniere, you should be aware of its limitations. Depending on the size you are working with, place an inch or two of pebbles on the bottom before putting the pot inside. Also, be sure the dress-up pot is large enough. There should be one and a half inches of air space all around. You must also be very cautious about watering. Check frequently to see that the runoff is not rising in the container and drowning your plant.

You are probably making a mistake if you insist on using one of these glazed containers as a flowerpot—at least I wouldn't recommend it. But if you do plant directly in a waterproof container, be sure to put an inch or two of chipped charcoal on the bottom before adding any soil. Charcoal will help prevent the soil from becoming sour. Again, you must be very careful to avoid overwatering. This is another situation where occasional "acupuncture" may be a way to get air down to the roots of your plant.

Metal Planters

Containers finished in copper or brass usually have a steel frame and are generally heavy enough to have great stability when filled with earth. As with plastic pots, use caution in watering. Some pots come in a black iron finish and are frequently styled to look well in a Spanish or Mediterranean setting. My friend Louise Riotte has a particularly decorative hanging planter that somewhat resembles a post lamp. This, secured to a wall by its bracket and filled with trailing greenery, is truly a conversation piece. There are "cage"-type wall planters which are equally dramatic. The old standing bird cages also make attractive holders for hanging pot plants. Wrought-iron planter carts make attractive and practical stands for potted plants. Like the old-fashioned tea cart, which they resemble, they make it easy to move plants from a warm room to a cooler one at night.

Urns

Antique lead and iron urns, once a must for all the gardens and balconies of Georgian-style houses, are now being copied in aluminum, cast stone, and fiber glass. If your home has that Georgian feel, one or several of these may be an excellent choice. Just remember that metal is a conductor and that your plants will probably be more comfortable if they have a liner of some sort to prevent the roots from chilling or overheating.

Washtubs

Don't overlook the possibilities of planting in an ordinary galvanized washtub. For a large plant this could be home for quite a while. To make it longer-lasting, paint the tub inside with roofing paint. To make it decorative, you can stencil a design on the outside or use decoupage to cover it. We know a young couple who have an orange tree planted in such a tub. They keep on hand several tubes of acrylic paint and a small brush, and whenever they are entertaining they have their friends sign their names all over the tub. The tree seems to respond to all the attention—the last time I saw it the whole tree was covered with tiny fruit! Washtubs have handles, but if you have a plant in one, I suggest you place it on a castered stand and move your planting outside on sunny days or for a few weeks "away at camp" in the summertime.

Wooden Shoes and Barrel Halves

Plants grow well in wood, and there are any number of shapes and sizes of "wooden shoes" that would be a perfect fit for your plant people. And speaking of wooden shoes (the kind that come from Holland), they make an ideal pair of planters for a couple of prized tulips!

Sooner or later, if you grow large specimen plants, you will have to consider barrels, barrel halves and wooden tubs. If you are a do-it-yourself hobbyist you may even find happiness in making your own tubs and built-in type of planters for gardening indoors. If not, you will find plenty to choose from at local shops.

Wooden tubs are most often used instead of flowerpots for growing plants that need more room. Such plants are aloes, acacias, cycads, citrus trees, bay trees, flowering maples and palms. If you have a large room or a greenhouse where a large plant will look good or have room to spread out, you may want to consider one of these. Or you may want to consider a tub for an aggressive plant that is completely outgrowing its alloted space.

If your plant is large enough to require a container with a

Container

diameter of twelve inches or more, or even ten or eleven inches, a wooden tub is often a better choice than a flowerpot of the same size. Such tubs may be either square or round—your plant pal won't care, all he wants is room. Most tubs taper toward the bottom and are usually bound with bands of copper or some other metal. It is very important to consider the type of wood that's used for these tubs. Florists often use inexpensive tubs of light construction, such as pine bound with wire. These can house a plant for only a short time, so probably will not be very practical for your purposes. Since changing the home of a large tree or shrub is something you won't want to do very often, plan to have it remain as long as possible in the first container you place it in.

Such woods as redwood, cypress, oak, or hickory, which are water-resistant, will be far longer-lasting. They will not rot easily, are almost always of superior construction, and are bound with stout steel bands or, in the case of square ones, bolted together with steel rods. If you don't like their color you can paint them. It's even a good idea to paint the interior as well—just make sure you use a nontoxic paint that won't injure the plant. If the man in the house happens to have a blowtorch, have him char the inside. This will increase resistance to decay. Or, as with your clay pots, spray your tubs with a substance that contains silicone, such as a clear plastic shoe guard. *Do not, under any circumstances, paint the interior with creosote.*

Large wooden tubs should never be set directly on the ground or floor. If they don't come equipped with legs, either make some or raise them off the floor with bricks or other supports. They must have this air space underneath or the base of the tub will decay quickly and drainage of excess moisture will not be possible. It's not a bad idea to use old skate boards, or better yet, a frame with casters on it, so you can move the tubs easily. Plants in tubs enjoy a summer outside in the sun as much as you do.

Strawberry Jars

Strawberry jars can be used for many plants other than strawberries. These jars are made of earthenware and are equipped with pockets on the sides to hold soil that is in contact with the body of soil in the pot. They are used effectively for patio decorations in the Southwest and also have great possibilities for home

Herb-Planted Strawberry Jar

decoration. Choose a size that is in proportion to the space you have available. What you will put in it depends on your personal preferences. I have seen such jars looking beautiful with African violets, dramatic with cacti and succulents, and lacy and aristocratic with trailing green plants planted in the side pockets.

Bamboo and Log Containers

In the tropics, sections of bamboo, two or three inches in diameter, each containing a node (the joint of a stem), are often used for flowerpots. But if you use these, it may become necessary to chop off any growth buds from the base of each section—or your pot will begin growing! This also happens sometimes when you use small pieces of tree as pots or containers.

Hollowed-out logs and even wicker baskets can be used to hold soil for house plants. Orchids, particularly, look great and are easy to grow in these containers.

Feather Rock Containers and Others

One of the latest fads is to grow plants in hollowed-out chunks of feather rock. These sell at Neiman-Marcus in Dallas for as much as fifty dollars, but you can buy the rock hollowed out for two or three dollars and plant it yourself. When I showed how to do this on NBC-TV's "Dinah's Place," Bessie was inundated with letters requesting directions. You can grow any type of house plant from orchids to cacti in these rock containers. After planting, set the rock in a tray filled with water and gravel.

Just about anything that will hold earth can, has been, or will be used as a flowerpot to hold a cherished plant. Some people put their trailing plants inside bird cages, others commandeer pieces of driftwood. Handleless cups are used for tiny plants, and all sorts of small dishes are filled with African violets. Use your imagination.

Pot Sizes and Shapes

Just as there is a wealth of pot shapes to choose from today, there is also a superabundance of sizes. And the relationship of form to size can be very bewildering. The square pot of, say, four inches will hold more soil than a round pot of the same size. You'll notice that more square pots can be placed next to each other on a windowsill than round ones. But don't make a practice of jamming them next to each other unless they are tapered enough at the bottom to allow air to circulate. The round clay pots are better for this kind of placement, because they allow for better aeration, which will help hold down the incidence of disease.

In a standard pot the inside measurement top to bottom is usually the same as the inside diameter: a four-inch pot will be four inches from top to bottom and roughly four inches across the top. A *three-quarter pot* will be wider than it is tall, and a *box* or *tray* is only half as deep as it is wide. Easter lilies, azaleas, bulbs, African violets and other gift plants are often put into three-quarter pots by the growers.

Whenever you read instructions that tell you to use a certain pot size for a certain plant, you can be reasonably sure they are correct. Someone has obviously already taken the trouble to find out that such-and-such a size will provide the correct amount of soil, root room, and drainage area for each particular plant.

Tufflite and Styrofoam pots and trays come in both white and terra-cotta (as do their matching saucers). In terra-cotta the pots range from 4 to 6 inches round, and the saucers are also from 4 to 6 inches. In white the pots range from 2¼ inches round to 10 inches, and the saucers from 4 to 10 inches. These pots are particularly desirable because they are strong and shatterproof.

Also, they don't develop the growth of green algae and fungi, but they do "breathe," just as clay pots do. They seem to have all the advantages and none of the disadvantages. However, they are as light as a feather, and you may prefer the stability of the heavier clay pots.

Some plants, such as poinsettias, can get along with shallow soil because their root systems do not go very deep. Even so, these plants are often put in pots of a larger size (deeper) simply for the sake of looks. The taller pot gives them a more balanced appearance. With such plants the amount of soil is not too critical. All plants are not created equal, and some are just naturally a lot less fussy about their environment than others.

Something we like to do at the Bakers' is to dress our plants individually. We give each plant a pot best suited to his or her personality. This should be determined when the plant is matured and has reached the final pot size in the progression of potting up. Of course the color, shape, and style of the container should also be chosen with an eye to the place it will occupy in the house.

Actually, all this business about pots is not half as complicated or mysterious as it sounds. At best I can only generalize. When you decide exactly what kind of plants you want to grow, ask the nurseryman or florist what pot sizes work best. If you plan to specialize—that is, grow one particular kind of plant—the first thing you will probably do is hunt for information about your specialty. Whether it happens to be African violets or aspidistras, you will probably find that someone has written an entire book or a number of books about it, and measured everything, so there is no guesswork left. If you take these books out at your local library and read them, you will probably go on to become an expert yourself. Good reading and good growing!

Now let's find out when you should pot and repot, and how it is done.

Repotting

If you have been giving your plant friends a little of your love and attention and have carefully followed the proper cultural practices for them, you will probably have a pretty good idea of when the time has arrived to move them to larger pots. Generally speaking, the best time to do this is at the close of their *resting* season. This is usually in late winter. Actively growing young plants, such as those raised from seeds or cuttings, or even small ones dug from flower borders in late fall, can be transferred to larger pots any time when the roots become so crowded that growth becomes checked. You should keep a close watch on your plants at all times to be able to detect this. Repotting will give the roots additional room and a supply of new soil. Its frequency depends on the rate of growth of the plant.

When you see new leaves forming near the soil level, as in the case of ferns and aspidistras, or new shoots beginning to spring out at the tips of branches, or young leaves forming with vigor on the dracaena, you can figure that *new growth* is beginning. This is most likely to take place after a fairly long period of dormancy. With most plants, the spurt of new growth happens in spring or early summer.

Now is the time to examine the plants to determine whether or not repotting is necessary. Do this by removing the plant from its pot as I described earlier in this chapter. Don't hold on to the plant and yank at it—you wouldn't like to have your hair pulled, would you? Now, if the ball of roots you are holding in your hand is densely matted, the crowded condition will be obvious and a shift to a larger pot is indicated.

The first step in repotting is to make sure that you have on hand clean pots of a suitable size. If new clay pots are used, soak them in water overnight to make sure they don't absorb water the plant needs. Usually a clearance of half an inch to an inch and a half between the ball of earth and the side of the new pot will be about right. If the pot is too large, the soil will remain too wet

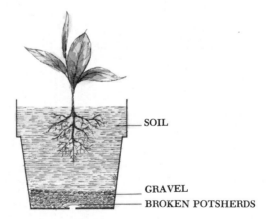

SOIL

GRAVEL
BROKEN POTSHERDS

and there will not be sufficient aeration. Make sure that there will be adequate drainage by covering the hole on the bottom of the pot with a piece of broken flowerpot, concave side down. Add an inch or so of small pebbles or flowerpot chips. On top of this place some organic material such as coarse compost, moss, or flaky leaf mold to a depth of about half an inch. This will keep the finer soil from sifting through and clogging the drain hole. The more carefully you do this—and it must be done with each repotting—the more likely you are to prevent waterlogging.

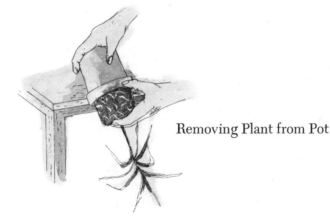

Removing Plant from Pot

Remove the plant from its pot and rub off any loose surface soil. Disentangle the crocks from the roots of the plant if it has grown into them. This will probably damage the roots somewhat, but it must be done. Sometimes you will find that the roots have even grown through the drainage hole and must be drawn back. This will do still further damage if they break off. I suggest you sacrifice the pot in this situation, but if you have to break off some root tips, don't despair, do the best you can. Put a little soil in the new pot over the coarse organic material you have already placed there, and put in the plant, bringing it up to the correct height. Put in a little more soil if needed to accomplish this. This should be about an inch below the rim of the pot—depending of course on the pot size—so that watering can be easily handled.

Always repot a plant at the same depth that it was growing before. With the plant set at the correct level, continue to fill in the soil about its roots. This soil, by the way, should be similar to the type in which it had been growing. (Remember, this is not a sick plant, just one that has been growing and becoming larger and needing more space.) Settle the soil by jarring the pot on the bench, then pack it down with your fingers to the same density as that of the old ball. Or use a potting stick for this simple operation. Level the surface of the soil with your fingers to smooth it.

Always keep in mind that repotting soil for plants at or near maturity should be of a quality to keep them in a healthy condition rather than to encourage continued growth. Most of us don't have the time or inclination to go on repotting plants indefinitely. After moving them once or twice you may want to give certain plants to friends or relatives.

Certain plants, such as aspidistras, cacti, Christmas cacti, and palms grow quite slowly and require infrequent transplanting. Types of plants that make rapid growth, such as begonias and geraniums, need transplanting at least once a year, and even more often when they are young. More frequent transplanting is required by young plants than by older ones of the same kind. There are also certain plants that need to be pot-bound. It's a way of forcing geraniums to bloom and it is the time-honored way to create dwarf plants and such ornamental dwarf trees as the bonsai.

Transplanting Seedlings and Cuttings

If you plan to transplant seedlings or cuttings, give them ample amounts of water on the day before you intend to do the job. This will result in a condition of turgidity (or swelling) of the plant tissues and will enable them to withstand the shock of transplanting better. With plenty of moisture in their system they'll have time to reestablish their roots in their new environment. This will also result in more earth clinging to their roots as they come out of the seed pot or flat. And cuttings will have more rooting medium coating their roots. The watering operation will give more protection to the plant and it will be less apt to dry out on contact with the air.

You can judge when seedlings are ready for repotting by looking at their leaves. About the time the third, or true leaf shows on each plant, it is ready to be moved to larger quarters—either to a larger flat or a small pot of its own. Cuttings may be potted about the time the roots become half an inch long. Don't wait until they are too long, as this increases the possibility of damage and makes potting more difficult.

To facilitate this job, have the soil before you on your bench.

Place the empty pots and drainage material on your left and the seedlings or cuttings on your right. Use the same soil mix as the plants are already growing in. Put some drainage material and a small amount of soil into the first pot. Then carefully lift the seedling or cutting from the flat by prying beneath it—never by pulling it out. Put the plant into the pot. Hold the young plant at the correct height—*the same depth at which it was growing before transplanting*—and continue to add soil around it until it is about a half inch from the rim of the pot.

You should now thump the pot lightly on the bench to settle the potting material and then tamp the soil around the stem of the plant. Do this carefully; seedlings are often brittle, especially when they contain a large amount of moisture. Use your thumb and forefinger for this job and be gentle but thorough. The purpose of this part of the operation is to eliminate air pockets.

Don't Put Them in Pots Too Big for Their Feet!

When I was a boy many parents would buy their kids shoes that were too big, hoping they would grow into them. The result of this is that a lot of adults my age are walking around with weak ankles, fallen arches, and bad feet. Don't make the same mistake with plants. Tender young seedlings or cuttings should not be placed in containers that are too large for the immediate needs of their roots. You will have a tendency to overwater the too large pots and leach away the needed nutrients before the roots grow enough to occupy the entire soil area. Often this overwatering will cause the soil to sour. Most successful gardeners have learned that young plants should go progressively from one pot size to the next. Only when they outgrow the pots they're in should you move them again.

If you are planting several seedlings or cuttings, make sure you give each a uniform depth of soil. This way each will receive the same amount of water each time you water without your having to make special adjustments in the amount for a particular plant.

Make sure the pots are set level on the bench and that the soil at the top of the pot is level. Only about a quarter inch of space is needed at the top of these small plants. But as the pot sizes increase, a little more space will be needed each time. However, I recommend that you never let this space be more than an inch or you will be tempted to overwater. After potting up your cuttings or seedlings, water the soil thoroughly and do not repeat until the soil surface becomes dry. Be careful to keep the newly potted plants from direct sunshine for several days to a week.

Drafts and Droughts Can Be Damaging

Sleeping or standing in a draft can be just as damaging to a young plant as it is to a person. To check for drafts, simply place a candle in a saucer and light it. Place the candle in the spot where you intend to put your plants and watch the flame. If the flame is blown out or blows in one direction for a long period of time, don't make the spot a home for your foliage friends, especially these young ones, or they'll catch cold and perish. Many people make the mistake of putting their kitchen plants too near or in direct line with their refrigerator door. When this door is opened, a chilling blast rushes out. This is very harmful to plants. Both young and old plants that are placed in a draft can catch cold. When you see the edges of the leaves turn brown or black, look out! Move your plant at once and be sure not to replace it with another plant in the same spot.

Drought is just as much an enemy of young plants as a draft. Either can check their growth at this critical period, and they may never regain their vitality. Tender young plants need to remain succulent in this early growing period. You will have to be especially watchful at this time. If the spot where you place them has a particularly dry atmosphere, check them often. Never allow the soil to become hardened or constricted.

Repotting an Established Plant

The correct time to repot an established plant is something that you will learn mainly by experience. Yet there are ground rules for this also, and (surprise!) sometimes it is desirable to repot into a smaller container instead of a larger one. You should do this when the roots are unhealthy and have not fully occupied the soil in the pot they were in. This condition may have been brought about by previous overpotting (placing the plant in a pot too large for it at some stage of growth), along with overwatering. It is even possible that the drain may be clogged by earthworms.

Such a plant may or may not be worth spending your time on. Your decision to try and save it will depend on its condition, its value to you (it may be an old friend or an expensive plant), and whether or not becoming a doctor or a nurse appeals to you. Some people enjoy restoring sick plants to health and regard this as a test of their gardening know-how. Others would rather just discard them.

Here's How To Repot a Sick Friend

Shake all the soil away from your sick friend's roots. Do this carefully and avoid injuring any root that shows signs of life. Take a sharp knife and remove any dead or injured roots. Make the cut through healthy tissue back of the injured portion. Now take a pot large enough to contain the roots with no danger of overcrowding and prepare it by putting in an inch or so of broken shards, pebbles, or broken brick. This will ensure that the plant will have good soil drainage. Place the roots in the pot and hold the plant at the correct level with one hand as you sift soil about the roots with the other. Move the roots up and down a little as you pour in the soil so they will not bunch up.

Do not repot in a rich mixture of soil. Use equal parts of compost, sand, and garden soil which have been sifted through a ¼-inch sieve or hardware cloth. When the soil is up to the brim of the pot, jar the pot on the bench and tamp the soil down with your fingers, just as you did when you were potting your seedlings. This will leave adequate room for watering, which should be done thoroughly. Do not water again until the soil is completely dry. Plenty of air is necessary for root vitality, so future watering should be just enough to keep the soil barely moist until the plant becomes well established and begins to form new roots. If growth continues to be good, resume normal watering.

Each sickly plant should be regarded on an individual basis. If the plant makes only a feeble effort toward new growth, perhaps, sad as it may seem, it would be more humane to inter it. If it is not actually diseased, place it on the compost heap and comfort yourself with the thought that it will have life again in a new form. Mother Nature's way is a life-or-death affair, a continual process of birth, life, death, and rebirth. If one of your plants happens to die, don't take it personally or think that somehow you have failed as a gardener. If, on the other hand, your plant seems to be making a real effort toward new growth, talk to it encouragingly and give it every chance to regain its lost vitality.

Pot-Bound Plants: A Chinese Puzzle?

There was a time in not too distant Chinese history when it was the fashion to tightly bind the feet of young ladies. This practice was supposed to keep their feet small, dainty, and beautiful. Actually it made them deformed, and the result was that these gals couldn't get around at all by themselves and needed constant attention or they would starve to death. It would be an understatement to say that they showed a considerable lack of vitality! Well, the same thing happens to your plants when the roots become pot-bound. They are unable to function properly, waste the food you give them, and show the same lack of vitality as those Chinese girls of yesteryear.

How can you tell when your plant is becoming pot-bound? As always, experience is the best teacher. One telltale sign is a miniaturization of the new-growth foliage and a gradual dying-off of the foliage closest to the soil. From this you can tell that your plant is doing everything it can to survive on restricted rations.

Don't be afraid to "knock out" the plant under suspicion. You can do this occasionally, and it's very seldom that harm is done by such an operation. If the plant is okay (roots not crowded), scrape away a portion of its bottom soil and replace this with fresh soil, then put it back in the pot it came from at the very same height it was planted at before. The plant won't be upset. On the contrary, it probably will enjoy all the attention and have a quiet laugh at your expense, seeing you do all that work for nothing! If, however, the root structure is beginning to look cramped and new root tips are sticking out of the ball everywhere, get out your potting soil and pots and go to work.

Repotting a Healthy Friend

The time for repotting a healthy, established plant is when the pot is crowded with roots to the extent that the available plant-food nutrients in the soil are exhausted.

If the plant in question is one for which a small pot is more desirable than a larger one, either because of ease of handling or the space that's available, you might want to consider topdressing the soil instead of repotting. This can be accomplished at your potting bench or kitchen table. It consists simply of loosening and removing the soil on the surface of the pot and replacing it with a richer mixture consisting of approximately 50 percent loam and 50 percent compost to which a small amount of bone meal has been added. Before adding the topdressing, be sure to examine the plant and make sure the drainage hole hasn't become plugged. If it has, remove the plant and remedy the trouble.

If the pot is so full of roots that little or no soil can be removed from its surface, then it definitely needs more space. It is almost always best to move the plant up only one pot size. If you go beyond this, you must be very careful not to overwater until the plant is growing well again. Try to remember that when a newly potted or repotted plant goes into an overlarge pot, you must restrict fertilizer for a time or the plant will have more food than it can cope with—which is like giving too much candy to a baby!

Au Revoir

If you are fortunate enough to have a greenhouse or that old-fashioned but very handy place called a conservatory, your larger plants will flourish there for a while after they have outgrown more favored locations around the house. But eventually the time will come when you and a plant pal will have to say goodbye to each other.

My "house plant expert" friend Louise Riotte tells the story about a friend of hers who cherished a rubber tree for many years. During that time it went from one large container to another even larger, and so on. Finally it became necessary to have containers specially built to hold it. In these it was faithfully moved outdoors in the summer and back indoors in the winter, straining the backs of family, friends, and employees. At last the day came when something had to be done! Its sentimental owner had its last and final planter box built for it, a very beautiful one, and donated the tree to the local hotel, where it was placed in the lobby. Here it was admired and commented on.

For a time the tree seemed to be doing well, but it gradually pined away. Louise says she doesn't know whether it was smoke, the unaccustomed light, or if it missed its former owner, but die it did. The original owner did not witness its demise. He couldn't bear to look in on his old friend in its last pangs and so never entered the lobby while it lingered. One day it just wasn't there any more. None of the man's human friends ever mentioned it again.

A Summer at Camp

As soon as spring arrives at my house the kids begin to spend more and more time out of doors. Like most parents, Ilene and I believe this time spent in the fresh air and sunshine is very good for them. And in many cases "a summer at camp" outdoors will be just as beneficial for your plants.

As you can see from what I have written several times in earlier chapters, it is very difficult to draw a fine dividing line between house plants and outdoor plants. In many cases they are interchangeable. And plants vary so much in their environmental needs that those that may safely winter-over outdoors in one part of the country will freeze and die farther north. Also, many plants grown originally in small pots frequently outgrow these to the point where they must be placed outdoors—if the climate is favorable to their growth—or discarded altogether. Some flowering pot plants, such as chrysanthemums, can be put outside when they are spent. These plants are reasonably hardy and may safely be planted in the outdoor garden. If they prosper they will make nice cut flowers for the house when their blooming time comes round again.

Of course the type of container your plant is growing in will have something to say about whether it will summer outdoors or not. Clay, plastic, or wood containers stand outdoor weather very well. Metal containers aren't usually as durable; soil weight may cause them to buckle, and if placed in the sun they may gather excessive heat. Large planter boxes and tubs made of wood are heavy and can be difficult to move. Since they are so heavy, consider putting them on "roller skates" before you plant them. Castered frames that will hold most tubs and barrel halves are available at garden centers or may be easily constructed by a handy do-it-yourselfer.

Some plants will benefit by being sunk into the soil during the summer. You can do this by burying them right up to the pot rim, but without removing them from the pot. This practice

Citrus aurantifolia
Persian Lime

might create a problem in the fall when you dig the pot up and discover some of the roots have left the pot and grown down through the drainage hole in the bottom. In that case you may have to do some root-pruning and repotting. Dwarf citrus trees will often get a real shot in the arm and renew their vigor and beauty if they're placed outdoors during the warm season of the year. But in the north these must be brought back in again when the cooler weather approaches.

There probably aren't any chestnut trees left, but under a spreading shade tree is an ideal spot for summering indoor plants outdoors—particularly if the tree is one that does not have extremely heavy foliage and deep roots. In this kind of location, pots can be plunged into the soil up to their full depth. They will receive the full benefit of filtered sunlight and refreshing rainfall. Place your shade-loving plants under such a tree on the north side of the house and dig a hole deep enough for them to sit in. If natural rainfall isn't available or sufficient, they will have to be watered. It may also be necessary to spray them for insect control. Here's a tip. If you turn the buried pot a quarter turn every couple of weeks it will help keep the plants from rooting through the drainage hole.

When I recommend plunging pots into the ground I am referring to clay pots and possibly some plastic ones that will hold up to this kind of treatment. Don't try to do this with expensive glazed pots, wooden or metal ones. Instead, change plants in these types of containers to "summer shoes" of clay or plastic. In the fall, when the temperature begins to drop, lift out the pots, clean them off, and bring them back into the house. You will be surprised at how healthy they look after their summer away at camp.

Soils, Pots and Containers for Cacti and Succulents

As with other types of house plants, it is almost impossible to talk about containers for cacti without also discussing soil requirements. You may be under the mistaken impression that cactus plants grow in pure sand. Nothing could be farther from the truth. These plants require a nutritional soil that's suited to their particular needs, which are usually quite different from those of such tropicals as African violets and other shade-loving plants, which prefer acid soils.

A loose, well-drained soil is necessary for most plants. For cacti, good drainage is even more important than it is for most other house plants. Pick one of the two soil mixes I have already recommended for cacti. Remember that succulents can take a mixture somewhat richer than most cactus plants. Succulents, like cacti, grow in the warmer, drier regions of the world, so let's consider their pots and potting requirements together.

For true desert cacti it will be necessary to add more sand and some gravel to the mix. For jungle species, such as Epiphyllum, an entirely different mix is required. This species is often referred to as the orchid cactus but it isn't related to orchids. If you want to have lush green stems and big, healthy buds, you must use an acid soil and good drainage, so use a planting mix of equal parts of compost, aged steer manure, and silt or sand. If you add a teaspoonful or two of bone meal, the plant will develop strong roots. You won't need more fertilizer for at least three years. Epiphyllums should never be fed high-nitrogen fertilizer because of the danger of burning the stems.

These plants do especially well in hanging baskets, where the long, cascading growth is unusually attractive. Some of them have a stiffer type of growth that looks well in a container if it is supported by a trellis. Clay pots, redwood tubs, or even tin cans will make fine containers. Allow the plants to become slightly pot-bound; this will encourage the growth of a greater number of flowering buds.

Rhipsalis is another jungle species that will do well on a mixture of one part shredded fir bark or osmunda fiber and one part garden loam. As with epiphyllums, the ingredients must be mixed thoroughly, and the texture should be loose and friable so it will quickly drain excess water but still provide moisture for the roots.

Garden centers now sell prepared soil that contains all the necessary ingredients for good growth of these succulents as well as for other types of cacti. One advantage of these packaged soils is that they are already sterilized.

Succulents and the hardier types of cacti may be grown in many different types of containers. They are often displayed in pieces of feather rock, but the usual clay pots, wooden tubs, and boxes also show them off to advantage. An inexpensive terra-cotta pot is both practical and attractive, and these come in many sizes.

Many cactus lovers like to display their plants in cachepots, which look something like jardinieres, because they come in such attractive shapes and colors. These pots are often glazed and are fine for cactus as long as they have drainage holes. Be careful when you water these, because moisture can't escape from the sides. Since cacti are plants that need such small amounts of water, a glazed pot can actually be an advantage if you are a traveler who needs to be gone from home for long periods of time. Neat, lightweight, inexpensive plastic pots are often used and may be especially pretty if chosen in a decorator color to harmonize with the room. They are also easy to clean.

Whatever you do, don't choose a pot that's too large for your cactus. Not only will it look lonesome but it will not thrive well for the same reasons as I have given before in discussing too large pots for other plants. If the container is large, plant some companion cacti so they can gossip among themselves. Also, remember that too small pots will increase your problems of caring for cacti and succulents as they will dry out more rapidly than larger ones. And cactus does need water; just use moderation when you provide it.

To Pot and Repot Cacti and Succulents

Cleanliness is just as necessary for cactus as for your other house plants, so remember the dictum: Scrub all with hot water to make sure they're free of dirt. Always use containers equipped with drainage holes or your cactus or succulent will be likely to drown or the roots will rot.

Just as I recommended with other house plants, you should use decorative pots or pot covers only if the cactus and succulent plants you place in them are first put into clay or plastic pots that are well drained and there is enough room between the two containers to allow air to circulate freely. Put several inches of gravel at the bottom of these decorative pots and bring water up to a level just below the top of this gravel layer. Be careful at all times not to overwater. Even if the pot is resting on the gravel, too much water will be detrimental. *Cacti must never sit in water.* Pots intended for either cacti or succulents should always have one large or several small shards placed over the drainage hole. Be careful not to accidentally push these out of place when you put the potting soil in, and recheck their placement with a probe after you have potted up these plants.

Make a small mound of the prepared mixture in the container and place the plant on it. Check to be sure it will be neither too low nor too high when the rest of the soil is filled in around it. If this mound seems about right, spread the cactus roots downward and fill in around them with the mix until the container is full. Be sure the plant is not sitting too high as you complete the job. If it is too low, gently press it upward, handling it with gloves or wrapping a collar of rolled-up newspaper around it. Since the soil is still loose, this will not injure the plant if you do it *carefully.* Settle the soil by tapping the bottom of the pot on a hard surface such as a table or potting bench, but don't pack the mix tightly.

Most cacti of the types found on or near deserts are sensitive to excess moisture. For this reason it is good to replace the top inch of soil with a layer of gravel. This will keep the base of the plant from coming into contact with moist potting soil. Leave the plant for several days before watering. Be sparing of water even then, and give little for the next few weeks. This will give any broken roots time to heal. They will start to rot if they get too much moisture.

Succulents require much the same sort of treatment when being potted as cacti. They are a lot of fun to grow, and my kids especially like *Sempervivum tectorum,* commonly referred to as "hens and chicks."

Succulents are particularly attractive when grown in strawberry jars. In time these containers may become almost solidly encrusted with plants. When you pot in these jars, you can use a growing medium of pure chopped sphagnum moss. *S. tectorum* is one of the hardy succulents and may be left outdoors in the wintertime. Most succulents, however, thrive best under desert or semidesert conditions and in homes. They are ideal house plants for people who are pressed for time or must be away from home frequently. Their unusual forms and growth habits enable them to live on a minimum of moisture while exposed to high temperatures and direct sunlight. They require soil that drains well and plenty of fresh air. Evaporation of moisture from their fleshy, odd-shaped foliage and stems is far less than from the thin, broad leaves of plants living in humid regions.

Thick, fleshy plant parts are characteristic of succulents. These store moisture for long periods of drought. Many plants, like the sempervivums are rosette-shaped; leaves are usually thick, dwarfed, and sometimes angular or tubular. As mentioned in the chapter on these plants, many of the succulents are shrubs and in their native habitats attain heights of ten to twenty feet. However, there are numerous small varieties suited to culture as house plants. Among these are aloes, cacti, crassulas, gasterias, haworthias, kalanchoes, sansevierias, and sedums.

Watering Succulents and Cacti

When determining your watering schedule for succulents and cacti, consider the type of soil, the kind and size of the pot, and the needs of the plant itself. Succulents are an in-between type of plant, midway between cacti and the shade-loving plants that require acid soil and moist conditions. They need more water than desert plants. These are plants that live at the edge of the desert and have adjusted themselves to this environment for centuries. Water your succulents *sparingly* all through the spring and summer and about twice a month in fall and winter. *Never water these or any other kind of plant on cold, gray days.*

Succulents ordinarily rest during the winter months and begin growing in spring and summer. When you notice new growth, begin to increase the amount of water in each watering. Do this slowly—don't water too often. Always be sure that drainage is not plugged in any way. Never use cold water; tepid water is best. Cacti and succulent plants are especially sensitive to cold water. A large clay pot about ten inches in diameter will hold moisture for several days. A smaller one may dry out in a day or so. Remember, too, that clay pots evaporate moisture much more rapidly than glazed pots or plastic ones. This may be to your advantage or disadvantage, depending on your watering habits and the amount of time you have for working with your plants.

Another factor in watering is the location of the plants in your home or on your porch or patio. If the location is sunny or constantly exposed to drying winds, plants will need more water than those placed in cooler, shadier locations. Most cacti of the desert type need sunshine. Jungle types should be protected; the direct rays of the sun will burn the stems and cause them to turn yellowish-green. If they must be placed in an area where the sun reaches them for long periods of time, the sunlight should be filtered. While such plants may be placed outside during the summer months, they should be given winter protection. Temperatures under 32 degrees will be harmful to the succulent stems. If you live in an area where the winters are severe, place them in a window garden, under artificial light, or in a home greenhouse.

Summary

Only general rules can be given about the potting and the subsequent care of the many different types of cacti and succulents. These plants vary greatly as to cultural and environmental requirements. So if you decide to specialize in growing either desert or jungle types of cacti or succulents, I would suggest you obtain books at the library that will give you specific and extensive information about the type you enjoy the most. But there is one definite rule about watering either succulents or cacti of any type that is reasonably safe to follow: *When in doubt—don't.*

21

Propagation:
Family Planning for Plants

Very often we would like to have more of a good thing—and this is true of house plants. Fortunately, since many house plants are propagated by seeds or cuttings, we needn't wish in vain. A cutting is a portion of a plant—the stem or leaf—without roots. If it is properly cared for, this cutting will develop into a new plant. Cuttings may consist of a single leaf or a piece of stem with a leaf attached, but a terminal portion of a stem is the most common.

End, or Terminal, Stem Cuttings

Stem cuttings should be made only from healthy shoots that are neither soft nor weak. Terminal stem cuttings usually are three or four inches long, but some kinds, like those of English ivy, may be longer. Foliage on the lower one-third of the stems of each cutting should be removed so no leaves are below the surface of the rooting medium.

Recut the base of the cutting with a sharp knife or razor blade. This is necessary, because a poorly cut surface retains many crushed and torn cells that favor the entrance of soil-borne organisms. The cut should be one-fourth inch beneath a node (this is the bump or joint on a stem from which leaves develop).

Sectional Cuttings

Sectional cuttings are made by cutting stems above and below each node so that sections of stem about one inch long may be obtained. Cuttings are good for propagating such plants as English ivy, philodendron, dieffenbachia, dracaena, and geraniums.

Cuttings don't have leaves. A leafless stem section of dieffenbachia or dracaena is usually placed horizontally, with the upper end exposed. Portions of stems containing leaves may be positioned into the soil in just the same way as terminal cuttings, or they may be placed in a horizontal position, like stem sections without leaves.

Leaf Cuttings

It's possible to develop a new plant from a cutting made of a single leaf. Leaf cutting works to propagate such plants as African violets, begonias, gloxinias, peperomia, kalanchoes, sansevierias, and most succulents. Sometimes more than one plant grows from one leaf. Portions of rex begonias and sansevieria leaves may give rise to several new plants.

Planting Your Cuttings

Terminal and sectional cuttings may be planted in clay pots containing sand, sand and peat, or vermiculite. Vermiculite is sterile and weed-free, but if you use any mixture of soil, or soil and vermiculite, you should sterilize the soil. After placing vermiculite in a pot, do not pack it or aeration will be lost. The base of the cutting can usually be pushed into vermiculite without injuring the stem. Sand and mixtures of sand and peat should be firmed before inserting the cuttings.

Cuttings should be inserted into the medium just deep enough to ensure their stability; one-half to one-third of their length is considered sufficient for most. The medium should be moistened before the cuttings are inserted. Make a hole with a pencil just slightly larger than the cutting is round and insert it. Make sure the cuttings are far enough apart so that each one will receive some light on the leaves. Spacing them close together won't create a big problem if you are careful about this. When the cuttings are all in place in the flat, the rooting medium should be firmed around the base of each cutting. Water again so the soil mix will settle and collapse any air pockets that might have re-

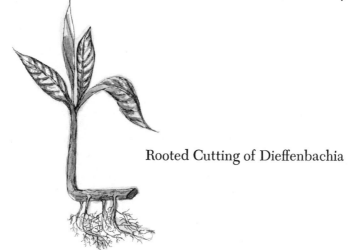

Rooted Cutting of Dieffenbachia

mained at the base of any of them. *Do not overwater.*

If you are a new gardener who has a little difficulty in recognizing plants from the shape of their leaves, take the time to label your flats of cuttings. This is especially important if you are working with cuttings of several different species and your flats are all the same size and shape. If the surrounding air is saturated with moisture, there will be less loss of water from the leaves because of transpiration and this will give the cuttings a chance to carry on with their moisture content until they have formed roots that will supply their needs.

A Propagating Case

A good way to supply the necessary humidity is to put the cuttings into a propagating case. This is simply a closed case for the rooting medium. It is something very handy to have, because it will prevent too rapid evaporation, and it is far easier to root cuttings in such a case than in an open flat, where more care is needed to prevent them from drying out. You can use something as large as an aquarium. This can be converted into a propagating case by placing in the bottom a soil mixture or vermiculite layer of several inches, and also making provision for drainage holes in the bottom. A removable glass top will conserve moisture and prevent wilting. A terrarium, usually smaller, may be used in the same way, and a large brandy snifter may be used for covering a small pot.

You may even use something as inexpensive as a coffee can. Fill this with the soil mixture. Water thoroughly and *then* punch holes in the bottom of the can and allow it to drain. Using a pencil, make a hole for the cutting and insert it. Put a plastic bag over the top large enough to completely cover and secure it with a rubber band. Make sure that the soil in the can doesn't dry out. When new growth begins, remove the bag and give the plant filtered sunlight, which should be increased gradually to full sun.

A Proper Rooting Medium

Cuttings should always be inserted in soil suitable to the individual species of plant—if you know what those soil requirements are. For some this may be sharp, gritty sand, for others mix in some damp sphagnum moss to provide organic material. Still others may need a layer of sand on top of the soil. With most cuttings, no matter what the medium used, except vermiculite, it should be packed firmly in the container. It is important to bring the base of the cutting into close contact with the rooting material. After you make a hole with your pencil, make certain the cutting touches the bottom of the hole, then pack the potting material close. A thorough watering will settle the rooting medium.

The Lust for Life

If you are new to this kind of a project, now's the time you probably are beginning to worry. Will my cuttings grow? I wonder if I did anything wrong? Etc., etc., etc.

You may be a clumsy gardener, but you can be assured of one thing—every one of your cuttings is filled with a determination to live and will do all it can to make the project work out successfully. Its outlook is definitely positive, and it will unleash all its faculties and strength to overcome any clumsiness or mismanagement on your part. It is this same lust for life that often causes newly set fence posts to sprout, and iris consigned to the rubbish heap to spread its roots and dig them down into the soil or debris around them. Because of this factor, inexperienced gardeners usually have beginner's luck with the cuttings they take. Of course, as my Grandma Putt used to say, "In gardening, luck's all right, but it never hurts to *know* what you're doing!"

Watering and Ventilation

If your cuttings are covered, very little water is lost to the outside air, and therefore very little water will be needed for a time. Keep a careful watch and add water only if a stage of dryness seems to be approaching.

While conditions of moisture and humidity are desirable for the cuttings, for about 90 percent of the time *ventilation* is still very necessary. Remove the glass from the propagating case (or the plastic from the coffee can) occasionally for five or ten minutes. Do this once every twenty-four hours if at all possible. Wipe off the condensation on the glass before putting it back. This will eliminate the presence of *too much* moisture. If atmospheric conditions are overmoist—which sometimes happens on rainy days when the air itself is overcharged with humidity—mildew and decay may show up. If this happens, ventilate more freely than recommended above. Remove any leaves showing signs of deterioration. Also remove any sick-looking plants in the propagating case. And of course remove any dead or fallen leaves that might encourage the spread of a fungus.

The Move into Some Bigger Shoes

Cuttings should be removed from the rooting medium as soon as their roots attain a length of one or two inches. Pot them up separately in a soil mixture best suited to their plant type but with a little more sand. We don't want our little fellers to get sick because of overfeeding, but there must be enough good soil to prevent them from becoming starved and stunted. Try to remedy this with a feeding as soon as you notice that the cuttings are having a problem. Too rich a mixture, however, combined with overwatering, may cause them to rot. How are you going to know? Experience, plus a little experimentation and keeping a close watch, will be your best teacher.

When Are They Ready?

It's important that you pot your cuttings as soon as they have made roots a couple of inches long. But don't keep digging them up every few days to look! Instead, watch the upper portion of the plant. It may give you a clue by looking extra perky and alive, almost as if it is very pleased with itself over a hidden accomplishment. It will have every right to feel that way.

When a sufficient period of time has elapsed and you suspect that roots have formed, give one or two of your plants a gentle tug. If they resist, it is quite probable that roots have formed. To determine this for certain, dig around the cuttings a little distance from the central stem. If you find roots have formed, the cuttings are ready for transplanting into their first real home. If roots are not apparent, or you think they are too small, pack the mix back firmly around them, watering a little to settle the earth and prevent air pockets. Rooting time varies from one plant to another— some may root in two or three weeks, others, especially those with woody stems, may take much longer.

Potting and Care for Your Well-Rooted Cuttings

Cuttings should be potted up in containers that are no larger than necessary to hold the roots comfortably—no crowding, but no extra room either. We've gone over this before, but it bears repeating. After watering thoroughly, keep the young plants shaded for a couple of weeks until they have a chance to become established and form additional roots. Spraying them daily or using a mister will help them get settled, especially if the atmosphere is dry. There is always a brief shock when a plant is first transplanted. Recognize this, and give it time to recover.

Why Propagate from Cuttings?

Perhaps the best reason for propagating your plants from cuttings instead of seeds is that plants grown this way are *identical* to the parent in genetic makeup, or inheritance, and are actually an extension of the original plant. Professional growers say they are "true to type," and, in theory at least, this extension may be carried out to infinity without any variations occurring. Seeds, on the other hand, may be very variable, producing a number of different plants even if they are grown from the same seed pod.

Plant scientists theorize that all plants have what is called a cambium layer. This is the soft formative tissue that gives rise to new tissues in the stems and roots of the plant. Even annuals, such as marigolds and others, possess this layer and may be rooted for blooming indoors. Especially fine petunia plants may be rooted from cuttings. Tender perennials are often propagated as bedding plants from cuttings. Propagation from cuttings is of special importance with plants that are difficult to grow from seed.

Plants That Grow Best from Leaf Cuttings

Some plants root very easily from leaf cuttings. Examples of these are African violets, gloxinias, rex begonias, and peperomia. If you plan to root piggyback plant, it will be necessary to cut off the mature leaves with two or three inches of leafstalk. Insert these in the rooting medium so that the blade of each leaf will touch the surface. You may also root this plant in water by the wax-paper-and-tumbler method described on page 289. Let the blade of the leaf just touch the surface of the water. Be sure that the water level does not drop. Rooting leaves of African violet and gloxinia are much the same (in soil), but it will not be necessary for the blade to touch the surface, like the piggyback or peperomia. It is at the *base* of the leafstalk that new plants are formed.

Tolmiea menziesii
Piggy-back Plant

Snake plant, or mother-in-law tongue, is one of the easiest plants to root by leaf cuttings. Sansevieria, the scientific name for

Sansevieria zeylanica
Snake Plant; also Bow String Hemp

Sansevieria 'Haknii'

Sansevieria trifasciata laurentii
Variegated Snake Plant

this plant, is so tenacious in its desire to live that it is almost impossible to kill it. Just cut the leaves into lengths of about three or four inches, keep them right side up, and insert them for about half their length in the rooting medium.

While Sansevieria will readily form new plants by this method, there is something that you should know. If your original plant is one of the fancier types, with a cream-colored stripe or border on the leaves, this will not be reproduced by the leaf-propagating method, and the children will not resemble the parent in this characteristic. If you want the children to look exactly like Mama, you must propagate by root division. That is, the crown, or rhizome, of the original plant must be divided. Otherwise you will have plain Janes, all green without any markings.

Rex Begonia

You may propagate rex begonias in several different ways. *Begonia rex* and its hybrids are those beauties with ornamental leaves. They have short rhizomes, or rootstocks. From these arise the long-stalked, ovate and frequently wrinkled leaves, which are about five to six inches long. In these plants the leafstalks, the veins, and in some varieties the leaves themselves are covered with fine hairs. To make a leaf cutting, try to choose a mature leaf in good, healthy condition, and detach it from the mother plant. Turn it upside down, and cut notches in the veins, close to where the latter cross, or on the lower surface of the leaves. Do this with a sharp knife. Use sand or sand and peat moss as a rooting medium. Turn the leaf right side up and make a hole in the sand to receive the stalk. Place the leaf so that it is lying flat on the sand.

For best results use a propagating box of some type so the moisture will be retained during the rooting process. Cover the box with a glass pane and watch. Young plants will soon form near the notches, and underground rooting will also take place. Soon the plantlets may be dug up and potted singly in small pots. Care for them and they will grow into nice new plants to take the place of the older ones that are outgrowing their alloted space.

Another method sometimes used for rex begonias is to cut a leaf into several triangular pieces, each two or three inches long and each piece containing a good-sized vein. Insert the end nearest the vein to a depth of about half an inch in the rooting medium. Now cover as outlined above.

Ferns

Some ferns develop plantlets on their fronds. Others, with creeping rhizomes, are easily propagated by division. Even ferns that grow outward from their crowns will usually spread and can be propagated by division. Plantlets of ferns may be detached or the entire frond may be laid on moist sand and the little plants allowed to grow in much the same manner as those on the leaves of *Begonia rex*.

Plants That Propagate Best from Rooting Runners

Some of the most interesting house plants are those that root from runners. And probably the most entertaining of these is the spider plant, which literally seems to be jumping away from the parent plant as if it had a separate life of its own. And so it has, if you give it the opportunity to take root. These plantlets, which are produced on the ends of its flower stalks, will sometimes slip quietly into the pots of nearby plants and make themselves at home. Sometimes they become well established before you're fully aware of what has happened.

If you see these new plantlets forming and want more of this plant, give it something in which to place itself. You may handle these runners by filling small flowerpots (either clay or plastic, or even tin cans) with a mixture of loam and leaf mold (compost) and a little sand. Pin the runner down to the pot with one of those paper or plastic-covered wires used in grocery stores for closing plastic bags. (They are usually found in the box when you buy sandwich bags or they may be bought separately.) I like these better than the hairpins that other gardening books advise, because with these there is much less danger of damaging the plant. As soon as roots have formed to the extent that the plant can operate on its own, sever the stem attached to the parent plant. That is all that is necessary. It's kinda like cutting the umbilical cord and separating a new baby from its mother.

BOSTON FERN

Another plant that roots from runners is that ever-popular standby the Boston fern. The runners of Boston fern are those stringlike, fuzzy growths that appear in profusion around the base of the plant. Unless you want to propagate from these, cut them off. If you want them to grow, allow them to root by sinking the mature plant in the ground and letting the runners grow into the surrounding soil. After they have made several leaves, dig them up and pot them. Water well until established. Here again, these new plants may serve you better, because they are smaller.

Saxifraga sarmentosa
Strawberry Begonia

SAXIFRAGA SARMENTOSA, THE STRAWBERRY GERANIUM

The strawberry geranium, sometimes called the strawberry begonia (although it is neither a geranium nor a begonia), is another runner rooter. It may be grown outdoors in mild climates or used as a house plant in more severe ones. It is an easy grower and will thrive under greenhouse benches or in out-of-the-way corners. It is a favorite window garden plant of those who enjoy plants but don't have much time for pampering them.

The plant gets its common name, strawberry geranium, because, like the strawberry, it is a trailing plant and produces runners. The leaves of this plant are coarsely toothed, hairy, reddish underneath and marked with white veins on the upper surfaces. The branched flower stems rise to a height of one or two feet and are covered in summer with white flowers. *S. sarmentosa* variety tricolor, a newer type, is handsomely marked, its leaves having creamy white and rose-red variegations, but it is not as easily handled or propagated as the older variety. Strawberry geraniums can be easily propagated by separating the rooted runners and placing them in ordinary soil. Give them light shade; even when fully established they should not be put in full sunlight. This is an excellent plant for hanging baskets, which show off its trailing growth to great advantage.

Softwood Cuttings

Softwood cuttings are what Grandma Putt used to call "slips." She was mighty knowledgeable about getting these to grow. Back in the old days, especially in pioneering parts of the country, there were no established greenhouses or florists as we know them today. House plants were loved just as much then as now—perhaps more so, because they were a link with homes and cultures left behind when a move was made to another part of the country.

These green, or softwood, cuttings were greatly prized, and exchanges were frequently made between friends as a means of expanding the variety of plants that could be grown in the average home. After your mother married and established a home of her own, I'll bet your grandmother gave her a supply of these stem-tip cuttings, or "side shoots" as they were sometimes called. They were made by snipping them off the main stem of the plant with the thumb and forefinger, without the use of a knife (which experts now recommend).

These slips are almost always easy to come by, and many house plants can be propagated this way if you happen to have a gardening friend. Gardeners are noted for their generosity, and no doubt you'll be able to reproduce most of your friend's plants by obtaining such cuttings. The best time to ask is when the plant needs to be cut back. Such pruning is very good for many house plants, making them more shapely and encouraging new growth. There are no hard-and-fast rules, but if plants are pruned in the spring at about the time they are to be moved outdoors, such cuttings will frequently grow to a good size by fall. They should be well developed before the first frost, when they will have to be brought inside, and will make very nice plants for indoor display.

Plants from which softwood cuttings can be made are cactus, chrysanthemum, dahlia, dianthus, hibiscus, kerria, penstemon, petunia, salvia, sedum, verbena, vinca, and zinnia, to name a few. The most common examples of such cuttings are those made from fuchsias and geraniums. As I have said, the spring is the best time for this—when new growth appears.

How to Take Geranium Cuttings

One of the best ways to illustrate how to make a softwood cutting, or slip, is to use our old friend the geranium as an example. Choose an older plant. Lift it in late fall before freezing weather, and keep it as completely inactive as possible. Give it just enough water so that it won't dry out. If it is kept at a temperature of 45 to 50 degrees it will remain as nearly dormant as possible. Reduce the light intensity and don't give it any fertilizer.

In early spring the old plant will be encouraged to put out new shoots as you increase the light, water, and warmth. In a few weeks strong new shoots will be produced which are true soft-wood cuttings. After several new leaves have formed, make a clean diagonal cut with a sharp knife. Cut three-inch to four-inch lengths—depending on the plant—just below a leaf or node (the spot where the leafstalk emerges).

The cut is made on a slant because this will expose more of the cambium layer to the rooting medium when the cutting is inserted in the pot. Each cutting should contain at least two buds. Any lower leaves, flowers, or buds should be removed. Never let the cutting dry out while this is being done. Once the cutting is made, encourage it to root by placing it in a moist rooting medium. This should be well drained, light, and airy and have the proper humidity. If cuttings are placed in a propagating box, they may be set close together or even touching.

The Right Rooting Medium for Geranium Cuttings

The choice of a rooting medium is important, as some plants do better in one than another. To be efficient, rooting material should hold moisture, supply good drainage, and remain well aerated. Sand is most often used, but it drains so rapidly that it's not unusual to have to water your cuttings two or three times a day to keep them from drying out. The greatest hazard in rooting cuttings is wilting from lack of moisture or too much light. Another problem frequently encountered is damping-off, the fungus disease that rots the stems right at the surface of the soil. It is usually caused by overwatering, so be moderate. I will say more about damping-off later in this chapter.

Peat Moss, Perlite, Vermiculite, and Coarse Sand

The essentials for quick rooting are better supplied if you mix the sand with peat moss to improve its water-holding capacity. Also, peat moss is acid in reaction, and it's been discovered that roots will form more rapidly in an acid medium. If you can, buy peat moss that's been imported. This type is less likely to be contaminated with weed seeds and other extraneous matter. If you can't get imported peat, check the domestic type for any possible contamination and for acidity. (The pH factor should be below 5.0.) Wet the peat moss thoroughly before mixing it with sand.

Another excellent rooting material is perlite, which holds moisture well and remains aerated better than vermiculite. Roots will grow quickly in this material, which is obtainable from most garden centers. You will probably obtain better cuttings if you water once with an ammonium sulfate solution before the cuttings are inserted.

Still another rooting medium for cuttings, good for all-purpose use, is a mixture of equal parts of vermiculite and coarse sand. If you decide to use this, sterilize the sand before making the mix by pouring boiling water through it.

It's Not All That Difficult

Not all plants are difficult to propagate, and some will root readily in a flowerpot, coffee can supplied with drainage holes, and even clean milk cartons (which also must have good drainage). A plastic refrigerator bag over the plant, secured with a rubber band around the pot, can, or carton, will make it a miniature propagating case. You can also try a trick that Grandma Putt taught me: invert a glass jar over a slip—just keep it out of the sun.

To Dip or Not to Dip

All sorts of hormone dips are on the market. Whether or not you will use one—or which one—depends on your attitude toward such things. If such a dip is prepared, place only the lower end of the stem in it. Hormone dips of this kind are intended to give cuttings an extra supply of certain growth-stimulating chemicals. These occur naturally in most plants, and this is an acceleration of the process, which takes place more slowly if the dip is not used. In my opinion it is an advantage to achieve quicker, more nearly complete rooting even with easy-to-root plant varieties. And sometimes you can root difficult species that perhaps could not otherwise be propagated from cuttings.

There is a trick that is well worth knowing if you want to try using a hormone solution when working with softwood cuttings such as lantana, fuchsia, heliotrope, or geraniums, which tend to rot easily when they pick up too much moisture. To avoid this, make your cuttings in the evening and allow them to lie overnight out in the open so the cut end will dry a little by the next morning. Dip this dried end into the hormone powder and place it in the rooting medium in the usual manner.

Those Half-Hard Cuttings

Half-hard cuttings are greenwood cuttings that have become hardened by more mature growth. They are cuttings made from the current year's growth which have begun to firm up but are not yet really woody. You can check this stage by bending over a shoot. It is still considered green if it crushes instead of snapping. It shouldn't bend—it should snap clean. If it hangs together as it bends over, it has advanced too far toward woodiness. Half-hard cuttings are ideal for roses, which are easy to propagate by this means. Shoots that have just completed blooming are just right for taking as cuttings.

How to Take Rose Cuttings

Take a pot or coffee can and hold a small piece of pipe or heavy cardboard tubing in the center. Put equal parts of sand, loam and compost well mixed together, into the container to within an inch of the top. Now fill the tubing with coarse sand and start withdrawing it, tapping lightly as you go. Moisten the newly mixed soil.

Take your cutting from half-hard new wood, leaving three sets of five leaves. Cut off the old flower. Think of the base of this cutting as square rather than round. Take a sharp knife and press it onto the stem just enough to penetrate the outer skin. Do this three times at about half-inch intervals on each of the "four sides" of the stem—all on the lower two of the cutting. Blot the excess moisture from this area and dip into a rooting compound. Tap off the excess and rub it into the cuts you have made. Using a pencil, open a hole in the center of the wet sand and insert the cutting. Pack the sand back firmly around it. Now water the can until it is thoroughly soaked and won't take any more. If you are using a coffee can, make holes in the bottom of the can, set the container up on two bricks and allow to drain freely. Insert four plastic drinking straws around the rim of the can and pull a plastic bag over it. Secure the bag around the sides of the can with a rubber band. The object of the straws is to tighten the bag so that the condensation that forms will drain back into the soil, making it a self-watering microclimate.

Place the can in semishade, and don't remove the bag until the cutting starts putting on new growth. Of course, you will have to see that the soil doesn't dry out. If necessary, remove the bag, add water, and then replace the bag. As growth begins move the can into more and more sunlight. In warm weather your rose cuttings should become well rooted in about three weeks.

All half-hard cuttings should be rooted in shade, whether they are roses or other plants of similar growth characteristics, such as azalea, camellia, forsythia, hibiscus, hydrangea, gardenia, mahonia, or spiraea. All of these can be rooted by the method just described.

Hardwood Cuttings

Most gardeners understand the term "hardwood cuttings" better than any of the others, and these are probably the easiest to recognize. They are sections of mature stems from which the leaves have dropped in the fall. Their big advantage is that they have stored within them the food for the next year's growth. We can trick them into using this food to form roots. Cuttings of the last season's growth are best for this purpose. They are cut in the fall of the year and stored in bundles—tied together and buried in damp sand. At the time of the interment the polarity of the twig is changed: the end that was downward on the bush is placed uppermost in storage. In other words, store your cuttings vertically during the winter, with the stems pointing opposite to the way they grew in nature. In the spring, when these twigs are unearthed, the cut end, which has usually callused over, is planted and will form a mass of roots.

Air Layering

House plants that don't receive as much light as they would like are notorious for growing leggy. Such a plant that has grown

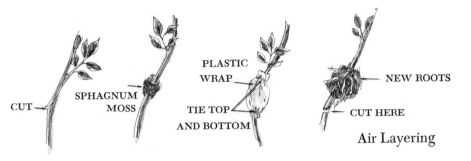

CUT — SPHAGNUM MOSS — PLASTIC WRAP — TIE TOP AND BOTTOM — NEW ROOTS — CUT HERE

Air Layering

completely out of bounds is usually an excellent subject on which to try out your skill of air layering. This is a good way for you to prune the plant back to a reasonable size and at the same time obtain a new plant or two very quickly.

In air layering, the cutting is not detached from the parent plant until roots have actually formed on it. Such plants are not called upon to operate on their own until they are actually very well able to root for themselves. Once you cut them and plant them as individuals, they will be off to a flying start. This method of propagation is receiving a lot more attention since plastic bags have come on the market. These bags make the operation a whole lot easier.

The method is quite simple. Let's use a rubber plant as an example, since this is one of the easiest plants for an amateur to air-layer successfully. Lay the plant down on its side on a batch of newspapers. Cut a notch upward at the place where you would like the roots to form. This usually works best about ten or twelve inches from the growing tip, but really depends on the size of the plant you are working with and the size you want the new plant to be. Cut one-third of the way into the stem and place a match or toothpick into the slot so the cut will be held open. Scrape away the cambium, or outer layer of the stem, for an inch or two around the cut but not completely around the stem. Never go more than half or three-quarters of the way around. After you have completed cutting through the stem and have inserted your peg (match or toothpick) to hold the cut open, you will notice a milky excretion of sap at the damaged area. This is exuded by the plant to heal the wound. Wipe it away with a paper towel.

Moisten a handful or two of sphagnum moss and wring it out lightly so most of the water will be retained. Wrap the moss around the wounded area and tie it firmly in place. The moss must never be allowed to dry out while rooting is taking place.

Cover it with polyethylene or cut out the bottom of a small plastic refrigerator bag and slit it along one side and wrap this around the moss. Tie it securely at the bottom, but leave a small opening at the top so water can be added if necessary. Water the mother plant sparingly while the air-layering material is being held in place. This will encourage rooting to take place where the plant is obtaining moisture. It will take six weeks to two months for most plants to fill the moss with roots. When this has taken place, sever the rooted tip of the plant from the parent stem and place it in a pot, being careful not to disturb the roots.

What Plants Can Be Propagated Best by Air Layering?

Many plants that are difficult to root from cuttings, such as dracaena, dieffenbachia, croton, India rubber plant, and philo-dendron, may be quite easily rooted by air layering. Air layering can be good gardening fun for you and the kids. As the roots form, they can usually be seen plainly through the clear plastic wrapping. This method of propagating plants has been practiced for centuries in the Orient and is also known as Chinese layering or pot layering. You may air-layer a plant any time of the year, but spring, when new growth is most vigorous, is usually considered the best time.

Dividing That You May Multiply: Taking Division Cuttings

The growth habit of many plants makes division cuttings the most natural method of propagation. This is best accomplished with most species in late winter or early spring. If you examine such of your plants as African violets at this time, you may notice that they have begun to split themselves up into several crowns. Ferns, sansevierias and aspidistras are also good subjects for division. This is one of the easiest forms of propagation and the one which the inexperienced gardener is most likely to accomplish easily.

Division consists of separating these multiple crowns, or roots, each with a tuft of foliage, and then potting and growing the divisions as separate plants. To do this it may be necessary to pull, split, or cut the plant apart, depending on the species and its way of growing. Choose a time when the plant is not in flower. Take the soil ball out of the pot and try to pry the crowns apart without any more root injury than is unavoidable. A cut here and there with a sharp knife may be necessary. The best time to do this is when new growth is just becoming apparent. After the divisions are made and the new plants potted up, water sparingly for a few weeks and shade them from overbright sunlight. If you have access to an outdoor area, set them under a tree where the light will be filtered.

ASPIDISTRA: THE UNIVERSAL PARLOUR PLANT

If you're one of those people who has become an avid antique collector, you might want to add a real Victorian to your collection. The aspidistra, sometimes called the "cast-iron plant" because of its ability to withstand adverse conditions, was considered the plant of plants. In the last century everybody had to have one— they were practically a status symbol. And they eventually became so popular that they went out of style. We will consider it here because it is an excellent example of propagation by cuttings. Our grandmothers cared for their aspidistras diligently, sponging their leaves and faithfully setting them out of doors if a rain shower seemed imminent. As a matter of fact, back in the old days, without quite knowing why, many people recognized the beneficial aspects of rainwater as opposed to the water that came out of their wells. Ladies caught rainwater for washing their hair. It is a well-known beauty treatment for both plants and people.

The aspidistra will remain in good health year after year, successfully coping with drafts, droughts, gas fumes, and mistreatment in general. If it is progressively repotted, it will eventually become as large and unwieldy as was the famous rubber plant. Dividing it every three or four years is the best answer.

Before attempting to divide an aspidistra, give it several good waterings. Turn the plant out of its pot by giving it a good hard slam on the bench to loosen the soil. Using a sharp knife, split apart the rhizomes, which are usually just showing on the soil surface. Cut so that each piece has at least four or five leaf stems. This is optional and will result in more plants. If you want just one or two good-looking mature plants, use eight or nine leaf divisions instead.

Whatever the number of divisions you decide upon, put each into a pot large enough to contain the roots without crowding, and firm the soil. Before you pot the rhizomes, take note of the way the leaves are turning. For a pleasing effect, use care in placing the rhizomes, wedging them with soil so the leaves will be as near vertical as possible. If necessary, hold the leaves in place with thin plant stakes. Aspidistras should be placed near windows but not in direct sunlight, for they are deep-shade plants in their natural environment and have a low respiration level.

Root-Divide Root-Bound Plants

The roots of some ferns, such as pteris, adiantums, and others, including maidenhair and Boston, will grow into dense, fibrous masses in time, completely filling their pots. Such plants have become root-bound. They may be divided by separating the matted roots with the fingers. This method is often used by commercial growers who want to have as many plants as possible. However, since most of us don't want a great many plants, cutting the mass up into larger pieces is quicker and more desirable.

Give your root-bound fern in its pot a hard thump and take out the plant. Cut off a couple of inches from the bottom of the

Pteris cretica
Pteris Fern

roots. Then, using vertical cuts, separate the plants into the size you want for repotting. This method, like that used for aspidistras, will give you as many new plants as you want or have pots for. The rest can be discarded.

Propagation by Seeds: One of Mother Nature's Miracles

So far we have been talking only about vegetative methods of propagation—cuttings of hardwood, softwood, root division, and so on—that is, propagation from existing plants. But plants, like people, have the characteristics of two sexes, and no matter how much the hybridizers continue to fool around, it still "takes two to tango." Many plants can be propagated by seeds very successfully. They may even produce better plants and can be handled more conveniently if this method is followed.

Seeds are the ovules of flowering plants and are contained within an ovary. Pollen grains effect the fertilization when they come in contact with the stigma (this is the part of the pistil of a flower which receives the pollen grains and on which they germinate). As the seeds germinate they send down long tubes through the style into the ovary. These pollen tubes contain nuclei, which join (fuse) with the nuclei of the ovules, and fertilization takes place. The ovules then develop into perfect seeds capable of producing new individual plants.

During the dormant period after fertilization the embryo of the new plant is protected by a surrounding seed coat. Inside, it has enough food in and around its seed leaves (cotyledons) to start active life and keep the seedling nourished until roots and true leaves are formed and begin to function on their own. Germination takes place when the seed comes into contact with moisture and the enzymes within it begin to break down. As they break down, the stored food elements become available, and these assist the forming of the plant cells and tissues. As the embryo increases in size it begins to swell from the moisture it has absorbed. Soon it begins to insist on being "born." The new plant bursts through its water-softened seed coat. The part containing the seed leaves will "leap" for the surface, and the part containing the rootlets will dig deeper into the ground. All this has been neatly calculated by Mother Nature, and this is the way she wants things done.

In addition to adequate moisture, other things must be favorable, such as air and temperature. Both of these must be in correct balance for whatever plant is being grown. Darkness or subdued light also plays an important part.

Seeds have something else going for them. They are relatively inexpensive, and you can have many more plants *and a greater variety of plants* if you can exercise the three P's and go this route. Planning to grow new varieties can be almost as exciting as actually planting the seeds. Most gardeners get a tremendous bang out of "fireside gardening," or "baby shopping," and can scarcely wait for the new seed catalogues to arrive each year. You can spend many happy hours going through dozens of these books making lists, scratching out and starting your planning all over again. After a while you will begin to realize that you will need a larger house—or greenhouse—unless you begin cutting your dream lists down to size. You will take a special pride in watching your tiny plants grow from seeds to maturity, pride in the knowledge that you, personally, brought it all about. Makes you feel like a proud parent!

Sports May Make You Another Luther Burbank

When you practice any form of vegetative propagation you will get the same type of plant as the one from which the cutting or root division is taken. But with seeds something entirely new may develop—something that no one has ever seen before. These atypical plants are called sports and are often the result of natural hybridization. The difference may appear in the color, the shape, or the form—as, for example, the doubling of a single variety.

Growing plants from seeds can be fun, but it isn't much fun to come in some morning all cheerful and happy and see that your little pals have fallen over during the night, victims of damping-off. This is a condition caused by various fungus organisms living in the soil and may take place even before your seedlings emerge. In that case the seedlings either do not reach the surface at all or reach it in such a weakened condition that they can't survive. Or it may attack after the seedlings emerge. The young plants may be doing fine for a while, and then, quite suddenly, fall over and shrivel up. This problem is most likely to arise with plants that are raised indoors, and there are several ways to avoid it.

The first possibility is to sterilize the soil by baking or steaming. Second, you can use vermiculite for germinating your seedlings, which is presterilized and inexpensive. However, this soilless mixture has its limitations. The young plants must be put into it with more nutrients, enough to permit them uniform and sustained growth. You had best not wait very long to supply this food or your seedlings will get a pinched, starved look and gaze at you reproachfully. There is still another way, and by following this plan you can germinate flowers, vegetables, house plants—even trees and shrubs. This method works for any species or types of plants that are suitable for growing from seed.

Make a Mini-Greenhouse, or Incubation Unit

Start with a clean, shallow container, not over two inches deep. The container need not be elaborate. Look around the house and you will find something—I often swipe one of Ilene's pie tins. You can make a handy container by stapling a milk carton at the open end and cutting it down to size. If you can't find anything suitable, go to your nearest garden center and check some of the inexpensive plastic garden flats. While you are there, buy enough milled sphagnum moss to fill your containers right up to the rim. If you can't find the moss there, try your florist. The moss he is most likely to have is the type called "coarse," which will do, but you will have to break it up by rubbing it through a sieve. This can be a pain, so let the kids do it for you. In any case, milled sphagnum moss is the only medium for germinating seeds that I would recommend for this method. The reason for this is that *sphagnum moss will not support any fungus disease,* such as the damping-off organism.

Thoroughly moisten the moss and squeeze out any excess water. (If you use hot water, the moss will become very absorbent.) Fill your containers loosely—do not pack, or firm up, the material. Small seeds such as petunia, African violet, or snapdragon shouldn't be covered. Larger seeds—calendula, aster, zinnia, for example—will germinate more quickly if the seeds are covered with a 1/16th-inch layer of loose, moistened moss. If you have a mister, use this to gently moisten the medium immediately after sowing the seed. Mark each seed container with the plant name and the date of sowing. Take a piece of plastic wrap large enough to completely encase the container—top, bottom, and sides. Fold the wrap and seal any loose edges. What you have now is an incubation unit. The moisture contained in the chamber will condense on the plastic wrap, forming there as droplets and falling back onto the growing surface, keeping the supply largely constant.

The unit should be placed in a dark but warm spot. If it is placed over a baby's vaporizer or warm-air register, the seedlings may emerge within twenty-four to twenty-eight hours! If you can't give them this last treatment, keep the unit in a room at a temperature around 85 degrees. Check within twenty-four hours. Seeds may have germinated, or you may see a green or white fuzz on the surface of the moss. When the seedlings become really visible, move the unit to a partially lighted spot—near a window but not in direct sunlight. Now you may lift one or two edges, but otherwise leave the cover intact.

Watch carefully. If you see signs of drying, add a fine mist of water. After a few days the seedlings should be moved to a cooler location. Here the day and night temperatures should not exceed 65 degrees. If the seedlings are kept too warm they will grow leggy, and this tall and spindly growth will be extremely brittle, making them difficult to transplant without breaking the stems. Keep a close watch, and remove the plastic film completely when the second set of leaves appears. Transplant the seedlings immediately into small pots filled with soil or into wooden flats. Bear in mind that they need more room, *but not too much room*; don't put them into pots any larger than necessary. Pry up the seedlings gently, using a kitchen fork or spoon. Any moss clinging to their roots should be left on. Water the transplants immediately after potting. Keep them in a cool but well-lighted spot.

You may plant your seedlings outdoors after the date of the last frost in your area. If you don't know when this is, check your local Ag station. If the seedlings are intended for house plants, put them in their permanent location and transplant them when they need more room. Remember, just move them up to *the next-larger pot size.* Many seedling varieties will benefit if you fertilize them once a month with a well-balanced, water-soluble fertilizer, which is obtainable at garden centers. The moss and the container may be used again to germinate more seeds.

Getting Cuttings to Root More Quickly
—Water Rooting

Many cuttings will root more readily if the bottoms of their stems are placed in water instead of soil. African violets, pothos, philodendron, English ivy, and many other plants will respond to this method. Here is a trick often used for rooting cuttings in water. Choose a tumbler, jar, or brandy snifter and cut a round of waxed paper about two inches larger in diameter than the top of your container. Fill the container with water. Now take a knife and cut a hole or slot in the waxed paper, place it over the top of the container and secure it with a rubber band. Then push the stem of the cutting through the slot until it is submersed in an inch or two of water. Keep an eye on the water; as it evaporates, add more. Place the container in a warm, light room, out of direct sunlight.

As soon as the roots have formed, the plant should be potted. It will adjust better to the soil at this period of growth than if you wait until the leaves develop. Plants that have been rooted in water should not be left there too long, because water-formed roots are modified so that oxygen may be extracted from the water instead of the soil. When the time arrives to pot them in soil, they suffer a serious shock, since they must readjust to their original medium. Sometimes this readjustment will not take place in time and the plants will die.

Cuttings rooted in water are difficult to transfer to soil because of the turgidity or brittleness of the roots. The high moisture content causes them to break easily. Transfer the cuttings carefully, doing as little damage as possible during the operation, and then water them thoroughly in their new home. If they continue to prosper, gradually water them less until they're on a normal watering schedule. Water-rooted plants will be slow growers at first, because the roots are struggling to adjust themselves and to get the necessary oxygen, essential to all plant growth, which they must have in order to live and grow.

As I mentioned before, all plants are *not* created equal, and some are hardier in respect to water-rooting than others. Success is most likely with such plants as oleander, pandanus, English ivy, Wandering Jew (sometimes called "lady in a boat"), and Chinese evergreen. If you root these in water, the roots are likely to be profuse, and you must be very careful not to bunch them up when

Aglaonema commutatum
Chinese Evergreen, Variegated

you put them in pots containing soil. Sometimes cutting back an over-full top of a water-grown plant will help that plant to become established in soil. After trimming a plant in this way put a glass or a plastic refrigerator bag over it, which will help it to retain moisture.

Generally, however, most plants will root better in soil than in water, because their stems will often rot in water before new growth begins. Creating a moist atmosphere for soil-rooted cuttings is probably better, on the whole, than water-rooting and should result in a more successful growth of plants.

Spores Are the Seed of Ferns

For me, growing ferns from spores is one of the trickiest projects in gardening. I really think it's easier to buy started ferns and leave this to the experts. But if you would like to try it, you can use the method outlined above for seeds in sphagnum moss. It might be fun just to see if you can do it!

Spores are produced in tiny cases in lines or dots, usually on the under part of the fern frond. It's important that you collect these spores at just the right time—when the spore cases are beginning to split open. The only trouble is that you may have to use a magnifying glass to determine this accurately. If you think the time is right, cut the spore-bearing frond into half-inch pieces and lay them, spore side down, on moist sphagnum moss. The exceedingly small spores will drift and sow themselves. When they have removed themselves, take up the portions of the frond. Another way is to gather fronds that are bearing ripe spore cases. Place these in a plastic bag and keep them in a warm, dry place. In a couple of days the spores will be discharged. Now is the time to scatter them thinly over the moss.

Cover your experiment with the plastic wrap, as I explained before, and keep the spores moist. Don't open the unit until the leaves are visible. As the spores germinate they will form a delicate plate of green tissue. On the underside of this the reproductive organs will be formed. It is only after fertilization that the young plants will begin to grow. When you see this happening, start to uncover the unit and admit a little air.

Incubators with Bottom Heat

For years commercial growers have known that the use of bottom heat will speed up seed germination. Somewhere along the line, probably by trial and error, someone discovered that the best soil temperature for seed germination is 10–12 degrees above the customary growing temperatures. And they also stumbled on the fact that heat from below was the best way of starting seeds without damaging other plants growing in the same room.

Many nurseries and garden centers now offer cold frames and miniature greenhouses that come equipped with or have optional automatic heating cables. These have a built-in 70-degree soil thermostat. One company sells an electric soil-heating cable with a thermostat that activates when the soil temperature falls below 74 degrees. This kind of cable can give you a head start on the regular growing season.

Because of the very fact that seedlings germinated with bottom heat grow so fast, you must make provision to give them some light within four to six hours after they begin to peep through. If you're careless about this they will go on reaching and soon will be standing on their tiptoes, looking like basketball players stretching for the goal. If this goes on long enough they will become like limp bits of string and will never regain that stocky, sturdy appearance associated with well-grown plants. If you are one of those lucky enough to have a sunny window that faces south, part of your problem is already solved. Take off the covering you placed over the seeds when you planted them which was meant to filter the light, and let in a little sunlight.

Growing plants from seeds or cuttings or root divisions is a great experience and good fun, but it's hard not to get carried away. Pretty soon you will find yourself up to your neck in pots. Don't be stingy—you can make a lot of friends by giving some of your "babies" away.

22

To Love and to Cherish

In most gardening books this is the chapter that usually bears the depressing label "Pests and Diseases" or "Trouble!" Maybe I should call it something like that, but somehow I believe the title above is more appropriate. By this time you have come to love and cherish your plants as members of your family circle, and like the other family members, you will want to love, cherish, and protect them from harm.

Of course, plants, like people, do get sick, and insects sometimes trouble them. But often their distress is not a result of either of these causes. The plain truth is that house plants were very probably the first victims of environmental pollution. Consider the fact that plants come to us from all corners of the world and we, in our clumsy way, try to force them to grow in an environment that is so unsuitable that it may damage their health, stunt their growth, or even kill them.

The greenhouse is the best place to grow plants indoors. Temperature and humidity can be controlled to suit the needs of the plants grown there. Even tropical house plants prefer a temperature of 62 degrees (average), but most of us want our homes heated to 70 or 75 degrees or even more. The warmer we keep our homes the less humidity we have and even desert plants need a rather moist atmosphere to thrive in. Since you and your plants *must* share the same house or apartment, I've already suggested various ways in which you may effect a compromise.

All through this book I have tried, sometimes very repetitively, to give specific directions for pots, soil mixtures, potting, temperatures, light requirements, and humidity. Following those recommendations will, I believe, help you ward off most insect pests and disease organisms. For the most part, plant pests and diseases steer clear of healthy, flourishing plants, which will fight back. They prefer plants that are in a peaked and weakened condition from poor culture. But since plants do get sick sometimes despite all your efforts to the contrary, try to develop a bedside manner. This will help you spot the trouble quickly and act just as quickly to remedy it. Finding the cause is half the battle. I will try to help you, but in many instances the best I can do is speak in generalities.

A plant may be unhealthy for several different reasons:

1. Perhaps there is a fungus, virus, or bacterium that is causing either local or general infection.

2. An insect or pest of some sort, such as a snail or a slug, is gnawing or chewing away at its vitals.

3. Or maybe it is suffering from physiogenic disease, which simply means that you have not provided it with the correct environment. This trouble may be caused by air that is too hot or too dry; too much or too little light; too much or too little water; or, perhaps a cold, wet draft blowing on its leaves. Perhaps, unthinkingly, you shocked it by pouring cold water on it instead of bringing the water to room temperature first.

Once again, a strong, healthy plant is much less prone to attack by diseases or insects—and much more able to withstand and overcome a temporary setback from these troubles.

If a plant is already weakened by our failure to meet its natural cultural requirements, it is quite likely to succumb. We then blame the virus or the insects for killing our plant. The truth is that it just didn't have the strength to resist. Remember, plants in pots are already at a disadvantage in their fight for life, struggling to live in an unnatural environment, even though you are doing everything in your power to make them feel at home. My Grandma Putt used to say, "Think perpendicular." By that she meant to remind me that the environment *below the ground* for the roots is as important as the environment affecting the aboveground portion of the plant.

If you are at all in doubt about the needs of a particular plant, look up that plant in a good gardening encyclopedia or try to find a book about your specialty in your local library. Librarians, like gardeners, are very kind people, and they will do all they can to help you. Don't guess—know.

Make sure the soil mixture you are using is the right one. Remember that a pot is a very limited area; if the nutrients the plant needs are not provided for it, there is no other way it can search for them. Water your plants in the morning with tepid water. Be sure you water the soil and not the plants. Begin feeding with the right fertilizer at the proper time. House plants respond to spring just as outdoor plants do. When they begin to make new growth and come into bud and flower, they are working very hard and they need more food—just like growing children.

And, like children, their health must be watched, and they need to be doctored occasionally. What do you need to know to become an effective healer? First of all, you must cultivate your powers of observation, really *see* what you are looking at. Watch especially for changes in the leaves. Do they droop? Is there a change in color? Is there something on them that wasn't there yesterday?

Fungus and Bacterial Diseases

Diseases caused by fungi and bacterial organisms are infrequent among plants grown in homes, because the low humidity in homes usually harms such disease organisms more than it does house plants. But if you notice spots and speckles on the leaves indicative of leaf diseases, apply a garden fungicide.

Rot. Numerous soil-borne disease organisms are capable of causing stem, crown, and root rot. Stem rot causes portions of the stem to become discolored and soft and eventually to die. The best treatment is prompt surgery. Cut away all diseased tissue, dust the cut surfaces with powdered sulphur, and keep the plant somewhat dry. Try to avoid wetting stems and foliage when stem rot is prevalent.

In stemless plants, such as African violets, rot may affect the center, or crown, of the plant, causing it to decay and become wet and slimy. Treatment is to remove all decayed parts, dust the plant with sulphur, and keep it comparatively dry.

Root-rot diseases are caused by various fungus organisms and are more serious than either stem or crown rot. All soils in which flowers or vegetables have been grown recently contain some fungi. The damage from root rot is aggravated by overwatering, crowding of plants, and poor drainage. The most effective control is treating the potting soil with heat to kill the soil-borne organisms. Small quantities of soil for home use may be sterilized by the method I have described before. For convenience I will repeat it here. Place the soil in a shallow pan and heat it in an oven with a temperature of 180–200 degrees. Leave it in the oven for thirty minutes. The soil should be moist but not wet before being placed in the oven and should be stirred several times to avoid baking. As a further precaution, wash and sterilize all containers in which plants are grown.

Powdery mildew. This is a fungus disease characterized by a grayish-white powdery, or mealy, covering on stems and leaves. It infects kalanchoe, African violet, begonia, primrose, and numerous other house plants. It usually occurs when the atmosphere is stagnant and too humid. Good air circulation is a preventive. Dusting with sulphur will cure the disease.

Where the Pests and Bugs Come From and What They Do

It is difficult to imagine where the numerous insects that attack house plants come from. You would think that sheltered indoors and protected as they are, they would be free from such troubles—but they're not. It is for this reason that you should be particularly careful about new plants brought into the house. Keep them segregated for a week or two. It may save you a lot of trouble.

Insects or diseases may be carried in with cut flowers; they may enter through open windows or doors; and many times they are brought into a home on clothing. Of course none of us realizes that he or she may be a sort of plant Typhoid Mary or Diphtheria Dan just by taking a walk in someone else's garden, but it can happen.

Once in, the tiny insects may multiply very rapidly and infest a number of plants. If they escape early detection and become established, control is much more difficult and considerably more plant damage occurs. The most common damage to house plants is caused by *sucking insects,* which draw sap from the plants. The loss of juices interferes with normal growth, development, and flowering.

Be curious. Examine the undersides of the leaves of house plants every week or two and carefully examine the stems. Insects are much easier than diseases to detect. But detection of the insect is not enough; it is also important to be able to identify the insect in order to apply the proper chemical control measure. For instance, a stomach poison is required for chewing insects; sucking insects avoid such poisons, and a contact spray is necessary for their control. A spray effective against aphids will be completely inadequate if it is applied to a plant infested with thrips.

Spider mites. Red spider mites—also known as red spiders— are tiny round creatures that are barely visible even when full grown. They attack most house plants and inhabit the underside of leaves and spin delicate webs. These mites are usually red, but there are orange, yellow, and green ones also. You might have to use a hand lens to detect them. They are sucking creatures, and the insertion of their sucking mouthparts into the leaves gives the foliage a finely mottled, or peppered, appearance. In severe infestations the older leaves turn brown and much leaf-drop occurs. Also the plant growth is severely checked.

Red Spider

Red spider mites are well adapted to living on plants in a home and thrive where the air is hot and dry. They are easily controlled if discovered before the infestation is severe. Spraying or dipping plants in a solution of nicotine sulfate (1½ teaspoons dissolved in one gallon of warm water) is effective. If spraying, be sure to dampen the underside of each leaf. Repeat this treatment two or three times at weekly intervals. A Malathion spray or an aerosol *house plant bomb* (not household) is also effective. When using any spray bomb, be sure to hold it at least eighteen inches from the plant. Aramite, at the rate of one teaspoon of 15 percent wettable powder to one gallon of water, gives good control.

An effective method of preventing infestations of red spider mites and reducing those already established is forceful syringing or spraying of plants with clear water once a week, with particular attention to the undersides of leaves. Use sufficient force to break the webs and wash away the mites but not enough to damage the foliage. This can be done over a sink, in a bathtub, or out of doors.

Aphids

Aphids. Aphids are small green, gray, black, or red insects usually found clustered on new growth or buds or on the underside of leaves. Examination of stems and leaves will easily disclose the presence of these soft-bodied insects, which are oval and fringed with short white filaments. They live by sucking plant juices and are noted for their ability to multiply rapidly. As a result of their feeding habit the plant is weakened and its foliage is deformed.

Spraying or dipping plants in a solution of nicotine sulfate and soap, mixed as the manufacturer advises, should be done every few days until control is complete. Every aphid must be thoroughly wetted to cause its death. It is difficult to reach those hidden in the folds of immature leaves. Dipping the aboveground portions of plants in a solution is sometimes superior to spraying, because all portions of the plant come into contact with the chemical. Malathion is also useful against aphids.

Mealy bugs. Small cottony patches along leaf veins or at axils, where stems join the main branch, indicate mealy bugs. An additional symptom is a sticky secretion that forms shiny patches on the leaves. Mealy bugs are grayish-white, oval, and have numerous fringelike filaments radiating in all directions. These are sucking insects that may be seen without a hand lens. An extremely large infestation will cause stunting and eventual death of the plant.

Mealy bugs can be removed with a stream of water or a brush. In serious cases, sprays or nicotine-and-white-oil emulsion insecticides will control them. Another method of attack is to swab off the plant with alcohol-dipped cotton or spray. You may also dip the aboveground portions, using contact-type insecticide. Malathion is also effective on mealy bugs.

Scale. Scale is an insect that lives under an armor like a flat turtle shell during its adult stage. Only when young can these insects move about; thereafter they stay in one spot. Newly hatched scales are almost invisible. After inserting its proboscis (a tubular sucking organ) in a leaf or stem, a scale remains in one spot the rest of its life, sucking sap from the plant and growing larger. Mature scales usually are brown, while young ones are smaller, flatter, and pale green. Do not mistake spore-bearing organs of ferns, which are on the undersides of leaves, for the insect scales. Insect scales form less regular patterns than the spores. Scale insects seriously reduce the vigor of plants. Foliage turns yellow and the rate of growth is reduced. Like aphids, they excrete a sticky honeydew that coats the foliage and encourages growth of a black fungus that resembles soot.

To clean a plant of scales, dip it in a diluted solution of nicotine sulfate. Sometimes it is desirable to dip a piece of cotton in either nicotine sulfate or alcohol and rub off the scales. Malathion

Mealy Bug

Terrapin Scale

is effective in killing young scales in the crawling stage. You may also use house plant aerosol spray. Washing house plants at regular intervals helps control scales. Clean a plant of scale immediately when the first one appears.

Thrips. These are brown or black creatures that live in crevices of small leaves around the growing point of a plant. A magnifying glass helps detect thrips. They are slender, pointed at both ends, with bodies that lie close to the surface upon which they travel. Thrips have rasping mouthparts used to suck plant juices. The sucking of sap causes a streaky, silvery appearance on the attached foliage; eventually leaves become brown and wilted and may drop from the plant. Thrips are easily eliminated by dipping or spraying with a nicotine insecticide, as recommended for red spider mites.

Thrip

Cyclamen mites. These creatures are invisible to the naked eye, but under a microscope they appear as nearly transparent white or greenish. Since the African violet has become popular, cyclamen mites have become more prevalent. Stunted, distorted leaves and flowers are symptoms of cyclamen mites. Sometimes they turn leaf margins up in cup shapes. With African violets they cause a hard, stunted center growth and a sickly light color.

Cyclamen Mite

Discard affected plants; observe strict sanitation to prevent spreading; with most valued plants use a systemic insecticide in pot soil. A cutting should never be taken from a plant infested with cyclamen mite, because the new plant will certainly have mites.

Nematodes. Nematodes are tiny worms that are very difficult to see. If the plant shows any of the signs referred to and you cannot detect other insects or evidence of plant disease, you may suspect nematodes. Discard affected plants; start over with fresh soil. Plants troubled by nematodes have an unthrifty appearance characterized by misshapen new leaves, bumps on leaves or stems, cessation of growth, and root knots.

Hygiene and First Aid for Plants

Cleanliness is one of the most important factors in dealing with diseases and insects. If it becomes necessary to cut away diseased portions of plants, always cut back to healthy growth. Keep your pruning tools sharp. A smooth, clean cut heals much more quickly. Disinfect all tools with denatured alcohol after pruning diseased parts of plants. In cutting back woody plants, such as small trees, make small pruning cuts less than one inch in diameter. These usually heal quickly if they are smooth and at an angle so water does not stand in them.

You should treat wounds over one inch in diameter to prevent decay, disease, and penetration by insects while the wound is healing. The best wound dressing is asphalt varnish containing an antiseptic. An antiseptic prevents the spread of harmful organisms that may contaminate the treating material. Asphalt varnish containing an antiseptic is available at most garden supply stores. If you cannot get a dressing containing antiseptic, use ordinary asphalt varnish. Before applying plain asphalt varnish, swab the wound with alcohol or coat it with shellac. Apply the dressing as soon as the wound is dry. Asphalt varnish will not stick if the wound is wet. Coniferous evergreens usually seal small wounds with natural resin. If no resin forms, treat the wounds with asphalt dressing.

If it becomes necessary to discard diseased plants, never put them in with composting material. Burn or otherwise dispose of them. Disinfect the pots if they are to be used again, as well as the soil that will go into them. Methods for doing this have already been described.

Always examine a new plant carefully when it comes into your home, whether it is one you received as a gift or one that you bought at the florist shop. Do this even if it is your own plant that you have just brought in from out of doors. This takes a little time but can save a lot of trouble.

Battle Plan Against Bugs

Here is a partial list of some of the most popular house plants and the troubles that may possibly infect them—a sort of battle plan for bugs and blights.

AFRICAN VIOLET. Mealy bugs and mites. Chlorosis: This is characterized by yellow, irregular mottling on the leaves. Keep out of the sun. May be caused by wetting of the leaves.

AMARYLLIS. Mealy bugs. Bulb flies: These are maggots of the greater or lesser bulb fly, and they eat out the centers and destroy the basal plant. Treat with hot water at 110–115 degrees for four hours, or discard the bulbs. Red fire disease: Look for red spots on leaves, flowers, and bulb scales. Flower stalks and foliage will look bent and deformed. Treatment: Remove and burn any infected parts.

Aspidistra. Even the "cast-iron plant" occasionally develops problems. These may be leaf spots (apparent as white spots), brown margins on leaf blades and stalks, or pale spots on leaves. Remove any infected leaves and burn. Chlorosis: This is discernible by yellowing of leaves, and may be due to too much strong light. Relocate in shadier area.

Azalea. May be troubled by red spider or chlorosis: Treat as previously suggested. Lace bugs sometimes trouble azaleas: Leaves will be stippled whitish with brown spots beneath. Spray with nicotine sulfate and soap.

Begonia. Mealy bugs and aphids: Follow general directions previously given. Mites: Treat as suggested for African violets. Leaf nematodes: Characterized by discolored reddish areas in leaves that curl up and drop. Keep this plant separated from healthy plants. Avoid handling or wetting the foliage. Try dipping leaves in hot water (115 to 118 degrees) for three minutes. If grayish mold appears on leaves and flowers, it is probably blight. Avoid wetting leaves, and remove infected portions. Leaf-drop in begonias may be caused by wet, heavy soil, hot dry air, or drafts. Treatment: Cool room, high humidity and porous soil.

Calla lily. Leaves that are streaked or flowers that are badly formed and brown indicate root rot. Destroy plants and soil;

Zantedeschia rehmannii
Calla Lily

sterilize pots before using again. If bases of stems and corms are decayed, it is probably soft rot. Discard corms. Aphids: Treat as previously suggested.

Cactus. Cactus plants may be troubled by many of the same insects and diseases as other house plants and will respond to many of the same controls, but there is often a difference in the way they should be applied.

Aphids: Use nicotine sulfate or Malathion. Water the plants the day before using the preparation, and keep them shaded for a few hours after spraying. Mealy bugs: Same treatment as for aphids. Scale: If mild, remove with a toothpick. For heavier attacks use Malathion as above.

Root knot nematode: This tiny roundworm sometimes enters the roots of the plant, causing minute swellings that appear like beads. As they cause the root to rot, the plant becomes stunted and pale in color. If infestation has progressed, it may be necessary to destroy the plant. If it is just starting, a plant may sometimes by saved by trimming off the infected portion and repotting in sterilized soil.

Thrips and red spiders: Spray with Malathion as directed for aphids and mealy bugs.

Snails and slugs: Search out and destroy or scatter bait over the soil and then water.

Ants: Control with Malathion. Ants are seldom harmful, but tend to spread aphids.

Fungus diseases: Avoid cuts or wounds. Fungus infections sometimes cause a plant to rot at the base or to develop soft, decayed areas. Cut away and destroy infected parts. Disinfect tools. Dust wounds with sulphur or a fungicide.

If your plant has one of these problems, what to do about it:

If your cactus shows slow growth or no new growth at all: May be caused by compacted soil, too much water, or decay of root system. Repot in sterilized soil. Use more care in watering.

If it fails to bloom: Too much nitrogen in soil, or it may need a winter rest period. During this time it should be watered sparingly and kept in a cool but not cold place.

When you see fresh growth starting, resume watering and give the plant more warmth and light. Plants, like people, need rest, and cactus is no exception.

If flower buds drop: May be caused by a draft, too low temperature, or too much fluctuation in temperature. Try a move to a warmer, draft-free location.

If it has soft growth: Too much moisture, too little light, too low temperature. Water less, cut away infected parts and dust with Captan. Give more light.

COLEUS. May be affected by mealy bugs: Spray with nicotine sulfate and soap, use lemon oil, or wash off with water. If infestation is slight, remove with cotton swab dipped in alcohol. Black leg sometimes causes plants to wilt and may cause death; best to destroy infected plants.

CYCLAMEN. Mites: Treat as suggested for African violets. Yellowing and drooping. Remove to cooler location, give moisture by placing in a pan of water and allowing moisture to seep upward. Drain.

DIEFFENBACHIA. May be troubled by mealy bugs and red spider mites: Treat as previously suggested. Leaf spot and root and stem rots: Leaf spots caused by bacteria may have a water-soaked appearance, orange or reddish-brown in color. To control, avoid sprinkling plants and space farther apart so they may receive better air circulation. Remove badly infected leaves.

DRACAENA. Spider mites and leaf spots: Treat as directed earlier.

FUCHSIA. White flies: Spray with Malathion. Mealy bugs: Spray with a nicotine insecticide or Malathion. Sometimes troubled with sooty mold. This grows in white-fly honeydew. Control insects and this will disappear.

GARDENIA. Mealy bugs, white flies, and sooty mold: Control as previously given. Bud drop: Give cooler temperature in winter and more light. Chlorosis: Characterized by yellowing of leaves. Test soil pH; if too alkaline, water with ferrous sulfate as directed on bottle.

GERANIUM. May be troubled with white flies, mites, black leg, or blight. Treat as directed above.

NARCISSUS. Failure of buds to develop. May be due to starting too early, too high temperature, or need for additional water.

PHILODENDRON. Leaves drying out. May need more humidity

or may have root injury. Add charcoal to water or soil in which it is growing.

POINSETTIA. Mealy bugs and leaf-drop. Leaf-drop may be caused by too warm temperatures. Root aphids sometimes cause a problem; these are yellow-green, cottony lice. Loosen the earth ball and immerse in nicotine soap solution at 110 degrees. Root aphids are not easy to control, and every effort should be made to eliminate ants (if they are present). Mixing tobacco powder (ground-up stems and leaves sold at garden centers) with the soil at planting time and watering the roots of infected plants with a nicotine insecticide will help.

RUBBER PLANT. Scales and mealy bugs: Treat as suggested. Anthracnose: Characterized by tip burn and scorching of foliage. Cut off and burn infected leaves. May be caused by too much water or water allowed to stand on foliage.

Do Plants Relate to People?

Whether or not your plants are aware of your good intentions toward them is a subject of considerable controversy. I, for one, would like to believe that they are. Experiments are continuously being made on this aspect of plant science. Perhaps none were more exciting than those made by Cleve Backster, the renowned polygraph expert, in New York City in 1966–67. His studies seemed to show that plants not only do respond to people but they even have a sort of ESP! This, according to Backster, lets them know if they are being threatened by strangers and helps them prepare for the shock.

In the 1950s the Reverend Franklin Loehr wrote a book, *The Power of Prayer on Plants*, which recounted his experiments with two separate groups of similar plants. The first group was prayed over and given words of encouragement every day. The second was treated just the opposite—the plants were cursed daily. According to the good reverend, the prayed-for plants prospered, while the cursed ones were stunted and unhealthy-looking.

It is now an established fact that different types of plants respond differently to various stimuli. Begonias, for instance, are often chosen by plant experimenters who use the audio-response machine. The age of plants also seems to make a difference. Nursery-grown plants when removed from this environment and mixed with other plants become less sensitive as they mature.

Perhaps you have heard the phrase "like a vegetable" applied to persons lacking sensory ability. It has more truth than fiction, for vegetables have not shown themselves to be superior performers on the polygraph. Perhaps this is because they grow "under a threat" from the day they are planted. They appear to have adjusted to the fact that they will end up on the dinner table, and do not spend their time worrying about it. Instead, they devote most of their attention toward their roots, their seeds, or whatever part is going to propagate the species—or be eaten.

Recent research by a fourteen-year-old girl in Boston—which was also carried on in strict adherence to scientific principles—seems to contradict the experiments of Backster and others. We'll have to wait for further, more conclusive experiments to determine which school of thought is correct. I'm not a scientist, so I won't take sides until all the evidence is in.

The Green Thumbers: A Special Gift

Is it possible that a person's attitude is the true source of that gardening accolade, the "green thumb"? We all know people who can get anything to grow. Such people aren't always those that we in our ignorance may consider "beautiful." An elderly farmer, a withered grandmother, even a crippled child may grow terrific-looking plants. The gift is theirs, even though their knowledge of the scientific principles of gardening is slight or nonexistent. My Grandma Putt had this gift. She called it "the gift of love," and I think she was right. Truly the power of love is a strangely strong and motivating force, and if these green-thumbers have power, that is the source. You can count on it!

I believe that beauty is the house plants' reason for being, whether they are grown for flowers or foliage. They do not live under a threat, and their lives, sometimes for many years, are filled with joy and admiration and constant, loving care. If science has apparently been able to measure the degree of excitement that plants feel when human thoughts are turned toward them, tuning in on the emotions of those near them, why is it not logical to believe that they can return our feelings?

Some of the Old Remedies Still Work

We need not even now rely wholly on chemicals to combat many of the pests and diseases. We can still use remedial measures

that are just as effective today as they were when our grandmothers raised house plants in the bay windows of their living or
dining rooms

Spider mites. This is one of the worst pests on many ornamental plants. The mites are so tiny that it requires more than
fifty of them to span even one inch, and the little pests cause
yellowing of foliage, stippling and twisting of the leaf tips. If you
find these, try buttermilk and wheat flour (½ cup buttermilk and
4 cups wheat flour, preferably flour ground from untreated wheat).
Mix well and add to five gallons of water. This will destroy a very
high percentage of mites and the mite eggs as well.

A milk shower. Here's a goodie with skimmed milk. Try a
spray made with one part of this to nine parts of water. This is
particularly good for tomatoes—either those you grow in your
garden or some of the plants you may grow in the house under
lights. This solution is good against most diseases.

Vinegar on the azaleas. Azaleas like an acid soil, so what's
wrong with humoring them? Occasionally add 2 tablespoons of
vinegar to a quart of water and let them enjoy a treat. Some old-
time propagators believed that cuttings rooted better in an acid
soil than in one that was either neutral or alkaline. Because of
this they added vinegar to the beds where cuttings were rooted.
Vinegar added to the water in which cut flowers are kept will
help to prevent spoilage, retarding the development of fungi and
bacteria.

Hot pepper and garlic. These two seasonings, crushed,
steeped, and mixed with water to make insect sprays will rid your
house plants, as well as those outdoors in the garden, of pests.

A good warm bath. That soap-and-water bath for plants that
I am always advocating is still one of the best ways of all to keep
indoor plants healthy. Outdoor plants get the dust washed off
their foliage by occasional rains. Indoor plants, poor things, just
have to sit there waiting. The soap, entirely aside from the aspect
of cleanliness, is particularly useful against soft-bodied pests, such
as aphids.

Also, if you happen to be a smoker, use plenty of soap to
wash your hands before touching your plants. Many, such as
petunias, peppers, eggplants, tomatoes, and others are susceptible
to tobacco mosaic virus, which may be on your hands.

Summary

I don't think anyone has the right to say, "Do it my way," so I'm giving you a choice. Treat the problems your plants have with chemicals or try natural remedies. Either method may work better for you. Or sometimes one may work but not the other.

It is not easy even for an experienced gardener to always diagnose accurately what is troubling a plant, but observation will probably tell you more than I can. If a plant has been growing vigorously and it begins to develop any of the symptoms we've been talking about, obviously emergency treatment is indicated as quickly as possible. Don't let the infestation or disease get a stronghold and spread before taking remedial measures.

On the other hand, don't think that you must save every plant, or that you are a failure as a green-thumber if you don't. If you must discard some plants, don't feel guilty. Discretion is still often the better part of valor. Throwing away a badly diseased plant may save many others from the same fate. Not even a gardening "godfather" could cure everything!

Then, too, there are some plants that just never seem to have gotten a good start in life. Everyone who has raised seedlings has observed this. There are always big, husky fellows and runts. Sometimes the little guys never really catch up. It is very often the weak and spindly ones that are attacked first, and with insufficient strength to fight, they die. By that time the disease or pest has grown stronger and moves on to healthier plants to work its evil blight. So again I say, "Keep a constant watch." Even with insects, diseases, or environmental problems, eternal vigilance is still the price of liberty from the heartbreak of losing a good friend.

Index